SMART MO

LEARN THE ANSWERS TO THE MOST FREQUENTLY ASKED QUESTIONS PEOPLE HAVE ABOUT MONEY, IN-CLUDING:

- How much mortgage can I really afford?
- Is my bank safe?
- What's the best first real estate investment?
- Can I sue my stock broker?
- How long should I keep my tax returns?
- Do I need a lawyer to make a will?
- What type of checking account should I have?
- Should I borrow against my home?
- What's the difference between an IRA and Keogh?
- How do I know when to buy and sell stock?
- Is there an easy way to get a credit card?

AND HUNDREDS OF OTHER QUESTIONS—THE ANSWERS TO WHICH YOU NEVER THOUGHT YOU'D *EVER* UNDERSTAND!

$MART $MONEY

HOW TO BE YOUR OWN FINANCIAL MANAGER

KEN & DARIA DOLAN

BERKLEY BOOKS, NEW YORK

This Berkley book contains the revised text
of the original hardcover edition. It has been
completely reset in a typeface designed
for easy reading and was printed from new film.

SMART MONEY

A Berkley Book / published by arrangement with
Random House, with supplementary material provided by the authors

PRINTING HISTORY
Random House edition/April 1988
Berkley trade paperback revised edition/June 1990

ISBN: 0-425-12179-8

A BERKLEY BOOK® TM 757,375
Berkley Books are published by The Berkley Publishing Group,
200 Madison Avenue, New York, New York 10016.
The name ''BERKLEY'' and the ''B'' logo
are trademarks belonging to Berkley Publishing Corporation.

PRINTED IN THE UNITED STATES OF AMERICA

10 9 8 7 6 5 4 3 2 1

To our parents:
FRANK and MARJORIE DOLAN,
May they rest in peace

JAMES and NORMA ROBBIANO,
Without whom this book could not have been written

Contents

Prologue

If there is one lesson that small investors have learned from
the stock market crash, it is that they—and only they—are
responsible for their portfolios.   ASSOCIATED PRESS

Oh, no, not another money book! Why is it that everyone seems to be
writing about what I should do with my money? I haven't figured out the
difference between a money market account and a savings account yet, and
half the world is trying to sell me collateralized mortgage obligations and
Ginnie Mae funds. Where does it end?

Sound familiar? Maybe the better question is, Where does it begin?

At first blush, it would seem that the stock market crash of October 19,
1987, and the "correction of 1989" would turn many people away from a
money book. What a perfect time to publish a book about personal finance
that includes a good deal about stocks, bonds and mutual funds! No one
needs this book anymore because the Crash of '87 has chased away investors and would-be investors forever, right?

Wrong! Even if you were badly bruised and battered by the October
bloodlettings in the stock market, it is important to point out that *Smart
Money: How to Be Your Own Financial Manager* is not just a stock market
book. Fully two-thirds of this book deals with non–stock market issues. It
has been written to instruct you in the many facets of ways to save and
make money, not just in the small, narrow arena of stocks and bonds.

Our financial life has greatly changed since the days when a bank savings
account was investment enough. You put your money in the bank, received
an interest rate that bordered on the ridiculous, and felt confident that you
were doing as well as just about everyone around you. A few hearty souls
dabbled in the stock market while a few others bought bonds; but generally,

1

everyone's basic investment portfolio started at the local bank and, in many cases, ended there.

Today, like it or not, there are more investment alternatives available than ever before. Even if you want to avoid hearing about them, you can't get away from the daily bombardment of all sorts of old and new investment vehicles. The newspaper and magazine ads trumpet the good news of tax-free bonds, government securities, and mutual funds. Television and radio report the roller-coaster ride known as the Dow Jones Industrial Average, expose insider-trading scandals, announce corporate mergers and economic trends, and further confuse us by assuming that we know what everyone's talking about. Are they kidding?

Most books written about investing make the assumption that we have a fundamental understanding of an investment before we start reading the book, and yet, a recent poll showed that 90 percent of us don't even understand how to finance our own home!

To further complicate matters, banks, brokerage firms, insurance companies, mutual fund and financial planning firms are all in the same business today. The banks are underwriting bonds and providing insurance. Insurance companies are running mutual funds, brokerage houses are selling certificates of deposit, and mutual-fund companies are selling stocks. The one product the consumer wants and needs, an *education,* is unfortunately not for sale.

And yet, investing without a basic understanding of the world of money is like wading out into the sea without knowing how to swim. We admire the bravado, but we bemoan the number of bodies that wash up on the shore.

Over and over again in the course of our work, we have watched investors get into trouble—because they do not understand what they're doing *before* they do it. Yet it's hard to blame them. Many professionals in the business of financial products don't bother to take the time to explain alternatives fully, and the people who do try to explain things often do so in a complex manner. Furthermore, would-be investors often feel intimidated by the professionals or are afraid to seem ignorant and hesitate to ask *any* questions, never mind the right ones.

Yet there is a striking similarity in what people want to know about money. We talk to thousands of investors every year through radio and television programs and investment seminars and we hear the same questions over and over again. It is our hope that in this book we have put together a one-stop reference that answers these basic and most often asked questions in a way that will help you become financially fit. We've also tried to use the clear, understandable language our audiences have responded to, proving that investment and money subjects don't have to be dull and difficult to understand to be any good.

We'll cover a wide range of subjects—everything from annuities to zero-coupon bonds, stopping along the way to answer such questions as:

- How much insurance is too much?
- Where can I find inexpensive credit cards?
- How do I choose the best checking and savings accounts?
- When should I *sell* a stock?
- Can I really buy a home for no money down?

We've put many of the investment alternatives together in simple portfolios for various risk groups right in the beginning of the book, to save you the time and trouble of flipping through pages searching for them. We want to show you what a financial blueprint can look like before we uncover the workings of the many alternatives. From that point, we will go back to the beginning and explain fully what you must know about the alternatives before you invest. We hope you will then be knowledgeable enough to be your own financial adviser.

Lastly, we'll show you the pitfalls that an investor can fall into and suggest some easy ways to avoid the quicksand that can pull down the unwary investor.

Although we both believe the old maxim "Money isn't everything," financial security to the degree that your individual tastes and desires dictate is a most important ingredient to a happy life.

Put your greed aside. (We're all a little greedy.) There are no get-rich-quick schemes in this book. In fact, there are no get-rich-quick strategies in life that really work, although many financial professionals use greed as a prime sales tool to sell financial products. You won't make a fortune because you read this book, but you may see a consistent gain in your assets and save a fortune by avoiding mistakes that could cost you money.

Many people believe that money is power, but we believe that power comes with education. "The harder I work, the luckier I get." We're here to educate you to make good, sound investment choices based on knowledge of what you're doing.

So let's begin. The first stop on this money tour is a well-balanced portfolio.

1

Portfolio Planning

Our plans miscarry because they have no aim. When a man
does not know what harbor he is making for, no wind is the
right wind. SENECA (4 B.C.-A.D. 65)

Today's financial services firms sell investment products in much the same
way as your local supermarket sells food. Mutual funds, real estate limited
partnerships, unit trusts, stocks, bonds, and insurance are placed on shelves
for the shopper to look at, throw into the cart, pay for, and take home.

Today's financial product shopper travels from firm to firm looking for
bargains the way a grocery shopper goes from store to store looking for the
cheapest prices on meat and canned goods.

What this has produced for most people's investment portfolio is a pantry
heavily stocked with duplicate canned goods and very low on meat and
potatoes. Old Seneca said it perfectly almost two thousand years ago: A
plan with no direction is as bad as no plan.

In our opinion, both the financial services firms and the investor are to
blame; financial advisers, for offering investment ideas without knowing
what other investments a client has, and clients, for not telling the right
hand (one adviser) what the left hand (another adviser) is doing.

The purpose of this chapter is to outline some good, solid investment
portfolios. With the follow-up provided by the other chapters in this book,
we will try to turn you into your own financial manager or, at the least,
show you how to be less dependent upon brokers and planners and more
confident of your own ability to choose the right investments. Financial
security cannot be achieved by haphazardly pulling a number of different
investments together. Financial security is achieved by placing one brick on
top of another after enough mortar is in place.

4

Too many people to whom we speak are what we call knee-jerk investors. They go along jumping on hot tips or new ideas without seeing what the house they're building looks like with each new addition. Even the most experienced of builders uses a blueprint to build a house, and yet many of us construct a financial house without ever looking at a plan.

Unlike many advisers, we do not hold with the theory that different stages of life necessitate a completely different financial plan. In our opinion, a good foundation of investments in the early years can be built upon as time and circumstances change. We don't have to sell holdings to pick up new products. We should be able to add to what already exists, just as we might add a room onto our home to accommodate another child or a change of life-style.

The basic foundation blocks are the same whether you are a twenty-one-year-old single person beginning a career for the first time or a sixty-five-year-old married person with a family, who's about to retire. The basics *never* change. No matter what stage of life you're in, you always need liquid investments for emergencies.

Another popular belief is that younger people's portfolios can stand the addition of riskier investments, while older people should eliminate risky investments entirely. That's bunk. Risk knows no age. Some young people don't want any risk at all, and many older investors we have spoken with like to take a chance on occasion. Risk is for anyone who feels he or she can afford to take a chance with disposable income *no matter what his or her age.* The key point to remember is, you must understand what is considered risk and what isn't. Many people make investments believing that they are risk-free when, in fact, they're not. For that very reason, we include here a triangle that classifies the various investment alternatives as to their degree of risk.

THE DOLANS' RISK PYRAMID
(See Figure 1)

Now that you've had a chance to review what experts consider the degrees of risk in investments, let's begin the portfolio planning. We will begin at age twenty-one (or any age at which you personally can begin planning), unmarried, and without children, and build upon that base. We call it the beginning portfolio. With the exception of marriage and children, everyone can follow the same guidelines. Single or married, we all need the same financial security by retirement age. Married people with children to support and educate will find alternatives listed for those special needs. In three of the four portfolio groups we list three alternative portfolios for high-, medium- and low-risk investors. Your own ability to handle risk will dictate which portfolio is the one for you.

BEGINNING PORTFOLIO

This portfolio will take you up to the purchase of your first home, condo, or co-op. This purchase should be your first financial goal.

- Checking account—only enough to pay monthly bills.
- 50 percent money-market account or money-market fund or regular savings account
- 50 percent growth mutual fund (choose the degree of risk you can handle)

Life insurance is necessary only if you are married or responsible for someone else's support.

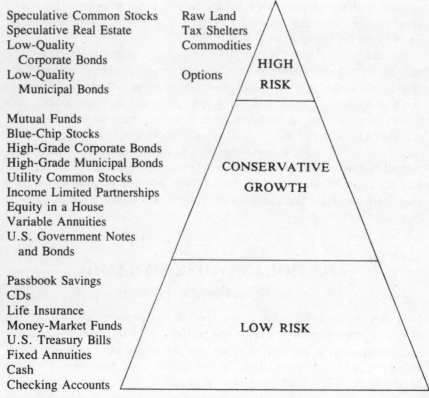

Speculative Common Stocks
Speculative Real Estate
Low-Quality
  Corporate Bonds
Low-Quality
  Municipal Bonds

Raw Land
Tax Shelters
Commodities

Options

HIGH RISK

Mutual Funds
Blue-Chip Stocks
High-Grade Corporate Bonds
High-Grade Municipal Bonds
Utility Common Stocks
Income Limited Partnerships
Equity in a House
Variable Annuities
U.S. Government Notes
  and Bonds

CONSERVATIVE GROWTH

Passbook Savings
CDs
Life Insurance
Money-Market Funds
U.S. Treasury Bills
Fixed Annuities
Cash
Checking Accounts

LOW RISK

FIGURE 1

SECONDARY PORTFOLIO

This portfolio should take you from the purchase of your home to the age of forty.

For couples with children to educate, 5 percent should come out of the highest percentage group in your portfolio choice for investment in U.S. savings bonds, Treasury zero-coupon bonds, and growth mutual funds.

- Checking account—only enough to pay monthly bills.

HIGH RISK

- 60 percent combination of: OTC stocks, new issues, growth stocks, options, leveraged real estate limited partnerships, long-term bonds (tax-free, if your tax bracket warrants)
- 20 percent combination of: short-term bonds, GNMA or government securities funds
- 20 percent money market or regular savings account

MEDIUM RISK

- 60 percent combination of: high-yield stocks, nonleveraged real estate limited partnerships, medium-term bonds (tax-free if your tax bracket warrants)
- 20 percent money market or regular savings account
- 10 percent GNMA funds or government securities funds, short-term bonds (tax-free if your tax bracket warrants)
- 10 percent cyclical and growth stocks, long-term bonds (tax-free if your tax bracket warrants)

LOW RISK

- 60 percent combination of: Treasury bills, short-term CDs, fixed annuities
- 20 percent nonleveraged real estate, blue-chip stocks, medium-term bonds (tax-free if your tax bracket warrants)
- 20 percent money market or regular savings account

PRE-RETIREMENT PORTFOLIO

This portfolio group can stay in place from age forty to age sixty-five or until you retire.

- Checking account—only enough to pay monthly bills.

HIGH RISK

- 50 percent combination of: OTC stocks, new issues, junk bonds, options, raw land, commodities
- 20 percent leveraged real estate limited partnerships, cyclical and growth stocks, long-term bonds (tax-free if your tax bracket warrants), variable annuities
- 15 percent money market or regular savings account

- 10 percent short-term bonds (tax-free if your tax bracket warrants), GNMA or government security funds
- 5 percent long-term CDs

MEDIUM RISK

- 45 percent combination of: nonleveraged real estate limited partnerships, high-yielding stocks, medium-term bonds (tax-free if your tax bracket warrants)
- 20 percent cyclical and growth stocks, long-term bonds (tax-free if your tax bracket warrants), variable annuities
- 20 percent Treasury bills, short-term CDs
- 15 percent money market or regular savings account

LOW RISK

- 45 percent combination of: Treasury bills, short-term CDs, fixed annuities
- 25 percent short-term bonds (tax-free if your tax bracket warrants), GNMA and government security funds
- 15 percent money market or regular savings account
- 10 percent nonleveraged real estate limited partnerships, high-yield stocks, medium-term bonds (tax-free if your tax bracket warrants)
- 5 percent options, OTC stocks, or new issues

As you get closer to retirement, pension and retirement plans should be reviewed and added to for security.

RETIREMENT PORTFOLIO

Although we think of age sixty-five as the standard retirement age, this group of portfolios will work for any age at which you retire.

HIGH RISK

- 45 percent combination of: long-term bonds (tax free if your tax bracket warrants), high-yield stocks, real estate investment trusts, options
- 35 percent medium-term bonds (tax-free if your tax bracket warrants), U.S. Treasury notes and bonds
- 10 percent GNMA funds, government security funds
- 10 percent money market and regular savings account

MEDIUM RISK

- 45 percent combination of: high-yield stocks, real estate investment trusts, medium-term bonds (tax-free if your tax bracket warrants)
- 25 percent U.S. government notes and bonds, immediate annuities

- 10 percent short-term bonds (tax-free if your tax bracket warrants), GNMA funds, government security funds
- 10 percent Treasury bills, short-term CDs
- 10 percent money market or regular savings account

LOW RISK

- 45 percent combination of: short-term bonds (tax-free if your tax bracket warrants), Treasury bills, short-term CDs
- 25 percent GNMA funds, government security funds
- 20 percent high-yield stocks, medium-term bonds (tax-free if your tax bracket warrants)
- 10 percent money market or regular savings account

In every portfolio classification we recommend that no less than 5 percent of your annual income be earmarked for retirement savings. For safety of retirement funds, we recommend that you consider investments in Treasury zero-coupon bonds, federally insured CDs, U.S. savings bonds, or—for the more aggressive—growth and income funds.

Many employers now offer special pension and/or profit-sharing plans that are well worth considering for a number of reasons. Among them is the fact that your contribution is, in many cases at least, partially matched by your employer. Such plans as 401(k)s, 403(b)s, and others grow tax deferred. Some plans also allow you to tailor your objectives by having several investment alternatives available.

These are basic plans for every stage of life. Some people will use portfolios that minimize risk while others will feel perfectly comfortable implementing the suggestions for high-risk investments. The choice is up to you.

No one plan is the best for everyone. A plan is good only if you personally understand the investments and feel comfortable with them. The ability to sleep at night—or, as we call it, the portfolio sleep factor—is just as important as how well the portfolio performs.

The portfolios you see here should help you to structure your own financial security. There's no denying, however, that taking control of your finances takes time and courage. The baffling array of new products and services available has made the job tougher. Even the old products have been changed and revamped for today. Therefore, it has become more necessary than ever before to learn as much as you can and take charge of your own financial future. No one will ever care for your money the way you will yourself. And, of course, if you do your own financial planning with aids like these portfolios, you'll never have to question the motives behind a particular product choice!

Portfolio planning doesn't have to be that hard or that costly. By using the guides we've provided here, you can do it yourself.

Now, let's go back to the beginning and review all the alternatives.

FOR FURTHER INFORMATION

Investing for Total Return
Peter D. Hurwagon
Probus Publishing

Portfolio & Investment Management
Frank J. Fabozzi, Editor
Probus Publishing

*Nest Egg Investing: How to Build a
    Secure Financial Foundation*
Helen I. Breunig
Dow Jones-Irwin

2

Dealing with Your Bank

When summoned to the bank for a meeting about his overdrawn account, James Thurber, the humorist, writer, and cartoonist, openly admitted that he never kept records of the checks he wrote. "Then how do you know how much money is in your account?" asked the bank manager. "I thought that was *your* business," Thurber retorted.

Banking used to be a pretty simple procedure for the consumer, if not quite as simple as James Thurber made it. Dealing with a modern bank, however, has become confusing and expensive. Competition created with the deregulation of banks has brought us many different types of accounts to choose from, and fees, according to the Consumer Federation of America, have doubled since 1979.

We now need to figure out the difference between a money market fund and money market deposit account; we wait ten days for a check to clear, or watch helplessly while an automated teller machine devours our plastic card.

A smart consumer can no longer expect the local bank on the corner to be all things to all persons. It is now necessary to use different banks for different transactions in order to get the best service at the lowest cost. We hate to have to say it, but you must shop around for bank fees and rates the same way you shop for everything else. It is possible to save yourself thousands of dollars by shopping for savings accounts and loans.

News of banks that have failed has taken the comfort out of banking for many of us. "How can I tell if my bank is safe?" is one of the most often asked questions we receive.

The rising number of bank failures and consumer complaints, as well as the number of banks that don't satisfactorily answer questions of depositors, has made it necessary to change the way we save our money, pay for goods, and finance them.

This chapter will show you how to determine if your bank is healthy; help you choose the best savings and checking accounts; and explain the many services now found in your local bank. We need all the help we can get in this confusing and expensive world of deregulated banks.

I went to a bank yesterday to open a checking account. By the time the teller finished telling me about the types of checking accounts available, I was totally confused. Can you explain the different types of checking accounts?

Sure. There are regular accounts, no-minimum accounts, NOW accounts, and SuperNOW accounts. NOW and SuperNOW accounts pay interest; no-minimum and regular accounts do not.

What is no-minimum checking?

Sometimes called a lifeline account, this is used to attract people who don't write many checks in the course of a month. No interest is paid on the balance. Sometimes the fees are *advertised* as lower than the fees for regular checking and NOW accounts. However, a survey conducted by the Consumer Federation of America showed that the fees are not significantly lower than for the other accounts. We only recommend no-minimum or lifeline accounts when you can't keep the necessary minimum balance required by the bank. Because the monthly fees and check charges vary so greatly from institution to institution, you have to shop around for the best of a bad deal! Avoid no-minimum checking.

How does regular checking differ from no-minimum checking?

Regular checking does not charge a monthly fee for service and transactions when a minimum balance is maintained. The minimum balance on regular checking varies greatly, from a low of $100 at some institutions to a high of $2500 at others. The average minimum is $500. As long as you maintain the minimum balance, you will avoid paying monthly service fees and check charges. This is a much better deal than no-minimum checking. However, if your balance drops below the required minimum, you will most likely be charged a service fee, which can be as little as $1.50 or as high as $15, and most institutions will also charge check fees at this time.

Where does a NOW account fit into this checking account lineup?

NOW accounts, offered by all banks and savings and loans, pay interest on the monthly balance when a minimum amount is maintained. The minimum amount required is generally higher than a regular checking account, and there is usually no service or transaction charge. If the minimum is not maintained, the fees may be higher than those of a regular account. Minimum balances range from $100 to $5000, although most institutions use a minimum of $500 to $1500, with $1500 being the most common. This is the best type of checking account to have. Shop around to secure the lowest minimum balance.

What is a SuperNOW account?

A SuperNOW account is a NOW account with higher minimums and a higher rate of interest. Although federal law allows the minimum balance of a SuperNOW account to be as low as $1000, most institutions require $2500.

What type of checking account do you recommend?

The best checking account is a NOW account. Our second choice, for those who can't meet the minimum-balance requirement, is a regular checking account. To find the best account, shop around and compare interest rates paid and minimum-balance requirements. SuperNOW accounts, in our opinion, are not as good a deal for the consumer. The minimum-balance requirements are too high and the interest rates paid not high enough to warrant tying up so much money in a checking account.

Would it be a good idea to price check charges at a few places to get a better deal on my checking account?

We like the way you think, but unfortunately, the cost of checks is basically the same from institution to institution. If you want to save a few dollars on checks, you may be able to do so by choosing a less decorative check. Other than that, check-printing charges really don't enter into consideration.

How much money should I keep in my checking account?

Keep only enough money there to maintain the minimum balance and to pay your monthly bills. More money than that is just not smart investing. Any excess funds should be placed in a savings account or other investment. The many other investment alternatives will be discussed fully in upcoming chapters.

I don't think I've ever been so angry in my life! I deposited a check from out of state in my account and after a week, assuming it had cleared, I wrote two checks on it. Now my bank tells me that the check hadn't cleared, so I'm stuck with two overdraft charges and a mess of paperwork. What can I do?

Take two aspirin and calm down! Check holds are a thorn in many people's sides. Ask at other banks and savings and loans in your area to find a shorter check-holding period. Some banks will even agree not to hold deposited checks if you can keep an equal amount in your savings account.

What does the bank do with the check deposit that causes such a long hold?

A bank must send the deposited check to the Federal Reserve branch bank by 10 A.M. the next day. The Fed will then credit the bank for the deposit. At that point, the bank is able to invest your money and collect interest on it. At some banks, unfortunately, the depositor can't touch the money during that period, which is called a float. Even though it's already in use, the bank maintains that the customer must wait until the check is cleared by the institution that issued it.

But if my check is sent to the Fed by 10 A.M. the next day and at that time cleared by the Fed, why can't I have access to the cash sooner?

Most banks maintain that they need to hold on to these funds to protect themselves against fraud or insufficient funds for payment until the checks are cleared by the issuer. They believe that without some kind of hold, people would deposit bad checks, draw against the credited funds, and then leave the bank holding the bag when the check bounces. Some banks, however, don't hold checks that long.

Do banks that release funds early really end up losing money from bouncing checks?

No, they don't. Recent federal studies showed that banks collect $25 in bad-check fees for every $1 they spend on processing bad checks or writing them off. One bank surveyed even admitted earning $170 million a year in interest from held checks!

Is there anything I can do to get deposited checks cashed more quickly?

Here are a few suggestions to help speed up the time:

- Ask for immediate payment for checks drawn on banks in your own area.
- Compare banking institutions for the best policies. A law passed in 1984 requires banks to provide a written statement on their check-holding procedures.
- When it becomes necessary, ask the banker for a wire transfer of funds or to call the issuing bank for confirmation that the check is good.

Are there any particular features I should look for when opening a checking account?

1. Compare checking costs.
2. Find an institution that has a short holding period on deposited checks.
3. Look for an institution that will contact you before bouncing a check.
4. If you prefer banking in one place, make sure the savings rates of interest are comparable to those at other institutions before opening any accounts.
5. Check the institution's ability to serve you efficiently. If there are long

lines in the lobby and few tellers' windows open, the service will be slow and aggravating.

6. Only take the services that you need. If the checking account comes with a credit card and a savings account and you don't want these, go elsewhere. Extra services usually cost you in fees or lower rates of interest.

I have a real problem balancing my checkbook. Consequently, I end up with checks that bounce. Is there any way I can solve this problem? My bank refuses to notify me before it bounces my checks.

Change banks for one that will notify you before it bounces a check! If you don't want to do that, you should ask your bank to give you a credit line. This will save you the problem and expense of bounced checks.

My bank has offered me a line of credit with my checking account. What is that?

A credit line is an automatic loan the bank will extend to you if you write a check for more than your account's balance. These loans are also called no-bounce checking, cash advances, advance accounts, or overdraft privileges.

Does a credit line just cover my check or does the bank lend me more than the amount of the check?

The answer to your question depends on the institution. Some lend the exact amount of the overdraft while others lend an amount in multiples of $100 or $300. If, for example, you are overdrawn by $253, the bank that lends in multiples would automatically lend you $300. We don't recommend this. Look for a credit line that lends only the exact amount. There's no need for you to pay interest on money that isn't being used.

How much will overdraft protection cost me if I have to use it?

The annual percentage rate (APR) on this type of loan is like credit card rates on unpaid balances, generally 18 to 22 percent a year. Some institutions also charge a monthly service fee or a per-loan fee when an overdraft is covered.

How do I repay the bank when I use a credit line?

How you repay varies greatly from institution to institution. Some institutions automatically repay the loan when you deposit new checks on the day of deposit. Others use the same method but wait until the end of the billing period. Some institutions require a formal payment on the loan after you receive a monthly statement, and others make an automatic payment from funds on the statement date.

Is it really necessary to have a checking account? I use money orders whenever I have to pay someone.

Ten years ago, money orders cost as little as 50¢. Today, however, they generally cost $1.50 and can be as much as $10. Even at $1.50 apiece, six money orders a month would cost you $108 a year. This can be far more expensive than writing checks on an account that requires a minimum balance and charges no fees. We'd recommend, even if you buy just a couple of money orders a month, that you look into a checking account to save yourself money.

How much money do you recommend I keep in a savings account?

Because emergencies do occur, we recommend that everyone strive to have at least three months' income in a savings account or money market account for instant liquidity or, in other words, so that you can get at your money immediately.

Should I open a regular savings account?

In our opinion, regular savings accounts are only slightly better than burying your money in the backyard! Many institutions are now charging fees on inactive accounts and accounts closed shortly after opening. Because regular savings accounts pay relatively low yields, fees and charges may end up being more than the interest earned. If you can't afford to meet minimum-balance requirements to open a money market account, which we will discuss in the next question, and you need the ability to withdraw savings occasionally, a regular savings account makes sense. We recommend that you check for the following features, however, before opening the account. Make sure the regular savings account has:

- the best prevailing interest compounded daily or continuously
- no charges for withdrawals within reasonable limits
- no- or low-minimum balance requirements for earning interest and no maintenance fees
- day-of-deposit to day-of-withdrawal interest computations or average daily balance
- federal insurance in the form of the FDIC-supervised Bank Insurance Fund (BIF) or Savings Association Insurance Fund (SAIF)

My wife and I have always used a regular savings account (passbook savings). The teller at the bank told me I should consider a money market account instead. What is that?

Banking institutions began to offer money market accounts in 1982 so they could compete with investment companies. Money market accounts usually require a minimum deposit of $2500, although some require a lot less. The institutions set the interest rates paid by these accounts weekly, although a small number change rates daily.

What's the difference between the money market account and a regular savings account?

The regular savings account rate of interest is fixed and does not change in response to the direction of interest rates. Money market accounts' rates of interest fluctuate. Most money markets also allow check writing, but they may limit the number of checks you can use per month.

Are money market accounts and money market funds the same thing?

They're not the same. A money market *account* (MMA) is offered by a banking institution and the rate of interest it pays is freely set by the institution. Rates can change daily, but they are generally adjusted once a week. Most institutions require an initial deposit of $2500. A money market *fund* (MMF) is offered by a firm regulated by the Securities and Exchange Commission. An MMF invests in short-term securities like Treasury bills, bankers' acceptances, and commercial paper and gets its interest rate from these investments. The yield of this type of fund changes daily and usually requires an initial deposit of $1000.

Would you recommend a bank money market account or a money market fund as a better investment?

Since they work basically the same way, we don't usually recommend one type over the other, although you should be aware that money market funds generally pay a few hundredths of a percent (basis points) more than bank money market accounts. We recommend money market funds over accounts only when there is a significant difference in interest rates. You should, however, consider the advantages and disadvantages of each for your personal situation.

Advantages of money market funds over bank money market accounts:

- generally lower initial deposits
- minimum-balance requirements usually lower
- no fees or charges if the balance doesn't meet the minimum requirements

Disadvantages of money market funds:

- no insurance by an agency of the federal government
- less accessibility than your local bank: money must be withdrawn by calling, writing a letter, or writing a check
- an increased difficulty in evaluating the account's performance: you must compare not only yield and features but the level of risk involved

How can I determine the level of risk in my money market fund?

Money market funds that invest in short-term securities are safer than those that invest in longer-term ones. To determine the maturity term of the securities, you'll have to read the prospectus. We describe in detail how to read a mutual fund prospectus in Chapter 6.

Lately the local banks and savings and loans are advertising automated teller machine cards. What are they?

These are plastic cards, like credit cards, that allow you to use a machine for the same services that were once provided only by a teller. ATM cards allow you to bank at any hour and at any branch with ease. In many areas today, you may even use your ATM card at other banks and stores, not just branches of your own bank.

Do all banking institutions offer the same services with ATMs?

No, they don't. There are several points to consider before you choose an ATM:

1. Does it offer the services *you* need, such as transfer of funds or late-night access to cash?
2. Are the ATM machines convenient?
3. Can you read the instructions and screen easily?
4. Does the ATM offer privacy when you transact business?
5. Are photos made of every transaction? Photos provide a record of all transactions and can be very helpful if your card is stolen and used by someone else. Unfortunately, only a small number of banks use this process at this time. If you can get this service with your ATM, it will be very valuable.
6. If you plan to use your card in high-crime areas or at night, is the area well lighted and accessible only to those with bank cards?
7. Does the bank charge you for use of the card?

How can I find out if I'll be charged for using my ATM?

Check the ATM agreement for section entitled "Fees," or call the bank's customer relations department and ask. If you already have a card, check your bank statement for fees. If you are charged, consider switching to another ATM.

How can I protect myself from fraud when using an ATM?

Don't write your ATM code on a piece of paper that you carry with you in your wallet or purse. It's amazing how many people do this. We also recommend that you avoid using it if you're in an area where there's a good chance of theft or risk. When you do use the card, make sure that you keep your private access code from prying eyes that may be in line behind you.

My ATM allows me to make cash deposits. Should I do it or go to a teller?

Please use a teller if it's at all possible. If the bank makes a mistake, there is only a record that you yourself created, which is very difficult to verify. Checks are a different story. There's always a written record of a check if it gets lost in the process.

What should I do if I lose my ATM card?

Report it to the bank immediately! If you report the loss within two days, you will be liable only for up to $50 of unauthorized transactions. After two days, your liability will increase to $500.

It suddenly dawned on me that I'm investing in certificates of deposit at my local savings and loan, but I really don't know what a CD is! Can you provide a definition?

We won't beat you up for investing in something you really don't understand, although we should! You should never put money into anything unless you know what it is. A CD, a certificate of deposit, is a debt instrument issued by a bank. This means that you lend money to the bank, for which it promises you a specified rate of return. The bank then invests the money it borrowed from you, hopefully at a higher rate than what you will receive. The bank pays you the specified rate and makes its money on the difference. CDs can be bought for as little as $500 and have maturities ranging from a few weeks to several years.

I live in Florida, where we have a bank on every corner. They all offer money market accounts and CDs, but the rates vary like crazy. How can I be sure that I'm getting the best CD and money market account?

By asking the different banking institutions some key questions before opening the account, you'll make the right decisions. Here are the questions to ask:

- *What is the stated rate on the account?* (The stated rate is the rate *before* compounding.)
- *Do you compound daily, monthly, or quarterly?*
- *What is the annual effective yield (the return in the first year)?*
- *Do different amounts deposited earn a different rate of interest?*
- *If I don't keep a certain balance in my money market account, will you charge a fee?*
- *If I close out my money market account within a certain time period, will you charge me a fee?*
- *What penalty do you charge for early withdrawal on a CD?*
- *When my CD matures, how much time do I have before you roll it over into a new CD?*
- *Will you notify me when my CD is about to mature?*
- *Are deposits here insured by FDIC?*

Please help. I was a terrible math student in school, and I feel embarrassed carrying a calculator to the bank to figure out how much a CD will earn. Is there a quick way to come up with the dollar amount a CD will pay me?

There sure is. *Ask.* When you are presented with an interest rate, just ask the officer to tell you in dollars and cents how much that will be. Find out how much will be in the account after one month and at the end of one year. It's always easier to understand rates when we can see them in dollar amounts.

Who should consider a CD as an investment?

CDs should be considered by someone who is unable to deal with a degree of risk and who can afford to give up instant access to the money for a period of time.

I found a great rate on CDs at a privately insured bank. Is this as safe as a bank insured by the FDIC's BIF or SAIF?

No it's not, and we strongly recommend that you avoid doing business with any financial institution that is privately or state insured. Stick with federally insured banks.

My mother invests only in CDs. Although she doesn't need the money, she always takes the interest payments instead of leaving them in the account to compound. I think this is a bad idea. What do you think?

We think you're pretty smart and your mother ought to listen to you! Since your mother doesn't need the interest checks that are sent out periodically, she really ought to leave them in the account. This will maximize the return on her investment.

What are the advantages of investing in CDs?

CDs offer a number of good features:

- There are no brokerage fees or other costs in buying them.
- When purchased in a Bank Insurance Fund (BIF)– or a Savings Association Insurance Fund (SAIF)–insured institution, they are completely safe.
- They are easily understood by almost everyone.

There must be some bad features connected with CDs. What are they?

You're right. Nothing is perfect. The disadvantages to CD investing are:

- a time-consuming hunt for the best rates
- substantial penalties for early withdrawal, which means they are not liquid
- lower yields than corporate bonds, mutual funds, and other investments, due to lower risk

Why do CD yields vary so widely from bank to bank and state to state?

Banks and savings and loans have come into the world of competition since being deregulated. The institutions that offer the higher rates are looking for as much business as possible. The institutions offering lower rates offer CDs more as an accommodation to depositors than to attract new business.

Do you have a suggestion to help me get the best return from my CD investments?

We do. Instead of buying one CD in hopes of guessing correctly the direction of interest rates, split the money into five equal amounts. Then purchase a six-month, one-year, two-and-a-half-year, three-year, and five-year CD. This strategy gives you more protection. If interest rates begin to rise, you have a six-month and a one-year CD maturing, which will allow you to invest at higher rates. If interest rates fall, you have locked in a higher return with the longer-maturity CDs. Instead of guessing, you can play the entire interest rate scene. To give an example, if you have $50,000 to invest, place $10,000 in each of those maturities instead of the entire $50,000 in one. This will also help you avoid early withdrawal penalties, by freeing up some money sooner.

Would you please give me a good definition of compounding versus simple interest?

Compounding is nothing more than interest paid on interest. Simple interest pays a one-time amount calculated on the principal amount.

I see ads for banks that say "compounded daily, monthly, quarterly, semi-annually, and continuously." Which is the best type of interest to get?

The best interest deal is continuous or daily compounding. To give you a better idea of why, let's show you an example. You have $10,000 to invest in a CD for one year at a rate of 10 percent. The following list gives you the type of compounding and the amount you would have at the end of one year.

simple interest	$11,000.00
semiannual compounding	$11,025.00
quarterly compounding	$11,038.13
monthly compounding	$11,047.13
daily compounding	$11,051.56
continuous compounding	$11,051.71

As you can see, the best bang for your dollar is in continuous and daily compounding.

The bank I do my CD business at has offered to renew my CD automatically at the current rates and for the same term when it comes due. Is this a good feature?

Automatic renewal sounds like a great feature to many CD buyers, but we feel it has a couple of drawbacks:

1. You may end up getting a lower rate of return than you could get somewhere else.
2. If you should find yourself in need of cash just after renewal, you'll pay penalties to withdraw it.

What do you recommend I do when a CD matures?

Redeem that CD on the day it matures, and if you don't need the money, reinvest it immediately at the highest rate you can find. That high rate may be at another banking institution, so shop around a few days in advance and you'll be ready to move quickly.

I have an opportunity to buy a variable-rate CD, which won't lock me in at the current interest rates. The term is for eighteen months and if rates go up, I'll do better than with a fixed-rate CD. Would this be a good investment?

It may be a good investment if interest rates go up, but you'll end up earning less if interest rates go down. That, however, is the calculated risk you take. We are more concerned about what the bank uses to determine rate changes and how often the rates can be changed.

Is there a rule of thumb in computing variable-rate CDs for changes in interest?

Most banking institutions change the variable CD rates once a month, but some adjust the rates weekly, and in at least one instance they can change daily. Obviously, the longer the rate holds, the better off you'll be.

If I decide to buy a variable-rate CD, what should the rate be tied to, to give me the best return?

The best formula you can find is the one that ties the interest rate to thirty month Treasury notes. The thirty-month notes usually have a higher yield than other, shorter-term securities.

What's the worst formula for variable-rate CDs?

The worst formula is found at banking institutions that leave changes in the hands of management. There's no way to track their formula. The second-worst deal is at banks that tie the variable rate to other products they offer.

What do you think about banks that offer a free gift with the purchase of a CD?

We think you should avoid them at all costs. They generally pay a lower rate of interest to make up for the price of the "gift."

I've been shopping CD rates for what seems like weeks and now I'm more confused and tired than ever. Is there an easier way than this to find the best CD rates?

There sure is. The highest CD rates in the entire country are tracked and published each week by:

100 Highest Yields
Box 088888
North Palm Beach, Florida 33408-9990
(800) 327-7717

Subscriptions are $84 for fifty-two weekly issues or $29 for eight consecutive issues. *100 Highest Yields* lists only federally insured banking institutions, for your safety and peace of mind. Every week, this publication also lists the top twenty money market–account yields, too.

Why do you two always stress that a person should deal with a bank that's federally insured and not state or privately insured?
The banking situation in Maryland and Ohio in 1985 showed that when one or two members of a privately insured system got into trouble, the entire system collapsed. Government agencies providing the FDIC's BIF and SAIF insurance have a much larger safety net. That's why we stress doing business *only* with federally insured banks.

Why are the BIF and SAIF better than private or state insurance?
They have lines of credit at the U.S. Treasury that can be drawn on if it runs out of funds. It may also go to Congress and ask for appropriations.

What's the difference between FDIC's BIF and SAIF insurance categories?
Although both agencies insure accounts up to $100,000, the BIF covers accounts at commercial banks and most savings banks; SAIF covers accounts at thrifts which typically are now or were formerly savings and loan institutions. Savings banks are also insured by SAIF.

Does the government provide the money for BIF and SAIF or do they get the money from somewhere else?
Both agencies assess their member banks for premiums which fund their insurance pools. It's rather like membership dues.

What's the first thing that happens when an institution insured by BIF or SAIF fails?
Contrary to what many people think, the FDIC and its sister agencies do not immediately start taking money out of their pools to pay depositors. Both agencies first appoint a government conservator who tries to get the institution's finances back into order to merge the troubled bank or thrift with a healthy institution.

What happens if the agency can't find an institution that's willing to take on a troubled member?
The second step, if a partner can't be found, might be to sell the assets and liabilities of the institution or liquidate them.

If that doesn't work, what happens?
The court of last resort steps in and pays deposits back to the customer

and closes out the accounts without any penalty. This is the step that would use the money in the insurance pool. But as we said, this is the last resort when other attempts fail.

A teller at my local bank told me that I can deposit more than $100,000 and still be insured. Could that possibly be true?

If the accounts are set up correctly, that is certainly true. In fact, it's possible for a family of four to insure up to $1.4 million. The strategy uses three types of accounts:

1. *an individual account*—your name alone
2. *a joint tenancy account*—two members of a family open an account in both their names
3. *a testamentary revocable trust account*—an account is opened in your name and is placed in trust for someone else

How could a family of four possibly insure $1.4 million?

Individual Accounts:	Husband	$100,000
	Wife	$100,000
	Child 1	$100,000
	Child 2	$100,000
Joint Accounts:	Husband/Wife	$100,000
	Husband/Child 1	$100,000
	Wife/Child 2	$100,000
	Child 1/Child 2	$100,000
*Testamentary Trusts:	Husband/In trust for Wife	$100,000
	Wife/In trust for Husband	$100,000
	Husband/Child 1	$100,000
	Husband/Child 2	$100,000
	Wife/Child 1	$100,000
	Wife/Child 2	$100,000
	Total:	$1,400,000

Using the same strategy just described, how much could a couple insure at one bank?

A couple would be able to insure $500,000. A family of three could insure $1 million. Again, we remind you to check with your lawyer, accountant, and financial planner before using this strategy employing a testamentary revocable trust.

What would happen if I opened up a five-year CD at a bank that fails while there are still three years to go?

If the bank is merged with another, financially stronger, bank, you may receive the agreed upon rate for the duration or you may not. Many times

---

*Testamentary trusts, also called a Totten trust in some states, are complex and may only be used with a spouse, child, or grandchild. You *must* consult a lawyer, financial planner, accountant, or all three before using this strategy.

the rate is dropped to a lower rate of return. If the institution's assets are liquidated, the CD will mature at the time of liquidation with no penalties to you. You'll receive a check for the principal and all the interest earned up to the liquidation at the five-year rate.

Compounded interest in one of my bank accounts has just pushed the account up over the $100,000 insurance limit. What should I do now?

Contact the bank and arrange either to have the bank send you the interest payments instead of leaving them in the account, or have the bank credit the interest to another account that isn't at the $100,000 limit.

Recent bank failures have made me very uneasy about putting my money in a bank. How can I check on the financial condition of a bank?

If the institution is publicly held, you can get a copy of the latest quarterly or annual report. If it isn't publicly owned, ask the institution for a financial report. Then, if you can't evaluate the report yourself, ask your accountant to study it for you and give you his or her thoughts.

Is there any other way to check the finances of a particular bank?

Private companies also rate banks for the public, for a fee. Although we don't recommend any particular company, here is the name of the least expensive that you can contact:

VERIBANC, Inc.
P.O. Box 461
Wakefield, Massachusetts 01880
(800) 44BANKS
(cost: $10 for an instant rating, $2 for each additional; $10 for a short-form report; $45 for a full research report)

If the bank that holds my mortgage fails, can I forget about making mortgage payments until the situation is cleared up?

Wouldn't it be nice if a failed bank meant a forgotten loan! Unfortunately, that's not the case. When a banking institution is closed or taken over by another management team, you continue the same loan agreement that you had with the original institution. That means you still have to make your payments to that same mailing address. Generally, the same rights you had before the closing would remain in place. However, you may be asked to pay immediately with an unsecured personal loan or a home equity loan.

How can I make sure that my money in the bank remains safe?

- Bank only at BIF or SAIF institutions.
- Check account balances periodically to be sure they haven't exceeded the $100,000 limit.

- Reread all account agreements to make sure names, addresses, and Social Security numbers are correct.
- Be sure trust agreements are drawn up correctly.
- Stay informed through the local newspaper about banking institution failures. When you find a local failure, find out how the depositors were affected.

By staying current with your banking affairs, you'll protect yourself from any surprises.

How can I tell whether my bank is federally or state chartered?
  Ask.

I'm having a small problem with my bank. We disagree over how much money is in my savings account. What's the proper procedure for making complaints?
  The order in which you complain is very important. You don't want to go over the head of a person who might be the one to solve everything for you. Start with the manager of the bank or S&L branch. If a solution can't be reached at this level, the next step is to determine whether it's a federally or state chartered institution. You'll also need to know if it's a bank or an S&L. You need this information in order to contact the correct department. For a federally chartered bank, contact the Comptroller of the Currency at (202) 447-1600. Ask them to send you a complaint form. If you're dealing with a federally chartered savings and loan, send a complaint letter to the Office of Thrift Supervision, Consumer Affairs, 1700 G Street N.W., Washington, D.C. 20552. For state-chartered banks *and* S&L's, you'll have to look in the phone book under "State Agencies" to contact the state banking commissioner. Your last resort is your lawyer or small claims court.

How do I write a letter of complaint?
  Be brief and to the point.
  Explain everything in the order that it happened.
  Use a typewriter, for easy reading.
  Include *copies* of pertinent documents. Never send originals.
  State the remedy you want.

It's been a few weeks since I mailed a letter of complaint about my bank, and so far I haven't heard a word. What do I do now?
  It usually takes several weeks before you hear back. The agency that received your letter has to send the complaint to the proper person, get in touch with the banking institution, and try to work out a solution. All this takes time. If you've been waiting for three weeks or more, however, call the agency.

Twice, now, I've been quoted one rate by a bank and received another. Is there any way I can keep this from happening again?

Get the rate you're offered in writing, and make sure the note includes the length of time that rate will stay in effect. There will be no arguments about who said what, with a letter in your hand!

Is there anything else I should know when dealing with a banking institution?

The most important point is to keep good records. You'll always have protection with the proper documentation.

How can I find out if my bank is safe?

VERIBANC, Inc., has started a new telephone rating service that allows you to instantly check the safety of your bank or S&L. Simply call 1-800-44BANKS. Cost: $10 for the first bank or S&L, and $2 for each additional institution.

What is a credit union?

Credit unions are nonprofit consumer cooperatives. They were first founded to provide better terms and lower loan rates for members than profit-making institutions offered. Today, their loan rates are about the same as commercial banks', but credit unions frequently offer members free credit life insurance and are often willing to make small loans to members in need. Credit unions are generally more lenient to borrowers who have trouble paying and sometimes pay dividends in the way of interest rebates at the end of the year.

Are credit unions available to everyone?

Unfortunately, they're not. Most are associated with unions or a specific company and available only to members or employees. Some credit unions have been formed for church groups and communities. We strongly recommend that you look for one of these in your area.

My neighbor was telling me about a share-draft account and how great it is. I thought I would open one, but my local bank said it doesn't have that type of account. Why not?

Share drafts are interest-bearing checking accounts similar to NOW accounts. Banks and savings and loans don't offer this type of checking. Your friend must belong to a credit union. Share drafts are offered by about 30 percent of all credit unions, and most place no charges on them no matter the size of the account.

Do credit unions have the same check-holding policies as other institutions?

Generally, they don't. Most credit unions won't hold your check, but the few that do will hold local checks for three to five days and out-of-town checks for seven to ten days.

Should I open a savings account at a bank or at my credit union?

Since you're fortunate enough to be a member of a credit union, we recommend you open a savings account there. Credit unions are more likely than other banking institutions to meet the requirements for beneficial compounding and good rates. They are also likely to offer you free life insurance for the amount of your deposit, usually up to $2000, and many of their yields on savings are higher than other institutions' rates. We are big fans of credit unions and wish they were available to more people.

SUMMARY

There are a few facts of life that never change: taxes will always go up; each day that we live, we get a little older; and as long as there are designer jeans, teenage girls will buy them (just ask our daughter)! As the old saying goes, "The more things change, the more they remain the same." The author of those lines wasn't talking about today's banking industry.

The good news is that many of the changes in our banks and savings and loans are for the better, but they are not all better for the consumer. Before you commit your money, get to know the banker and the services. If you can't have access to your own personal banker, do your business elsewhere. Banks are *not* not-for-profit organizations, existing solely to provide safe haven for our money.

Because of the new competition in the banking world, we need to take the time to find the best rates and services available. Competition isn't necessarily bad for the depositor, but it does mean we must examine each institution carefully to find the right combination of high yield, individual attention and safety.

To find the best bank(s) for you:

- Compare rates. Track them for a number of weeks and see how they compare with others in the area.
- Check out the lobby. If there are long lines, don't expect quick and efficient service.
- Consider whether the bank is convenient. Find out if it's open evenings and weekends and if the cash machines are close to home or work.
- Put bank fees under a magnifying glass. Deregulation has forced banks into offering higher rates, which many try to balance with higher fees. Good banks will provide you with a list of fees and charges.
- Assess the services. Make sure the bank will fit your needs.

Smart investing begins with smart banking.

FURTHER INFORMATION
PAMPHLETS

The Basics of Interest Rates
The Federal Reserve Bank of New
  York
Public Information Department
33 Liberty Street
New York, New York 10045
(free)

Your Savings Options
The Consumer Federation of
  America
1424 16th Street, N.W.
Washington, D.C. 20036
(25¢)

*How to File a Consumer Credit
  Complaint*
Director, Division of Consumer
  Affairs
Board of Governors of the Federal
  Reserve System
Washington, D.C. 20551
(free)

OTHER SOURCES

Federal Deposit Insurance
  Corporation (FDIC)
Corporate Communications
550 17th Street, N.W.
Washington, D.C. 20429
(800) 424-4334

Board of Governors of the Federal
  Reserve System
Office of Consumer and Community
  Affairs
20th and C Streets, N.W.
Washington, D.C. 20551
(202) 452-3946

Consumer Information Center
P.O. Box 100
Pueblo, Colorado 81002

*Making Deposits: When Will Your
  Money Be Available?*
Publication 439V (50¢)

Your Insured Deposit
Publication 584V (Free)

3

The Stock Market

Anyone who thinks there's safety in numbers hasn't looked at the stock market pages.   IRENE PETER

The collapse of the stock market on October 19, 1987, and the following days of unprecedented volatility shook investor confidence in a way not seen in any other period of our history, except for the Crash of 1929. Many people, too cautious to invest in 1985 and 1986, were finally caught up in the frenzy of the June, July and August, 1987, gains of the Dow Jones Industrial Average and began shoveling their hard-earned dollars into stocks. No one wanted to miss the gravy train of quick and easy gains. Like a giant tornado, the stock market spun faster and faster, sucking up more and more people, most of whom were spit out and left wondering what had happened on October 19 and 20.

Did the Crash of 1987 put an end to the stock market and investing in stocks? No. If the Crash of '29, followed by the Great Depression, did not put a FOR SALE sign on Wall Street, it is foolish to think that the occurrences of 1987 and 1989 will put an end to stock investing. However, thousands of people have had the point brought home to them in hard and expensive terms that you *must* understand what you're doing before you invest.

There are groups of savvy, educated investors who managed to profit handsomely from the calamitous events of October 1987. Why? Because these investors understood the equity markets and knew what they were doing before they made a move.

As the dust settled and the media hype subsided the intelligent person looked for answers. We have written this chapter to provide some of those answers and to help educate and enable you to have a better working un-

30

derstanding of what makes the stock market tick. The Crash of '87 should be used not as an excuse to avoid all stock investing forever, but rather as the reason to learn more about what stocks and stock markets are so that you'll be able to take advantage of certain situations.

What is stock?

A share of stock is evidence of ownership in a corporation.

I often hear stocks referred to as equities. Why are they called that?

Stock is often called an equity because the word means "ownership."

Are there different kinds of equities?

There are two types of equity securities: common stock and preferred stock. All corporations issue common stock, but they don't have to issue preferred stock.

Are stocks guaranteed?

No, they're not. They are always unsecured, which means they are not backed or guaranteed by specific corporate assets.

What's the difference between common and preferred stock?

Common stock is the first security a corporation issues. It usually entitles the holder (owner) to vote in the election of directors, and it has the greatest management control in matters of capitalization, etc. Common stock generally offers the greatest overall rate of return for its holder, but it participates in earnings *after* the claim of other securities and, for this reason, has greater risk.

Preferred stock also represents ownership, but it generally carries no voting rights. It has a *fixed* dividend and takes preference over common stock. This means that dividends are paid to preferred stockholders first. Then, if cash is still available, dividends are paid to common stockholders.

You mention that common stock is riskier than preferred stock. Are certain common stocks riskier than others?

Absolutely. The volatility (price fluctuation) may vary greatly among groups of stocks. Stocks of young, growth-oriented companies tend to be riskier than those of the so-called blue-chip companies, which have established themselves over good and bad business and economic cycles. Younger, riskier stocks generally pay little or no dividend because the companies often choose to reinvest that money in expansion, equipment, and research and development. Of course, along with the risk comes the possibility of rapid growth.

What exactly is a blue-chip stock?

The term *blue chip* comes from the game of poker—blue chips have the greatest value! A blue-chip stock earns that designation by having:

- a history of paying dividends in good times *and* bad
- a history of solid yearly profits
- recognition as a leader in a particular industry (GM, McDonald's, Eastman Kodak, for example)
- strong prospects for continued dividend and earnings growth and good competitive position

Could you please explain what a stock exchange is? I feel stupid asking, but I don't really know.

Don't ever feel stupid asking. Remember, there are no stupid questions—there are only stupid answers! An exchange is a marketplace where buyers and sellers come together, although the exchange itself doesn't buy and sell for its own profit. Securities are bought and sold in an auction market. Brokers representing clients or their own account bid for and offer stock for sale.

Which is the largest stock exchange in the United States?

The New York Stock Exchange (NYSE). Established in 1792, more shares are traded on the NYSE than on any other U.S. exchange, and it is the best-known and most respected exchange in the world.

What is the American Stock Exchange?

The American Stock Exchange (ASE), another major exchange, also located in New York City, specializes in trading small- to medium-sized companies as well as a large number of oil and gas companies.

What is NASDAQ?

NASDAQ, also called the over-the-counter (OTC) market, stands for the National Association of Securities Dealers Automated Quotation system. Here, buyers and sellers negotiate trades, unlike in a stock exchange, where the shares are auctioned. Business on an exchange is conducted face to face on the floor of the exchange, while OTC business is transacted through a computer and telephone network of the various dealers. Many more shares are traded on exchanges than in the over-the-counter market.

What happens when I give my broker a buy or sell order?

A lot is accomplished, or should be, in a very short period of time!

1. The broker writes up your order on a ticket and hands it to a wire operator right in the branch office. This operator then enters your order into a computer or a form of teletype machine connected to the firm's main order room.
2. Upon receipt at headquarters, the order is then transmitted to your firm's order desk on the floor of the proper exchange.
3. The order is transmitted from the order desk to the particular trading booth reserved for that company's stock and handed to the floor broker.

4. The broker completes the transaction as quickly as possible and returns the transaction slip to the firm's order desk on the floor. From there, computers reverse the direction your order first took: from order desk to main office to branch office to your broker to you. Simple!

How long should it take from the time I enter the order until my broker receives confirmation of the trade?

When we asked this of an officer of the New York Stock Exchange, we were told that the exchange has the ability to turn the entire transaction around within two minutes. However, how long it takes the firm you do business with may be another matter! An efficient firm working with stock that is constantly trading may make the trade within two to five minutes on an average day.

On Black Monday (October 19, 1987) many investors didn't get status reports on their trades for hours, and some not for days.

How much does it cost me to buy stock?

Since May 1975, when the brokerage industry became deregulated, paving the way for discount brokerage firms, the commissions or transaction charges of full-service brokers have widely varied.

Is there a minimum number of shares I have to purchase?

There is no minimum, but the most common type of order is for 100 shares. This is called a round lot. If you don't buy a round lot, the commission will generally cost you more. In other words, 150 shares will be charged at a higher proportionate rate than 100 or 200 shares. The prices of odd lot orders are based on round lot prices and can't be executed until there has been at least one round lot sale in that stock. Often a 12.5¢ charge (one eighth of a point) per share will be added to the price you pay.

I thought an odd lot referred to some of the traders on the New York Stock Exchange!

What a wonderful thought, but not true! An odd lot is an order of less than 100 shares.

Are all stocks listed on an exchange?

No, they're not. Some stocks are listed in the over-the-counter market, which is a network of telephones and computers, and privately held stock is not listed at all.

How do I know where to find a stock?

Stockbrokers are furnished monthly with a book that lists almost all stocks and identifies where the shares are listed, be it an exchange or the over-the-counter market. If the stock is too small an issue or very infrequently traded, it will be necessary to check the pink sheets, a daily quotation sheet that lists the interdealer wholesale quotes for over-the-counter stocks.

Can I buy and sell stock quickly?

That depends on the stock you own or wish to own. Most stocks listed on the New York and American stock exchanges and many listings on NASDAQ are actively traded and therefore extremely liquid. The only time you will encounter trouble is with a stock issue that trades infrequently, or when there is an imbalance of buyers or sellers, such as investors experienced on Black Monday, October 19, 1987. In that case, you will have to wait until a buyer or seller can be found.

Not long ago, my broker told me that I was unable to purchase stock at the start of the day because of a delayed opening. Does that mean that the entire stock exchange hasn't opened or just my stock?

A delayed opening doesn't mean that the traders and brokers were late to work! The exchange opens on time every day. Simply stated, exchange officials may postpone the beginning of trading in a particular stock because of certain conditions, such as a major influx of buy or sell orders or pending corporate news, that may influence the movement of a stock.

How much time will it take me to learn about the stock market and how to invest in stocks?

A smart investor never stops learning. If you're serious about building your net worth through investing, then realize it can take at least an hour a day of reading and research to take control of your finances. But it's certainly worth the effort! Remember, *no one* will ever be more concerned about your money than you.

What is the Dow Jones Industrial Average?

The Dow Jones Industrial Average (DJIA) is the oldest and most widely quoted of all the market indicators. It is comprised of thirty actively traded blue chip stocks that represent approximately 15 to 20 percent of the market value of New York Stock Exchange stocks.

What does it really mean when I hear on the nightly news that the Dow Jones Industrial Average is up or down?

Unless you personally own every one of the thirty stocks that make up the DJIA, it doesn't mean a great deal. It is a broad indication of market direction. When you hear that the market is up twenty-one points, that simply means that this group of thirty stocks as a whole is up approximately twenty-one points in value. It's a market bellwether only. The DJIA could be substantially up one day and your particular stocks could be down in value.

How is the market value of a stock determined?

The market value of a stock is the price that someone is willing to pay for it. Many things affect what an investor is willing to pay:

- the dividend/earnings growth outlook
- the company's competitive position
- the value of the assets of the corporation
- investor sentiment
- supply and demand for the shares

Prices can also be affected by political and economic developments and other factors that may not be directly associated with the stock itself.

I understand where the market value of a stock comes from, but I have no idea what par value means. Can you explain?

Sure. Par value, or stated value, is nothing more than an arbitrarily assigned value placed on stock when it is first issued. Par value is a stable figure and never changes.

Then what is book value?

Book value is calculated every year and is arrived at by deducting a company's liabilities from its assets and dividing by the number of shares of stock outstanding. Book value will usually be a different amount each year.

What are penny stocks?

These are stocks that typically sell for less than $5 a share and are typically issued by companies with a short or erratic history of earnings and dividends. Generally, penny stocks are very volatile and are not listed on the New York and American stock exchanges because the companies do not meet capital requirements. In other words, the companies aren't large enough.

Where are the biggest profits made in penny stocks?

Many of the biggest profits made in penny stocks are made in IPOs (initial public offerings), better known as new issues. These are the first-time offerings of any stock of a company. Investors in these situations are usually not trying to buy into a company's long-term growth potential, but rather cashing in on temporary investor euphoria.

I hear lots of stories about people who make big profits by investing in penny stocks. Are the stories really true?

Like the fisherman's tale, these stories may or may not be! Don't believe everything you hear. You usually hear only the good news.

Does that mean that investing in penny stocks is risky?

It certainly does. In our opinion, penny stock investing is the most risky of all stock investing and should be avoided by anyone who can't afford to lose his or her investment. Don't forget: When you buy a share of stock worth $1, it doesn't have far to go down before it's worth nothing. A share of stock bought at $20 has a lot more room for error.

I understand how risky investing in penny stocks can be, but I'd like to give it a try. Can you give me some tips so I can invest wisely?

We'd be happy to steer you in the right direction.

- Check out the new-issues track record of the company bringing out the penny stock in which you're interested.
- Set a target price when you purchase the stock. If the stock doubles, take your profits and run! If it drops 10 to 20 percent, bail out. Don't get caught up in your own emotions. Set up and down limits and follow them.
- Don't expect the "hot" deals (issues with more buyers than stock available) unless you do a good amount of business with your broker.
- Invest only *high-risk* capital in penny stocks—money you can *afford* to lose, and no more than 5 percent of your portfolio.

Speaking of capital, how do I know if I can afford to invest in stocks?

That's a very thoughtful question. You must have the ability to take the risks of stock ownership. First, be sure you have adequate insurance and funds for emergencies and a roof over your head. In our opinion, these are the prerequisites before investing in the market. It's also important to have the temperament to own stocks. Many people cannot cope with the fluctuations in price. If you have trouble handling change and uncertainty, forget the stock market!

Is there ever a guarantee that a stock I buy will increase in value?

Absolutely not! Buying stock is risky business. Admittedly, by doing your homework you may be able to tip the odds in your favor, but stocks are not like certificates of deposit at your local bank.

My broker recommended a stock, so I bought 100 shares. The stock has gone down ever since! I originally paid $24 a share. Today my broker called again with the stock at $17 a share and said it's a great time to buy some more. What do you think?

We don't think much of his idea! Many people have been talked into averaging down with the idea that if a stock was a good buy at $24, it's an even better buy at $17. That could be a one-way ticket to nowhere. If the stock began going down immediately after you bought it and has continued to do so, then your broker isn't telling you something, or he never knew the entire story. Do some research on your own before you make any moves. There may be a perfectly legitimate reason for the stock's fall, but we wouldn't buy any more until we knew. You may end up considering to sell after you check it out.

How do people who understand the market decide if a stock is likely to increase in value?

Likely is the key word. Correctly evaluating a stock's growth potential is what separates the children from the adults. Here are some guidelines for intelligent stock picking:

- *dividends:* an excellent indication of a company's growth. Steadily rising dividends over a ten-year period are healthy. Look for uninterrupted dividend payments for at least ten years.
- *competitive position:* The company should be in a growth area of business or in a firmly established niche.
- *rating:* A Standard & Poor's rating of A or better is most desirable.
- *earnings:* The company should have shown improvement in at least five of the last ten years.
- *shareholders:* At least 5 million shares outstanding to ensure your ability to buy/sell shares at will.

Although there are many other recommended ways to choose stocks, we believe that the five checkpoints we have just mentioned are the easiest to understand and the most conservative way to go about investing in stocks.

Everyone seems to know when to buy a stock, but no one has ever told me when to *sell*. What are your thoughts?

This is a very common complaint. Brokerage firms are famous for making lots of buy recommendations but not nearly as many *sells*. While it is impossible to generalize when any individual stock should be sold, let's look at some guidelines.

- When a firm's research analyst changes the recommendation from buy to hold, you're being told, "Don't buy this stock." You aren't being told outright to sell, but this is a time to reevaluate the company. You may decide to sell after you do some homework.
- All the news you're hearing about your stock is *good*. Rumors are running wild. Remember that no stock has *all* good news to report. Some investors sell on good-news rumors because very often the uninformed investor buys on that good news, which typically strengthens the price of the stock.
- Disappointing earnings growth is a big indicator to consider when selling stock.
- When an anticipated event occurs, you may consider selling. Very often, a stock appreciates on the anticipation that an event (patent approval, earnings report, etc.) will occur. After the event or after nothing happens, the stock will very likely weaken in price.
- Watch the price action of a stock. If a stock drops through its fifty-two-week low (you can find that in the financial section of your local newspaper), you should consider selling.
- If you make a mistake and buy a stock that begins a downward turn soon after, cut your losses. Don't stick with a stock headed down because you are emotionally tied to it.

- Always set a high and low price for your stock when you purchase it. When the stock hits either set price, sell.

My broker quoted a stock as 5 bid and 5¾ asked. What does that mean?

The bid is the highest price anyone is willing to pay for a security at a particular time. The asked is the lowest price anyone will accept to sell shares at that time.

I called my broker the other day and asked him to buy 1000 shares of a stock I had been following. He asked me if I wanted to enter a market order or a limit order. I didn't know what he meant, but I was too embarrassed to admit it. Can you define these terms?

Before we answer your question, we want to take a moment to lecture! When dealing with *your* money, don't ever be embarrassed to ask a question when you don't understand. Although in your situation there was probably no damage done, in a swiftly moving stock you might have cost yourself money by not asking the difference between a market and a limit order. Here are the definitions:

- *market order:* An order for stock that is executed at the *current* price of the stock when your order is received. It is the quickest, most efficient way to get an execution. But if a stock is moving up rapidly, you may end up paying more than you expected. If you are selling, a plummeting stock price could cost you a good deal of money.
- *limit order:* An order to purchase stock or sell stock at a specified price or better. Less efficient than a market order, you will not buy or sell if the price isn't reached.

The average investor, not involved in extremely volatile stocks, will do as well entering a market order. Leave limit orders to well-versed investors.

I'd like to be sure that I pay only a certain price for a stock I'm considering buying. Is there a way to enter a limit order that will be good for more than a day if my stock doesn't reach the price I'm looking for?

There sure is. Tell your broker when he enters the order to make it a good-until-canceled order (GTC) instead of a day order, which is only good for that day. Your order will remain on the floor of the exchange until you get your price, even if it takes days or weeks.

What if I change my mind about the stock?

As the name suggests, your GTC limit order can be canceled at any time you decide. There is *no charge* for this service.

My broker recommends that I place a stop order to sell at a certain price every time I buy stock. He claims this will protect me from heavy losses. Is that true?

A well-placed stop order will give you some protection in your stock position. A stop order to sell becomes a market order once the stock's price reaches or passes the specific price stated in the stop order. For example, if you buy a stock at $50 a share and you place a stop order to sell at $42, if the stock fell to the $42 level or lower, your sell order would be triggered. However, the $42 stated on your stop order is not guaranteed. At $42, your order to sell is triggered and you will receive the *next* price. In a badly plummeting stock, the next price could be substantially lower. A stop order does not always get you out at a price you might expect, but it will get you out.

What would happen if I placed a stop order and the market had a very volatile trading day, which also affected my stock?

That's the principal problem with a stop order. If it is placed at a price too close to the current trading price, you might find yourself out of a position when you didn't want to be. If the stock itself was having a day of wide swings, the same thing would happen.

What is a utility stock?

A utility stock is evidence of ownership in electric generating plants, telephone companies, gas, water, or sewer systems—any company that operates public utility services.

My broker claims that utility stocks are appropriate for income-oriented investors such as myself. Is he right?

Yes, he is. Utility stocks usually pay dividends. These dividends will provide income for an investor. When interest rates are down, you will often find the dividend yield of a utility stock better than the yields on bank accounts and CDs. An added plus to investing in utility stocks is the potential growth of the underlying shares as well as periodic dividend increases, with well-run companies.

What's the downside to investing in utility stocks?

Two things can go wrong with a utility stock investment: 1) Lack of appreciation in share price. Because utility stocks are interest rate sensitive, they generally do not perform well in times of rising interest rates. This might cost you growth of your investment. 2) A dividend cut or discontinuation of the dividend could be disastrous to an investor. Dividends are based on the successful running of the company.

I buy utility stocks and blue-chip stocks for income. Do these companies guarantee always to pay dividends?

There are no guarantees. Dividends are paid out of earnings. No earnings, no dividends! Dividends can be suspended if profits are off and the board of directors decides that reinvestment of available cash is preferable to declaring a dividend. But it's not all bad news. Many fine companies have paid dividends for many years without missing a single payment. Your broker has a listing of corporate dividend payments in his Standard & Poor's stock guide. Check with him to see how long your company has paid dividends.

Are there any utility stocks I should avoid?

We recommend that conservative investors avoid electric utilities that have a nuclear power plant under construction or not already on line. We also suggest that you take a very hard, in-depth look at utilities that are now, due to large cash reserves, diversifying into business outside their normal sphere. We prefer the companies that stick to the business they know best.

Are utility stocks bought for growth or income?

Generally, an investor looks for income first and growth second when analyzing utility stocks. The best-case scenario is a combination of the two.

A stock I own just went ex-dividend, according to my broker. Does that mean it's paying an extra dividend?

Nice try! Ex-dividend doesn't mean extra dividend, but it's still good news for you. If you've owned the stock during the period the dividend was declared and five days prior to the ex-dividend date, then you are entitled to payment of the dividend. The fifth day prior to the ex date is called the record date. Any name listed on the record date as an owner of the stock is entitled to that dividend. If you purchase the stock during the five days between the record date and ex date, you don't receive the dividend. Ex-dividend merely means without dividend.

Would it be a smart idea to buy a stock when a dividend is declared and sell it the day the stock goes ex? You'd get to keep the dividend and not have to worry about the stock.

We're happy to see you thinking, but your idea just doesn't work. On the day a stock goes ex, the price is readjusted to account for the dividend. So you'd end up even, no gain at all, just transaction charges. We'll give you an example: Stock XYZ declares a dividend of 50¢ a share. You rush out and buy the stock at $25 a share. You hold the stock until the dividend is paid. On the day the stock goes ex, the opening price of the stock is no longer $25. It opens at $24.50, automatically readjusted to reflect that 50¢ dividend. You end up exactly where you started.

I'm an aggressive investor. My broker has suggested that I short some stock. What is that strategy, and should I do it?

Shorting stock is *not* for the faint of heart. When you short stock, you sell stock that you don't own. The technique is used most often to take advantage of an anticipated decline in the price of a stock. You borrow the stock from your brokerage firm and deliver it to the buyer. For this you are paid the current market rate at the time of the sale. Now you have the cash in your account. You're betting that the price of the stock will go down. If the price does decline, you then buy the same number of shares that you originally sold and return them to the brokerage firm, which expects the borrowed shares to be replaced. There is no time period for shorting stock. If the price drops significantly the next day, you may purchase shares for delivery to the firm.

Can you show a real example of stock shorting?

Let's say you sell short 100 shares of XYZ for $25 a share. The broker lends you 100 shares to deliver to the buyer from his inventory, another firm's, or someone's margin account. When the sale is complete, you receive $2500. Ideally, let's assume that stock XYZ drops to $15 a share. You cover your short sale by buying 100 shares for a total of $1500 and deliver the shares back to the broker. You've covered yourself and made a $1000 profit.

$$
\begin{array}{rcl}
\$2500 & = & \text{Sale of 100 shares @ \$25} \\
-\ \$1500 & = & \text{Cost of buying 100 shares @ \$15} \\
& & \text{to replace borrowed stock} \\
\hline
\$1000 & = & \text{Profit}
\end{array}
$$

We do not show brokerage commissions in any of our examples because the cost of doing business on stock trades varies so greatly from firm to firm.

That sounds great! But suppose the stock goes *up* in value?

Aha! There's the rub. Let's use the same example again. Should the stock appreciate to $30 a share, you've got a loss on your hands. You sold the stock short for $25 a share and received $2500. However, now you have to go into the open market and buy 100 shares at $30 a share to deliver to the lending broker.

$$
\begin{array}{rcl}
\$3000 & = & \text{Cost of buying 100 shares @ \$30} \\
& & \text{to replace borrowed stock} \\
-\ \$2500 & = & \text{Sale of 100 shares @ \$25} \\
\hline
\$500 & = & \text{Loss}
\end{array}
$$

If the stock price had gone higher, the loss would be greater! Shorting is dangerous. It's sometimes profitable, but *always* dangerous!

What is convertible stock?

Convertible stock is a preferred stock that pays a fixed dividend or rate of interest and can be *converted* into common stock at a specified price or conversion ratio. It typically trades in 10-share lots and has a par value ranging from $10 to $100.

Who should buy convertible stock?

You might consider buying convertible stock if you are looking for conservative income with a potential for growth. With convertible stock, you can capitalize on the growth of the underlying common stock shares by converting or you can sit tight on the income that is produced and not convert. It's like having your cake and eating it, too. Convertible stock allows you to play both sides of the fence. However, be aware that for a strict income investment, its dividend is usually less than a straight preferred stock.

I keep hearing about the attractiveness of owning shares in foreign companies. What are your thoughts?

Depending on many factors, the foreign stock markets can be very profitable, offering investors the opportunity to selectively diversify their holdings. Investors wishing to develop a well-rounded portfolio should consider investing overseas—5 percent to a maximum of 10 percent of their total portfolio.

Where can I buy and sell foreign securities?

Most large U.S. brokerage firms have the ability to transact this business. They have foreign offices and investment analysts who closely follow foreign markets in much the same manner as our U.S. market analysts. Reports on foreign stocks are now commonplace at many firms.

Do I have to subscribe to foreign newspapers to follow price quotes?

Thankfully, you don't. Many foreign stocks are traded on the U.S. exchanges, and their quotes are available in most major U.S. newspapers. Look under "over-the-counter stocks" and other minor exchanges. The big companies can be found listed in these two places. For other, less known, foreign firms, check with a broker at any major brokerage firm.

If I decide to invest in foreign stocks, should I find a broker who specializes in the overseas markets?

That type of specialized broker would be darned hard to find. The key to this type of investing is to use a strong firm with foreign branches and an international economist on staff.

What might be a potential problem in buying foreign stock issues?

The biggest problem most U.S. investors encounter when they buy individual foreign stock issues is the lag time that can sometimes occur with news concerning the company. If you're buying stocks in Japan and news comes out concerning a company, the Japanese investor will hear almost immediately and act. You might not receive the same news for a day or two, which could affect the stock price before you can react. For this reason, we strongly recommend investing in an overseas mutual fund instead of individual foreign stocks. For more information on overseas mutual funds, see Chapter 5.

What's the difference between foreign stock and an ADR?

ADR stands for American depository receipt. Like foreign stock securities, ADRs are fully negotiable registered securities of foreign companies and may be bought and sold by American investors. However, unlike a share of foreign stock, ADRs eliminate the need to ship shares between the U.S. and foreign countries. They are bought and sold on American exchanges. ADRs were originally devised to avoid delays in buy and sell transactions. These investments entitle an investor to all dividends and capital gains.

Are foreign stocks an effective hedge against U.S. inflation?

Foreign stocks can hedge U.S. inflation when the outlook for growth in the foreign economy and specific industry sector appears to be healthier than in the U.S. But gains from dividends and capital gains can erode with currency fluctuations.

May I borrow against my holdings in foreign securities?

Yes, many quality stocks from overseas may be used as collateral. Just like American stocks, foreign stocks listed on American exchanges are subject to the Federal Reserve's margin requirements.

Are my securities on deposit at a brokerage firm insured?

Most firms protect your account through the Securities Investor Protection Corporation (SIPC). That's the reference to SIPC you hear at the tail end of a financial services advertisement. SIPC provides funds for use, if necessary, to protect a customer's cash and securities on deposit with a SIPC member. SIPC is to the brokerage industry what FDIC is to the banking industry. The minimum coverage is $500,000 in cash and securities; however, some firms have customer protection up to $10 million per account. Ask your broker how much coverage you have.

I'm very confused by stock splits. Could you please explain them for me?

Don't feel that you're the only one. Stock splits confuse many people. A split causes an increase or decrease in the number of shares outstanding in a corporation but does *not* change the market value of the outstanding shares. When a split occurs, the dollar value of the share declines. Here's an example:

Company XYZ announces a two-for-one split with the stock at $50 a share. You own 100 shares of XYZ, which is worth $5000. After the two-for-one split, you will own 200 shares of XYZ, now worth $25 a share or the same pre-split total value of $5000. Your shares are now worth the same

amount, but you own twice as many. The hope is that the 200 shares will
increase in value and prompt another stock split!

What happens to my dividend when my stock splits?

Generally, the dividend falls in proportion with the split. But a cash-rich
company may not touch the dividend or, if the profits have been exception-
ally good, the dividend may be increased.

Why do companies split their stock?

In many circumstances, a company will offer a stock split to bring down
the price of the individual shares to make that stock more attractive and
affordable to investors, thereby helping the stock's price to rise more quickly,
they hope.

I thought I knew all I needed about stock splits. But my broker called today to tell me that my stock just had a reverse split. What the heck does that mean?

A reverse split *reduces* the number of shares of stock outstanding. Your
total number of shares will be fewer after this type of split, but the value
of your holding will remain the same. Let's give you an example of a
reverse split to make this clearer:

Company XYZ announces a reverse split of one for ten. Let's assume
you own 100 shares at $5 a share, for a total of $500. After the reverse
split, you will own 10 shares at $50 a share, worth the same $500. Your
market value remains the same, but the number of shares you own shrinks.

What's the strategy behind a reverse stock split?

Many companies employ reverse splits for the same reason that other
companies give stock splits—to make a stock more attractive to investors.
Just as a stock selling at $50 a share may be too rich for some investors'
blood, a stock selling at $5 a share may seem too speculative. By raising
the price of the stock, a company may induce investors to perceive that it
is financially more solid.

I own 500 shares of a drug company. A competitor is making a tender offer for my shares. What is a tender offer?

A tender offer is a public offer by another company to buy existing shares
from stockholders. The company offering to buy your shares sets specific
terms, such as price and time. Stockholders are asked to tender (surrender)
their shares for a fixed price, usually more than the current market value.
Often, tender offers are made subject to a minimum or maximum number
of shares being delivered.

Am I guaranteed the tender offer price?

There is no guarantee you will receive the company's offer. There are
potentially two reasons for this: 1) If the minimum number of shares is not

tendered, the company will withdraw its offer. 2) If the tender offer becomes oversubscribed (more shareholders tender than the maximum number needed), the company will return the unneeded shares to stockholders.

My brother has done very well investing in stock warrants and stock rights. What are they?

In a general sense, both rights and warrants give the holder the ability to purchase stock shares at a pre-stipulated price. Both are potentially valuable, depending upon the current market value of the underlying shares of stock. The major difference between the two is time. A right must usually be exercised in a relatively short period of time, while a warrant may have no time limit stipulated at all.

A lot of my friends are talking about the listed option market. What are options?

Listed stock options, commonly known as puts and calls, are contracts that allow an investor to control 100 shares of stock for a pre-agreed period of time for much less money than it would take to buy the 100 shares of stock.

What is a call?

A call entitles the option buyer to purchase 100 shares of a particular stock at a pre-agreed price for a specific amount of time—as little as a few days or for several months—no matter how high the stock price may rise. The call buyer is betting that the stock price will go up.

May I have an example, please?

Let's say that you believe Sears will appreciate in value during the next six months, but you are unwilling or unable to buy 100 shares at $55 per share, for a total of $5500. However, after checking the newspaper, you find that for $375, the option premium, you may have the right to purchase 100 shares of Sears for $55, known as the strike price, no matter how high the per-share price rises during the six months. Now, let's further suppose that you're right and at the end of six months Sears is now selling for $75 per share. The call option you originally purchased for $375 is now worth $2000, because the underlying 100 shares of Sears have appreciated $20 per share. You can either sell the call in the open market for $2000, a $1625 profit, or exercise the option by purchasing the 100 shares of stock at $55 per share. Most option buyers would sell the call at a profit and not exercise it.

That's all well and good, but what happens if Sears stock drops to $35 a share during that period instead of going up to $75?

That's one of the attractions of buying calls. Although the call buyer's profit is unlimited on the upside, the most an option buyer can lose is the amount of the premium—in this case, $375. The call buyer may have bet wrong, but his loss is limited, unlike that of the investor who bought 100 shares at $55 and now owns the same 100 shares worth only $35 per share.

What is a put?

A put gives the buyer the right to *sell* 100 shares of stock at a pre-agreed price (strike price) for a specified period of time.

Why would I purchase a put?

A put buyer is betting that the price of a stock will go down during a particular period—just the opposite of a call buyer, who looks for price appreciation.

Would you give me a put example?

Using Sears again, a six-month put with Sears at $55 a share might cost $325. This would entitle the put buyer to sell 100 shares of Sears at $55 per share. Let's assume that Sears goes down to $35 per share. Because the put owner may then purchase 100 shares of Sears at $35 per share in the open market and sell the shares to the put seller (writer), there is a profit of $1675, $2000 from the spread in stock prices minus the original option premium of $325.

What happens if Sears stock goes up in value?

If at the end of the option period the stock is higher than $55, the put buyer loses his $325 but no more than that.

If the price of a stock doesn't move during the specified period, who does make money?

The option premium is pocketed by the option seller, known as the writer. Very often, an investor who writes (sells) calls owns the underlying stock against which the call is sold.

Why would an investor sell calls against stock that he or she owns?

There are a number of reasons to employ this strategy. Among the most common is the goal of receiving option premiums, which add to the overall return on the stock position and offer at least a measure of downside protection. By that we mean: By receiving a $375 call premium on Sears for a six-month call, the investor is protecting 100 shares of stock against a $3\frac{3}{4}$-point drop. A $375 option premium divided by 100 equals $3\frac{3}{4}$ points of protection. Commissions charged for options and stock purchased are not included in the calculation.

Who would sell a put?

An investor who expects a stock to go up, and would thereby pocket the option premium, or an individual who would actually like to acquire more shares of a stock.

What determines the price of the option premium?

A good question and an important one! The option premium is determined by a number of factors, including:

- supply and demand
- time remaining in the life of the option (duration)
- volatility of the underlying stock
- the level of interest rates and other market factors

You can make a lot of money buying options, can't you?

Yes you can, if you are able to predict which stocks will go up (calls) and which will go down (puts) and *when* these things will happen. Timing is so important because you make money with options only if you own the option during a price climb or fall. Before or after doesn't count!

Are options risky?

Listed stock options may be either very risky or relatively conservative, depending upon the level of expertise of the investor and the option strategy used.

Who should deal in the listed options market?

Option trading is clearly *not* for everybody. Options are appropriate only for those investors who are willing to take time to learn this specialized method of investing It's also important to work with a broker or financial adviser who is experienced in option trading. He or she should be able to furnish you with the names of several happy clients. Options are a very tricky business and should be used only by the informed.

Where can I get more information about listed stock options?

A lot of free information is available from the New York Stock Exchange, at (212) 656-3000; the American Stock Exchange, at (212) 306-1000; and from the Chicago Board Options Exchange, at (312) 786-5600. However, in our opinion, the best single source of information is a book written by Lawrence G. McMillan, called *Options as a Strategic Investment*, published by the New York Institute of Finance, 2 Broadway, New York, New York 10004. You can write for it, or call (212) 344-2900.

My friend has his den loaded with charts and old stock quotes. He says he picks his stocks by using technical analysis. What does he mean?

Technical analysis is a method of judging a stock by supply and demand and charted movements of stock prices. A technical analyst follows the short- to medium-term prospects of a stock or commodity, generally using price cycles, charts of the history of performance, and a variety of data bases. The true technician is unconcerned with a company's balance sheets, assets, or earnings ability.

How does fundamental analysis differ from technical analysis?
They differ in just about every way! A fundamental analyst attempts to predict the future value of a stock by considering economic factors, such as interest rates, gross national product (GNP), inflation, and others. This type of analyst puts great emphasis on a company's balance sheet, assets, earnings, sales, and marketing trends.

It seems as if I receive a prospectus every other day from my broker touting new stock offerings that are coming to market. I think I'd like to do some investing in new stock issues, but I don't have any idea how to read the prospectus. Can you help?
The first bit of help we'd like to give you is, Don't waste your time reading a prospectus if you're not interested in that particular stock. It can cause undue eyestrain and lots of confusion! But if a prospectus does appear interesting, *don't* buy the stock without reading it. The prospectus is the most comprehensive source of information concerning a security. Here are some guidelines:

- Familiarize yourself with the prospectus summary. This will tell you what the company is and how much stock is being offered.
- Thoroughly study the section on risk factors. This section will give you all the things that might adversely affect the performances of the company, which would certainly affect the performance of the stock.
- The "Use of Proceeds" section will tell you how the money raised from the sale of stock will be used. Be sure you are in agreement with the anticipated use of funds.
- The "Management" section is a very important one to go over *in depth*. This will tell you who the officers and directors of the firm are, what their past experience is, their salaries, and any legal problems they may currently have or have had in the past. A company's prospects for success are only as good as the management team. Satisfy yourself that these are the people you want at the helm.
- Finally, read the auditor's report and the company balance sheets. If you can't understand them, have your accountant go over them. You want to be sure that the company is in the black before you get involved.

Don't be overwhelmed. Take it step by step before you commit your hard-earned money.

I own a number of stocks and, consequently, I receive lots of annual reports. They're beautiful to look at, but I haven't a clue how to read one! Any suggestions?
Those annual reports certainly are pretty. Awards are given for the most attractive ones! But beauty is only skin deep. Here are the five important sections to read:

1. *The chairman's/president's letter to shareholders:* This is important because it's supposed to be a realistic view of the company's short- to

long-term prospects. It's also the rationale behind that year's progress or lack of progress. This letter shows how the company looks at itself.

2. *The earnings report or income statement:* This is a summary of the year's sales volume and other income, costs, profits/losses, etc. It compares these figures with the previous year's.
3. *The retained-earnings statement:* This relates what share of company profits is being distributed to shareholders in the form of dividends and what money is being kept in the company. If the dividend is being reduced, you want to know why. Is it due to less profit or more retained earnings?
4. *The price/earnings ratio:* The P/E ratio is the current market value of the stock divided by the annual earnings per share. The annual report won't carry the actual ratio, so you'll have to figure this yourself. You should come up with a figure around the industry average. Other companies involved in the same business make up your company's industry group. If the P/E is lower, it might suggest investor wariness, but if it's higher, the stock might be overpriced.
5. *Footnotes:* All sorts of interesting information can appear in the footnotes. It is a little tedious going through this small print, but there might be one piece of information hidden there that would be very helpful in analyzing the company.

Don't forget: You can receive additional information on your stock holdings from your broker, financial adviser, or the investor-services office at the company.

If I hear P/E ratio one more time, I'm going to scream! Please give me an example so that I can understand it better.

You hear the term *P/E ratio* so often because it is one of the most important fundamental measures of a company's stock's growth potential. Before we give you an example, let's define it again. The P/E ratio is the current price of a stock divided by its earnings per share for a twelve-month period. Here's the example:

A stock selling for $25 a share has earnings of $5 for a twelve-month period. Its P/E ratio is 5.

$$\$25 \text{ divided by } \$5 = 5$$

You are paying five times what a share of stock earns. The more the P/E varies from the industry average, the more speculative the stock is. For example, if the industry average for oil stocks is 15 and your stock has a P/E ration of 40, unless you like to gamble, you might consider selling. Your stock is overpriced for its group. The P/E ratio, also called a stock's multiple, is one easy and effective way to compare stocks of varying prices.

What does the beta of a stock mean?

Beta is the measurement of a stock's volatility in relationship to the rest of the stock market. Volatility is the degree of price fluctuation of a share of stock. The Standard & Poor's 500-stock index has a beta of 1.0. Any

stock with a higher beta is more volatile than the market, while a stock with
a lower beta can be expected to rise and fall in price more slowly than the
overall market. For conservative investing, you should be looking at stocks
with a beta lower than 1.0.

What is contrarian investing?
There is an old maxim on Wall Street that says, "When everyone's buying, sell; and when everyone's selling, buy." In short, contrarian investors
believe that the little guy is usually wrong in picking the direction of stock
prices.

Contrarians sound pretty smart to me! How do they pick their stocks?
A contrarian will evaluate a situation many different ways. Here are a
few ways to go against the herd:

- Find out what stock groups are depressed and why. Some may be depressed only for emotional reasons. If this is the case, find a stock or
  stocks in a group with steady to growing earnings and dividends and a
  growth rate higher than the Standard & Poor's 500.
- When the price/earnings ratio and the price/book value are below the
  Standard & Poor's 500 average, there may be a buying opportunity.
- When debt is no more than 35 to 40 percent of a company's equity, a
  contrarian will consider buying.
- Contrarians don't chase trends. They're much more interested in dull,
  mundane stocks that are profitable!
- Above all, contrarians are patient!

What's the Standard & Poor's 500?
This is an index showing the change in total market value of five hundred
stocks in relationship to their base period of 1941–1943. It's composed
mostly of New York Stock Exchange–listed companies, with some American Stock Exchange and over-the-counter stocks. The S&P 500 represents
almost 80 percent of the market value of all issues traded on the New York
Stock Exchange. Like the Dow Jones Industrial Average, it is an indicator
of market direction and, in our opinion, a better indicator than the thirty
stocks of the DJIA.

**Can computer programs help me pick stocks with good growth poten-
tial?**
Yes. The number of stocks actively traded and all the related information
could fill a gymnasium! Computers can sift through all of this and reduce
the information to a single disk. However, before investing in a computer,
evaluate your needs and your *real* interest in investing. A good computer
system could cost you $3000 or more. Also keep in mind that comput-
ers are not gurus. The saying in computer circles is "Garbage in, garbage
out!" Computers are merely an aid in the decision-making process.

I'm comparing several stocks before I make my investment decisions. I'd like some qualified help. Is there one data service that you would recommend?

One service that we like very much is the series of publications available from Value Line, Inc., 711 Third Avenue, New York, New York 10017. Value Line sells a variety of services designed to tame the flow of paper work on many stocks. Its services aren't cheap, but they are good.

I want to subscribe to an investment newsletter. How do I pick the right one?

There are hundreds of newsletters from which to choose. The first thing you have to decide is what type of investments you are most interested in, and then you must determine whether you are conservative, aggressive, or growth- or income-oriented. Not every newsletter will fit your objectives. Then, before you commit money to a year's subscription, get a trial copy and *read* it thoroughly. Be sure that you understand the writer before buying a full subscription.

Is there some way I can find out how well or how badly a newsletter's recommendations did over a period of time before I subscribe?

There is a way. A frequent radio and television guest of ours, Mark Hulbert, tracks the results of more than a hundred investment newsletters. Mark invests a hypothetical $10,000 according to the recommendations of *each* newsletter he follows. He makes all the recommended changes, and at the end of the year, he tallies his results. He also rates newsletter performance on a monthly basis throughout the year. All these results are published in his *Hulbert Financial Digest* so his subscribers can know who has the best track record before they subscribe to a newsletter. Mark offers a five-issue trial for $37.50. You can reach him by writing or phoning:

> *The Hulbert Financial Digest*
> 316 Commerce
> Alexandria, VA 22314
> (800) 443-0100 Ext. 459
> (703) 683-5905 Ext. 459

It's well worth a try!

How can I get trial newsletters before I make a final decision?

The Select Information Exchange offers readers an opportunity to try fifteen different newsletters in its catalogue for only $7.97. You get one to five issues of each newsletter, and the $7.97 may be applied partially to the subscription price of the newsletter you choose.

Select Information Exchange
2315 Broadway
New York, New York 10024
(212) 874-6408

I've never invested before and I don't know anything about the stock market. There's an investment club in town that I've been asked to join. Would this be something for me or is it too advanced?

An investment club would be a great way to start. This club concept really works and often allows you to earn while you learn! Investment clubs are usually made up of people with no investment experience when they start and, usually, very little money. Most clubs have about fifteen members, who contribute between $25 and $30 a month. The group researches stocks and economic and investment conditions. After recommendations are made, the group votes on what stock or stocks to buy. Generally, every investment club has one or more experienced investors as members to help newcomers.

I'd like to join an investment club. How am I obligated, though, if I don't want to stay with it?

You're under no obligation to stay with a club. In fact, there's generally no time period involved. When you decide to leave, you will receive your pro-rata share of the portfolio either from cash on hand or from the sale of stock.

How can I start an investment club?

Contact the National Association of Investor Corporations, 1515 East 11 Mile Road, Royal Oak, Michigan 48067, (313) 543-0612. The NAIC will help you form a new club with sample forms and a how-to kit.

I'm really unhappy with my broker. I've finally decided to change firms and go with someone else. What's the proper procedure in transferring my account?

The firm to which you're transferring will assist you in the move. It will ask you to fill out a transfer-of-account form, which contains your list of holdings and other pertinent information. The new firm will then submit this form to your old firm. This *should* take from one to two weeks. If the procedure takes more than two weeks, complain to *both* firms! More than likely, the tie-up will be with the former firm. It may drag its feet in hopes of keeping your account.

May I buy and sell securities in my account while it is being transferred?

Yes you may, but contact your broker for the specific details.

My husband just died and I'd like to change the names on all our stocks to my name only. How can I do that and how much will it cost?

There are two simple ways to handle a name change:

1. Instruct your broker to have the firm handle this request. The firm will contact the transfer agent listed on the stock certificates, and with the necessary documentation, such as a death certificate, within a few weeks you'll receive new certificates with only your name on them. The cost of this differs among firms. It could cost nothing or it may cost as much as $50.
2. For no charge except postage and phone calls, you can effect the change yourself by contacting the same transfer agent listed on the certificates. This is usually a major bank. The transfer agent will instruct you in the proper procedure.

My wife and I have all our stock certificates in joint name with the right of survivorship. Is this the right way to do it?

There are both benefits and disadvantages to keeping your stock in joint name. It's up to you to decide whether the good points outweigh the bad. You can also refer to Chapter 15, entitled "Estate Planning," which discusses the proper method of ownership, but here's the way things stack up:

- *Benefits:*
  1. Upon death, speedy settlement of the estate.
  2. It bypasses probate.
  3. There are reduced administrative costs.

- *Disadvantages:*
  1. Both must agree to a sale of the securities.
  2. Paper work to reregister stock in a single name after the death of one.
  3. Paper work to reregister stock in case of a divorce.

I've misplaced a stock certificate for 500 shares of stock. I've searched high and low, but I can't find the certificate. Is there anything I can do or am I out the amount the 500 shares were worth?

If you truly have lost the certificate, notify the transfer agent immediately! Most often, a stop transfer will be placed on the account for three months. A stop transfer prohibits the stock from being sold. The company will ask you to file an affidavit of loss and you will have to buy a surety bond, which will cost you about 3 percent of the market value of the 500 shares. This surety bond protects the company from any financial loss. After you complete all this, the company will reissue new shares in your name. We would recommend after you have this all straightened out that you either make plans to leave your certificates with the brokerage firm or buy a bank safe-deposit box for future storage. Stock certificates are easily negotiable. They must be guarded in the same manner as cash.

Do you recommend that I keep my own stock certificates or leave them at my brokerage office?

We always recommend that you leave the stock certificates with the firm, known as leaving stock in street name. We have heard too many times about lost certificates.

Full-service brokerage firms charge so much more in commissions than discount brokerage firms. Do you recommend using a discount broker to buy and sell stock?

If you are making your own decisions concerning which stocks to buy and sell, by all means use a discount broker to save money on commissions. Full-service brokerage commissions are worth the price only if you have reached the decision to buy or sell because of firm research provided.

How do I choose the right broker?

See Chapter 10 for a full discussion of this question. A broker/financial adviser is as important to your financial health as choosing the right doctor is to your physical health.

Before investing in any stocks I did some studying about them. I believe I'm now ready to begin investing. The only thing that hasn't been explained is how to read a stock quote in the newspaper. Can you help?

Of course. Stock owners should check the prices of their stocks daily. It's important to understand what all those columns of numbers mean. Let's use AT&T as an example.

AT&T   1.20   3.4   26   63335 $35^7/_8$ $34^7/_8$ $35^3/_8$ $+^5/_8$

- AT&T is the company name, in this case American Telephone and Telegraph.
- 1.20 signifies the annual dividend. AT&T pays 30¢ per share four times a year, for a total of $1.20 a year per share.
- 3.4 tells you the dividend yield of the stock based on the closing price that day.
- 26 is the P/E ratio, which is explained earlier in this chapter. The P/E tells you that at the current price of AT&T stock, you are paying twenty six times the earnings per share of the company.
- 63335 refers to the number of shares (in hundreds) traded that day. In this case, 6,333,500 shares traded hands.
- $35^7/_8$ tells you the highest price the stock reached that day.
- $34^7/_8$ shows the lowest price the stock traded at that day.
- $35^3/_8$ is the closing price of the stock for that day.
- $+^5/_8$ tells you that the stock rose $^5/_8$ of a point, or $.625 per share, from the closing price the day before.

How much is an eighth of a point worth?

Every eighth of a point is worth 12½¢. Therefore, $^3/_8$ equals 37½¢; $^5/_8$ equals 62½¢; and $^7/_8$ equals 87½¢. The $35^3/_8$ in the AT&T quote means that each share of the stock is worth $35.375.

I bought some AT&T stock last week. My broker told me that its stock symbol is T. However, when I look in the financial section every day, I can't find T listed. Why?

When stocks are listed daily in newspapers, the stock exchange symbol is not used. All stocks placed in the daily newspapers use either the full name of the company or a shortened, recognizable form of the corporate name. It is easier to look for the company name in the alphabetical listing than to remember a large group of stock symbols. It's also important to understand that the business section of a newspaper cannot list every stock traded on every exchange, for lack of space. Therefore, only those stocks that trade widely and daily are given space there.

I don't feel confident in picking individual stocks. Is there another way I can participate in the stock market?

Yes. Mutual funds are for you. See Chapter 6 for a complete explanation of mutual funds.

SUMMARY

There's an old investment adage that says, "The only people who really make money are the people who *own* something." By investing in stocks, anyone with a few dollars can become an owner of a piece of corporate America and perhaps make a good deal of money. For every story of an investment gone sour, there are an equal number of success stories. There are profits to be made if you keep these suggestions in mind:

- Educate yourself *before* you invest.
- Don't jump on emotional bandwagons. Buy stocks that make economic sense.
- Have patience: Rome wasn't built in a day.
- When you make a mistake, admit it and *sell*.
- Don't be greedy. When you have a good profit, take it.
- Don't follow hot tips. They often lead to cold stocks.
- Set profit and loss limits when you first buy a stock, and stick with them. It's better to leave the game early and return to play another day.

Successful stock investing is a combination of smart planning and good timing!

FURTHER INFORMATION
BOOKS

Questions and Answers About
  Today's Securities Market
Nachman Bench
(Prentice-Hall)

Dividends Don't Lie
Weiss/Lane
(Longman Financial Services
  Publishing)

A Random Walk Down Wall Street
Burton Malkeil
(W.W. Norton)

One up on Wall Street
Peter Lynch
(Simon & Schuster)

The Prudent Speculator: Al Frank on
  Investing
Al Frank
(Dow Jones-Irwin)

Handbook of Financial Markets
Frank J. Fabozzi and Frank Zarb
(Dow Jones-Irwin)

The Mathematics of Investing
Michael J. Thomsett
(Wiley & Sons)

The Dow Jones-Irwin Guide to Using
  the Wall Street Journal
Michael B. Lehman
(Dow Jones-Irwin, 3rd Edition)

Stan Weinstein's Secrets for Profiting
  in Both Bull and Bear Markets
Stan Weinstein
(Dow Jones-Irwin)

NEWSLETTERS

Fundamental Analysis

The Addison Report
P.O. Box 402
Franklin, Massachusetts 02038

Dow Theory Forecasts
7412 Calumet Avenue
Hammond, Indiana 46324

The Prudent Speculator
P. O. Box 1767
Santa Monica, California 90406

Standard & Poor's—The Outlook
Standard & Poor's Corporation
25 Broadway
New York, New York 10004

The Value Line Investment Survey
Value Line, Inc.
711 Third Avenue
New York, New York 10017

Technical Analysis

The Chartist
P. O. Box 3160
Long Beach, California 90803

The Granville Market Letter
P. O. Drawer 413006
Kansas City, Missouri 64141

The Professional Tape Reader
P.O. Box 2407
Hollywood, Florida 33022

The Professional Investor
Lynatrace, Inc.
Pompano Beach, Florida 33061

Penny Stocks

The Bowser Report
P.O. Box 6278
Newport News, Virginia 23606

Penny Stock Preview
Idea Publishing
55 East Afton Avenue
Yardley, Pennsylvania 19067

Over-the-Counter Stocks

OTC Insight
P.O. Box 1329
El Cerrito, California 94530

Value Line OTC Special Situation
  Service
Value Line, Inc.
711 Third Avenue
New York, New York 10017

New Issues

New Issues
The Institute for Econometric
  Research
3471 N. Federal Highway
Fort Lauderdale, Florida 33306

The Value Line New Issues Service
Value Line, Inc.
711 Third Avenue
New York, New York 10017

MISCELLANEOUS

The American Association of
  Individual Investors
612 N. Michigan Avenue
Chicago, Illinois 60611
(312) 280-0170
AAII Journal—published monthly

Securities Investor Protection
  Corporation
900 17th Street, N.W.
Suite 800
Washington, D.C. 20006
(202) 223-8400

New York Stock Exchange
11 Wall Street
New York, New York 10005
(212) 650-3000
(many pamphlets available)

American Stock Exchange
86 Trinity Place
New York, New York 10006
(212) 306-1000
(many pamphlets available)

4

Bonds

The famous nineteenth-century playwright R. B. Sheridan was frequently in debt. One day, when his tailor got tired of asking Sheridan to pay the bill, he suggested that Sheridan pay the interest on it. Sheridan replied, "It is not my interest to pay the principal nor my principle to pay the interest."

Since the time of George Washington, bonds have been issued to raise money without giving up ownership. When we buy stock, we become owners of the issuing company and so become entitled to any dividends and fruits of corporate growth. When we buy bonds, we don't become owners. We merely become *lenders* to the issuer. Bonds have no growth potential for the owner, generally. They provide *fixed income* without growth, although in some cases there *is* capital-gain potential.

In the past, an investor could buy a bond and hold it until maturity without fear. However, in the past five to ten years, fluctuating interest rates have changed things.

Gone are the days when an investor could buy bonds, lock them away, and forget about them. Today's bond buyers have to be more sophisticated and flexible. Bonds, once considered a proper investment for widows and orphans because of their safety and predictability, have become less predictable and far more complex. This doesn't mean you should avoid bonds. It means you must take some time to understand their workings.

Bonds of one kind or another have an important place in everyone's portfolio. In this chapter we will answer the most frequent questions we have received to help you get a clear, understandable idea of what bonds are, how they work, and how you can get maximum return from them.

What is a bond?

A bond is a debt security. It represents a creditor of a company, *not* an owner. Before a company can pay dividends to stockholders, it must first pay interest to bondholders. If a company files for bankruptcy, the bondholder receives his or her share of proceeds from the sale of the company assets first. These claims are settled *before* the claims of any stockholders. For this reason bonds are called senior securities. A bond is basically an IOU that says if you buy a bond with stated face value (usually $1000), the issuing company or authority will pay you a set amount of interest twice a year and the face value at maturity—that is, the date on which the bondholder is repaid.

Why are bonds called fixed-income securities?

There's a simple answer to that. Most investors buy bonds because they can depend on a predictable, *fixed* flow of income from these securities. In other words, you will receive the same amount of interest every time it's paid.

Does a company make any promises to me when I buy a bond?

The company does unconditionally promise to repay to you the principal amount (face value written on the certificate) at a specific date in the future, called the maturity date.

Do some bonds last forever?

No, they don't. Bonds are normally issued with maturity dates that range from ten to forty years. The most popular maturities with investors and with the corporations are generally those in the twenty-to-thirty-year range.

In what denominations do they issue bonds?

Usually, bonds are issued in $1000 denominations.

My father-in-law buys a lot of bonds. He's always telling me to buy bearer bonds instead of registered bonds. What's the difference?

Bearer bonds, also called coupon bonds, are bonds issued without a record of the owner's name. Whoever holds the bond is considered the owner. It's a negotiable instrument. A registered bond is just the opposite. It specifically states the name of the owner on the face of the bond certificate and in the records of the trustee.

Why do some people think that bearer bonds are better than registered bonds?

Many people prefer the privacy that bearer bonds offer over the public nature of registered bonds, which list the bondholder's name in the records of the trustee.

Are there any other reasons why some investors prefer bearer bonds?

Yes, although we don't mean to encourage this line of thinking! Since there is no record of the owner's name, some people buy bearer bonds and avoid mentioning the fact to Uncle Sam in hopes of avoiding tax on the income the bond produces. However, the IRS has gotten wise to this practice, and your Social Security number must now be provided when you present a coupon for payment!

Where can I get bearer bonds?

Bearer bonds are no longer issued. The practice was stopped in June 1983. The only bearer bonds available now are those that were issued prior to that date and offered for resale in the secondary market.

How often do bonds pay interest?

The interest on a bond is usually paid semiannually throughout the life of the bond. Generally, payments are made on either the first or fifteenth of the month.

What does my broker mean when he talks about a bond's par value?

Par value refers to the face amount (principal amount) of the bond stated on the certificate. For example, a $1000 AT&T bond priced at par would be selling for $1000.

Is the price of a bond the same as its par value?

Not often! If you buy a bond that is newly issued at par, then the price will be the same. However, as soon as the bonds begin trading in the open market, their prices rise and fall in the same way a stock's price will. Once a bond begins trading, it can be difficult to find one with the same price and par value.

I bought some bonds the other day from my broker. He said they would cost me only $985 each. But when I received the confirmation slip from the firm, it had the price of the bond listed as 98½. Who's wrong?

Nobody's wrong. When bond prices are written, they are expressed as *percentages* of the principal amount of the bond. A little math will explain the misunderstanding. You paid 98½ *percent* of the $1000 face amount, or $985.

When I buy a bond, when must I pay for it? Sometimes it takes a month before I receive my certificate of ownership. Can't I wait until then?

No, you can't. Almost all bond transactions are made "regular way." Like stock transactions, regular way calls for settlement on or before the fifth business day following the trade. Even though you may not receive your certificate immediately, you are still considered the owner of the bond, and therefore you must pay within that time period.

When I sell a bond, how soon must I deliver the certificate to my broker?

You have the same five business days for delivery of the certificate as you have to pay for the purchase of a bond.

I know that a broker earns a commission when I buy or sell bonds, but I don't know how much or who pays, the buyer or the seller.

You pay the broker a commission on either the purchase or sale of bonds. The commission isn't as clearly defined as it is with stocks and mutual funds. The broker's commission is added into the price you pay when you buy or the money you receive when you sell. For example, a bond you plan to buy is quoted as 98½, or $985. Since most bond commissions range from $10 to $30 per bond, the actual price of it would be somewhere between $955 to $975. If you were selling a bond and the broker told you he could get you $1050 for each bond, he would actually be selling the bond to someone else for $1060 to $1080 apiece. You're paying a commission on either side of the transaction.

I bought my first bonds the other day. The broker said I was buying them at par, so I bought ten bonds, which I assumed would cost me $10,000. When I received the confirmation, I was billed for $10,144.40. Is the extra charge the broker's commission?

No, it's not. The broker's commission was in the $1000 per bond that you paid. The actual price of the bond might have been only $970, but the firm priced it at par ($1000) to pay the broker a commission and make a profit for itself. The extra charge you found on your bill is for accrued interest. Accrued interest is added to the cost of the buy transaction because as the new owner, you will receive the full interest payment on the next coupon date even though you didn't own the bonds for the full interest period. Since the seller owned the bonds for a piece of that interest period, he's entitled to his fair share. You pay him when you buy, so that you don't have to track him down when the check arrives.

I still don't understand exactly how accrued interest works. Can you give me an example?

We know how confusing it can be! The clearest parallel we can think of is land taxes on your home when you sell it. Most states collect real estate taxes in *anticipation* of the coming year. In other words, you pay taxes on your home before you use it. If you were to sell the house during the course of that year, the buyer would rebate (pay back to you) the amount of taxes you paid and weren't there to use. Accrued interest works basically the same way.

A broker called the other day. He was trying to sell me some bonds. They sounded pretty interesting. But when he called them debentures, he lost me! What's a debenture?

A debenture is like an unsecured loan. There is no specific asset of the issuer pledged against it. It's backed only by the corporation's *good name*. If the issuer defaulted, there would be no equipment, building, or property that could be sold to pay back bondholders. Debentures were popularized by AT&T and are the most common type of corporate bonds sold.

Are debentures the only kinds of bonds available?

Not at all. Corporate bonds called mortgage bonds are also available.

What's the difference between a debenture and a mortgage bond?

A mortgage bond has pledged against it a specific asset like land, machinery, or a building. It's like a secured loan. If the issuer were to default on a mortgage bond, the bondholders would be able to recoup their money through the sale of the asset that's been pledged.

Which type of bond has a higher yield?

Hands down, it's the debenture. Because there is no specific asset pledged against the debenture, there is greater risk. Don't ever forget the first rule of investing: The greater the risk, the greater the reward.

Are some debentures more risky than others?

Yes, there is more risk with some bonds than others. Remember that the good name of a company is all you have when you buy a debenture. So if you're interested in a particular one, you want to make sure that the name behind it is a secure one.

How can I check out the financial strength of a company without having to wade through a complex balance sheet?

Two major rating services, Standard & Poor's and Moody's investor services, evaluate the financial soundness of the issuer and make their ratings decisions after a thorough inspection.

How are bonds rated?

Standard & Poor's rates bonds from AAA (the highest rating), AA, A, BBB, down to D. Moody's uses Aaa, Aa, A, Baa, etc. A conservative investor should make sure that any bond he or she buys is rated *at least* BBB by S&P and Baa by Moody's. Your broker is able to give you (and should give you) the rating of any bond you're considering *before* you buy it.

Does an AAA rating from Standard & Poor's and Moody's guarantee that the company won't default on my bonds?

There is absolutely no guarantee. However, you can take comfort in the fact that no investment-grade bond (a bond rated BBB/Baa or better) has ever defaulted. But these two ratings services do change the ratings on issuers from time to time. That's why we recommend that all bond buyers check the ratings on their bonds periodically.

I've heard that interest rates affect the price of a bond, but I don't understand why. Can you explain?

Sure. During the life of a bond, its current market value (price) will fluctuate as general interest rates rise and fall. If interest rates go up, the value of the bond goes down, and vice versa. Simply stated, the market value of a bond moves in the opposite direction of interest rates.

If you buy a bond with a yield of 9 percent and interest rates go up to 11 percent, the value of that 9 percent bond drops because it's paying a lower rate of interest than a new bond would.

Let's suppose, using the same example, that interest rates go down to 7 percent. Your 9 percent bond now looks *great*, and it will appreciate in value because of investor demand for your higher-paying bond. People are willing to pay more for something they want. So you see that interest rates have the *greatest* effect on bond values.

What sets the level of interest rates being paid on bonds?

Basically, the current level of interest rates at the time the bond is issued is what determines the yields. The credit rating of the issuer also comes into play, because a less credit-worthy issuer must pay more than current rates to attract investors.

How are bond yields calculated?

The formula is really very simple. Just divide the annual interest paid on the bond by the price of the bond. Here's an example: Suppose you paid par ($1000) for a bond that pays $100 in interest every year. The yield on that bond is 10 percent ($100 divided by $1000 equals 10 percent).

Now let's assume you bought another bond that also pays $100 a year in interest, but this bond cost you only $900. Then your yield would be 11 percent ($100 divided by $900 equals 11 percent).

What's the difference between a bond's yield to maturity and its current yield? I thought they were the same thing.

They're not usually the same thing at all! If you can buy a newly issued bond at par ($1000) and hold it until it matures, your current yield and yield to maturity would be the same. But bonds are most often bought and sold for more (a premium) or less (a discount) than their face amount. As the price changes, so does the current yield. For example, if a bond pays $70 a year in interest on a $1000 face amount, the yield of that bond is 7 percent. However, $70 interest on a bond that costs you $1100 yields you only 6 percent because it cost you $100 more than the face value to get that yield and the yield is calculated only on the initial $1000. This is how yield to maturity is calculated. Current yield, however, is figured every day by that day's price (value) of the bond and divided into its coupon yield.

Okay, I think I understand current yield and yield to maturity, but how does yield to call figure into all this?

Before we muddy the waters any further, let's define what a bond's call provision is. This provision is a written agreement between an issuing corporation and its bondholders that gives the corporation the *option* to redeem the bonds at a specified price before their maturity date. Yield to call throws another potential monkey wrench into the works! A bond that yields a certain amount from issue date to maturity will yield a little less to an investor if it is called early. Yield to call is the rate of return that accounts for the cash difference between what the bond cost and the proceeds you may receive, calculated to the earliest date that the bond may be called away from you.

Would I be smart to avoid callable bonds?

Maybe and maybe not. A wise bond buyer always asks about call dates before he or she buys. We recommend that you *know* if and when your bonds may be called. If you're considering buying bonds at a premium (bonds that cost more than the $1000 face amount) because the interest rate is so much better than prevailing rates at that time, be aware that an early call at a price less than what you paid for the bond could cost you some money. Nevertheless, the rate may be so favorable you will want to buy the bond anyway.

How will I know if my bonds have been called?

If you own registered bonds, you will receive a notice about the call. If you own bearer bonds and you miss a notification in the financial section of the newspaper, you won't find out until you take the next coupon in for redemption. This could mean a loss of interest for you, because the issuer won't pay interest beyond the call date.

What's so bad about being called?

The major problem in being called is that you have to invest that returned principal at *current* rates, which generally will be lower than the rate of the called bond. Look for ten-year call protection; i.e., the issuer can't call your bond for at least ten years.

Can I get any protection from calls?

You can't buy an insurance policy, if that's what you want to know, but there is some protection for you. Bonds generally have an initial noncallable period, such as five to ten years after the bonds have been issued. You also have a degree of protection built in, because bonds are generally called at premium prices to help cover an investor's loss. The call prices decrease as the bond gets closer to maturity.

What do you mean when you say bonds are called at premium prices to help cover the investor's loss?

You are paid more than the $1000 the bond would be worth if held to maturity. The issuing company or agency does this because you will now have to reinvest that returned principal at lower interest rates than the rate you were receiving on the called bond. Remember, issuers call high-interest-paying bonds in times when interest rates are down, in order to save money. You are reinvesting returned principal in lower-interest-rate times and, thus, receiving less income. You have lost an opportunity for a better return.

Shouldn't the broker who sold the bonds to me tell me my bonds are about to be called?

Should—yes. But he or she may *not*. It's ultimately *your* responsibility to keep track of possible bond call dates.

How can I keep track of a bond's call dates?

There are two ways to do this. First, ask your broker to check his or her *Standard & Poor's Bond Guide* and give you a list of the call dates. Second, with list in hand, check the financial section of your newspaper on or around the dates of the possible calls. When an issuer calls in bonds, the serial numbers and the particular bond issue may be listed in the newspaper.

Is refunding the same as calling a bond?

No, it's not. Refunding means retiring a bond issue, using money that's been raised from the sale of new bonds. A call is accomplished with money already on hand within the company. Issuers can opt to refund all of an issue or only part of it. However, refunding is usually done on an entire issue. If it's worth the issuer's while to refund a portion of an issue, then it's generally worth it to refund the entire issue.

My broker told me that my bonds have a sinking fund. Is the company insuring ships?

Not unless ship insurance is part of the company's regular business! A sinking fund consists of cash or bonds that are deposited with the bond trustee. In this way, funds are always available with which to redeem bonds. This allows the issuer to retire gradually the entire bond issue without having to dip into cash reserves, which may be better used for other projects.

Who should buy corporate bonds?

Generally speaking, corporate bonds are most appropriate for income-oriented investors. But bonds are certainly appropriate for a piece of every investor's portfolio, particularly if you can find bonds priced at a discount, with a good rating—not easy, but sometimes possible.

What's the difference between a corporate and a municipal bond?

A corporate bond is generally issued by a corporation, and the interest the bond pays is fully taxable. A municipal bond, better known as a tax-free, is issued by an authorized issuing authority, such as a state, city, or governmental entity, whose interest payments are generally exempt from federal taxation.

Aren't some municipal bonds also exempt from city and state taxes?

That depends on where you, the buyer, live. If you buy a bond issued by an authority in your own state, *generally* the interest you earn will also be exempt from state and city taxes. If you buy an out-of-state bond, you will be exempt only from paying federal taxes. But there are a few exceptions to this rule. Bonds issued by Puerto Rico, the District of Columbia, and the U.S. Virgin Islands are exempt from *all* taxes, no matter where you live.

Who should buy municipal bonds?

The Tax Reform Act of 1986 made the distinction between taxable and tax-free bond buyers a whole lot more difficult. But let's talk generally. An investor in the 28 percent tax bracket or higher should consider municipal bonds. As with all taxable versus tax-free decisions, your accountant should also be questioned before you make your final decision.

Of course if your income is higher than these figures, you are even more likely a municipal bond investor, but bear in mind that not everyone in these income ranges should necessarily invest in municipal bonds. See your accountant first.

My wife and I make $51,000 combined income and we have an opportunity to buy a 8% tax-free bond or a 10% taxable bond. Are we better off buying the taxable bond or the tax-free one?

"Better off" must be defined as having more money in your pocket after taxes! Let's compare taxable and tax-free by calculating what's called the equivalent yield of the two bonds. Here's a quick formula to help you work the question out:

Your joint tax bracket is 28 percent. Deduct 28 percent from 100 percent = 72 percent. Now divide the tax-free yield (8 percent) by 72 percent.

The tax-free yield equals an 11.1 percent taxable yield. Simply stated, in your tax bracket you would have to buy a taxable bond yielding 11.1 percent to equal the "net" return of an 8 percent tax-free bond. In your case, go for the tax-free bond.

I understand that due to tax reform, some municipal bonds are no longer tax-free. Is this an ugly rumor?

Ugly perhaps, but not a rumor. So-called private-purpose bonds issued *after* August 7, 1986, are no longer exempt from taxes. These are issues where more than $15 million or 10 percent of bond proceeds (whichever is *less*) is used by a party other than a state or local government. To put that into plain English, the bonds affected by this ruling are industrial development bonds, single-family and multifamily housing bonds, airport bonds, and student-loan bonds. But *only* bonds issued after August 7, 1986, fall into this taxable/tax-free category. Check with your broker before you buy or before you pass up a bond.

What types of municipal bonds are available?
There are basically two types of municipal bonds: general obligation bonds and revenue bonds. A *general obligation bond* (GO) is backed by the full faith, credit, and taxing ability of the issuing municipality. Interest and principal on a *revenue bond* is payable only from the specific earnings of the project for which the bond was issued. For example, bonds issued to build a toll bridge may pay interest and principal to the bondholder only from the collected revenues that come from the tolls imposed on the vehicles that use the bridge.

My father buys only general obligation bonds. He refuses to invest in revenue bonds. Can you tell me why?
To some older investors, revenue bonds have a somewhat tarnished reputation because if the project fails, there is no other pot to go to for money. Your father may remember that in the past, a number of revenue bonds defaulted. Revenue bonds do offer a somewhat higher yield because they represent a greater risk.

I didn't think municipal bonds ever defaulted.
Unfortunately they do, but there haven't been too many cases. Since the late 1920s, only about 1 percent of all municipal bonds issued have stopped paying interest or principal (defaulted), a darn good record. Of that 1 percent however, 75 percent of the defaults occurred in revenue bonds, the most recent being the Washington Public Power Supply (WPPSS) bonds, better known as WHOOPS bonds.

I'm a very conservative investor. Can I get insurance on my bonds to protect me from default?
You sure can. There are agencies such as American Municipal Bond Assurance (AMBAC), the Municipal Bond Insurance Association (MBIA), and others who insure municipal bond issues to attract conservative investors.

How much does this insurance cost me?
When you ask the question that way, we assume you expect an insurance bill in the mail. But that's not the way it works. Generally, an insured bond gives you 1/4–1/2 percent *less* in its yield. You don't pay any direct cost. You give up a small percentage of the yield that you will receive. However, the price is worth the cost to many investors.

Is it possible to insure all the bonds I buy?
No, it's not. Bonds are sold either insured or uninsured. Insurance cannot be arbitrarily added to your bonds as you would insure a car or home.

I'm interested in buying either taxable or tax-free newly issued bonds. Where can I get a list of new bonds coming out?

Brokers in most brokerage firms receive a listing of available bonds on a daily basis. Just ask to be called when a newly issued bond fits the criteria that you have established with your broker.

How can I get a price quote on my particular bond?

Many bonds are quoted in the financial pages of your local newspaper. Here's how to read a bond quote:

AT&Ts 8¾ 00 8.6 170 102 101⅞ 102 −¼

- AT&T is the company symbol, in this case American Telephone and Telegraph.
- 8¾ is the coupon rate of interest per $1000 or $87.50 a year interest.
- 00 stands for the year of maturity, which is 2000.
- 8.6 is the *current* yield, calculated on the closing price.
- 170 equals $170,000, the dollar value of bonds traded that day.
- 102 equals $1020, the highest price the bond traded at that day.
- 101⅞ equals $1018.75, the lowest price the bond traded at that day.
- 102 equals $1020, the price at which the bond closed.
- −¼ equals $25.00; how much the bond lost in value from the close the day before. (If this had been a +¼, the bond would have gained $25 in value.)

My bonds are not listed in the financial section of my newspaper. Where can I get a quote for an unlisted bond?

Relatively current prices for bonds can be found in Standard & Poor's *Weekly Bond Outlook* and Moody's *Weekly Bond Survey*. Your broker/banker has access to these publications. So just ask!

On two separate occasions I've called a couple of brokers and asked for price quotes on bonds I was considering selling. Both times I was told that it would take time to figure out the price and they would get back to me. Why couldn't they give me a price immediately?

Unlike stocks, most bonds do not trade on an exchange. Therefore, when you call a broker and ask for a price on bonds you wish to sell, the broker contacts the firm's bond trading desk to ask for a price. Oftentimes, the buyer of your bonds will be your brokerage firm. Before the trading desk will give the broker a price, traders check with other firms to see what prices your bonds are getting in other trades, and they also check their own inventory to see how badly they want to have your bonds. This can take time, especially since your broker isn't the only one in the firm asking for bond prices and a trading desk isn't staffed with thousands of people.

Where can I buy and sell municipal bonds?

We suggest that you deal with a firm that *specializes* in municipal bonds. Remember, we are in an age of specialization. If you are unable to find such a firm in your area, deal with a firm's or bank's municipal bond department. You'll probably have to push hard to get that access, but it will be well worth the trouble. At the very least, do your municipal bond business with a broker who specializes in municipal bonds. Many brokers lack the expertise to advise you wisely, and unless they do a great deal of business in this area, they may not be able to get you the best bonds available.

Why do you recommend that I deal with someone who specializes in bonds? Aren't bonds traded widely and available to everybody?

It takes money for a firm to have a wide inventory of many different bond issues, and smaller firms just can't afford to do this. Often you will have a broker call and say, "I have some XYZ bonds available today." That means his firm's bond department made a purchase of a particular number of bonds and there are just so many available for sale. It's often a case of first come, first served. The more specialized a broker is, the better his or her chances of getting a certain bond issue for clients. It's the same with the firm. The bigger the firm, the better your odds of being offered a wider variety of bonds.

What are the commission charges for buying and selling bonds?

Charges vary from transaction to transaction and from firm to firm. It could cost you from $5 to $30 per bond for a smaller number traded or as little as $2 per bond for a large transaction.

When I buy or sell bonds, I never see a separate charge for the commission listed on my bill. I have no idea how much my broker is charging me. How can I find out?

In a word, *ask!* When you buy or sell bonds, the commission charge is built into the price you're quoted. Remove that commission from the bond price, and watch the yield rise! The only way you can determine whether you've paid $10 or $30 for that bond is to ask the broker. The information is coded on the quote directly in front of him. He knows immediately how much he'll make from the transaction. By asking, you'll know too.

I really don't feel comfortable buying individual bonds. Do I have any other choices?

You sure do. If you don't have enough money to diversify your bond portfolio over a substantial number of different issues for protection or you don't know enough about bonds to make an educated decision, then a couple of other options probably make more sense: *unit investment trusts* or *bond funds*. We'll do a full discussion of bond funds in Chapter 6.

What is a unit investment trust?

A unit investment trust (UIT) is a *fixed* portfolio of bonds. In other words, once bonds are placed in the trust, they are not removed or added to. The portfolio remains the same until a bond is called or matures. Therefore, unlike a bond fund, a unit investment trust's yield will remain the same as long as all the bonds remain in the portfolio.

How often do unit investment trusts pay interest?

Because the primary objective of a unit investment trust is income, you can receive a check every month, quarterly, or semiannually. The choice is up to you.

Unit investment trusts sound too good to be true! Is there any bad news?

Like most things in life, UITs have both good and bad features. Probably the biggest problem with UITs is their inflexibility in adjusting to the marketplace. In other words, while an individual bond price will rise and fall easily with interest rates and market demand, a unit investment trust is far more sluggish in reacting. Units tend to lose their value far more easily than they gain, and if you need to sell, you may find your units in the trust are worth a lot less than you paid for them. However, the good news is with the long-term investor. If you buy UITs and plan to hold on until maturity, you will find a predictable income and return of principal.

I invested in a bond mutual fund instead of individual bonds because I wanted a check every month. I know that individual bonds pay only semiannually, but I don't like the way my principal fluctuates in a fund. What can I do?

Providing you have enough investable cash, there is a way you can buy individual bonds and still collect an interest check every month. By diversifying your bond purchases over six different issues with different semiannual payment schedules, you can accomplish the check-a-month payment just as with a bond fund. Discuss this with your broker. Most firms offer the check-a-month plan with bonds in their inventory. For more fund information, see Chapter 6.

What are utility bonds?

These are bonds issued by utility companies that offer added bonuses to investors, the chance of capital appreciation as well as income, and, with a well-run utility, less fear of default. Utilities are somewhat safer than other corporations because of our continuing need for electricity and other services and because of the industry's monopolistic approach to its business activities.

When I told my broker I don't want to buy any bonds now because I think interest rates are going up, she suggested that I look at some variable-rate bonds. What are they?

Variable-rate bonds are also called floating-rate bonds. The interest paid on this type of bond fluctuates during its life because it is tied to other factors, like the prime rate or Treasury bill rate. Usually, the yields on variable-rate bonds are slightly less than fixed-rate bonds, but they do offer an investor the opportunity to get more yield if rates go higher. However, you must also keep in mind that if interest rates slip downward, so will the yield of the variable-rate bond.

I've been hearing a lot about zero coupon bonds. What are they?

Zero coupon bonds are bought at a deep discount (you pay *much* less than the $1000 face amount) and the issuer pays you *$1000* at maturity. *No* interest is paid out to you along the way. You are earning imputed interest that is added to the value of the bond and not paid to you until the $1000 face amount is reached at maturity.

Are zero coupon bonds safer than ordinary corporate or municipal bonds?

If you buy Treasury zero coupon bonds, you do have more safety than with corporate or municipal zeros, because Treasury zeros are backed by the full faith and credit of the U.S. government. But remember that on a day-to-day basis, the price of *all* zeros fluctuates much more widely than that of ordinary bonds.

Are Treasury zero coupon bonds the only kind of zeros available?

Corporate and municipal zero coupon bonds are also available. However, these zeros are more vulnerable to early calls. Take note that housing zeros issued prior to September 1, 1982, are especially susceptible. These bonds were issued in bearer form, and because the trustee doesn't know who owns them, there's no way to contact an owner if the bonds are called. Consequently, when a bondholder goes to collect what he thinks is due on maturity, he may find that these bonds were called years earlier and his interest stopped some time ago.

How does a zero coupon bondholder who owns this type of callable bearer bond protect himself?

Two ways offer protection. First, if you feel uncomfortable with the idea of an early call, always ask your broker if a bond being offered is subject to an extraordinary call. Extraordinary calls mean that the bond may be retired *at any time* without notice. If it is subject to this type of call, you may want to pass on it completely. However, if you do decide to go ahead with the purchase, use the second protection: Make sure that your broker keeps a close watch out for call notices. That's why you pay a broker!

Do you think that zero coupon bonds are a good investment to help fund my children's college educations?

We certainly do, particularly if you invest in Treasury zeros, which have a guarantee of the U.S. government to pay. Zeros allow you to lock in programmable future dollars for much less money today.

Are there any bad features to funding a child's college education with zero coupon bonds?

The Tax Reform Act of 1986 has put one potential fly in the ointment. Children under the age of fourteen are now taxed at the parents' rate on any investment income earned over $1000. Although zeros don't pay you interest directly, you still must report the annual imputed interest that these bonds produced, which means you will be taxed as though you had received the interest as cash in your hand. If a young child's investment income is small or the child is fourteen years of age or older, this ruling won't affect you at all. Check with your accountant before you proceed. If tax ramifications do present a problem, investigate a municipal zero coupon bond instead. There's no government guarantee, but a highly rated issue should pose no problems.

A friend of mine was talking about investing in convertible bonds. What are these?

Convertible bonds pay a fixed rate of interest and can be exchanged at an appropriate time for a specific number of shares of the issuer's common stock. Convertible bonds tend to hold their value better than common stock when the market goes down. When the market goes up, taking the common-stock price with it, the bond's value goes up, too. A convertible sells at a premium over the market value of the shares it can be converted into because the yield offered is higher and more secure than dividends available through common stock. It also sells above the market value of the common shares to discourage an investor from buying the bond and converting immediately, thus acquiring common stock more cheaply. Due to the growth opportunity offered by conversion, the yields of convertible bonds are generally lower than those of an ordinary bond of the same issuer.

I thought I'd heard of every kind of bond there is. But yesterday a neighbor told me he had bought a convertible zero coupon municipal bond. I told him he must have the name wrong. Is there any such thing?

There sure is, and it is a combination of some of the best features of a number of bonds, as its name implies. Convertible municipal zeros are tax-free bonds bought at a deep discount, like zero coupon bonds, that convert into regular interest-paying bonds when the $1000 face value is reached. For example, you might buy a 7.2 percent convertible zero for $500 today. Ten years from today, the bond would be worth $1000, at which time it would begin paying you 7.2 percent interest semiannually through maturity, which may be ten or twenty years down the road. You receive tax-free compounding for the first ten years and tax-free income for the rest of the bond's life.

What type of investor might benefit from a convertible municipal zero coupon bond?

The first consideration with any type of municipal bond is the tax consequences. Your income must be high enough to make sense investing in tax-free bonds. Once you've determined that tax-free is the way to proceed, this type of bond can be ideal if you are nearing retirement, because you can buy bonds cheaply now and program income when you retire.

I've heard about something similar to this, but I thought my broker called it something else. Is that possible?

It's very possible. Wall Street loves to put catchy titles on new products. This type of bond is marketed under names such as GAINs, LIMOs, and FIGs, to name a few.

What is an escrowed bond?

The funds needed to pay holders of the bond are placed in securities held by a third party until the contract conditions are met. The money is invested in Treasury securities and the bonds generally pay 85–90 percent of the comparable Treasury yield. In our opinion, you'd be better off buying the Treasury bond for the full yield.

Speaking of Treasury securities, could you please explain the different Treasury investments available?

See the next chapter for a detailed explanation of the many government-backed investments in which you can participate.

What is a junk bond?

A junk bond is a bond with a credit rating of BB or lower. These bonds are issued by companies with questionable financial strength or that don't have long and successful track records of sales and earnings. Junk bonds are more volatile than a higher-rated bond and pay a higher yield because they offer the investor a greater risk of default.

I really like the higher return offered by junk bonds. Would you recommend investing in them?

No! Junk bonds should be used only by the most educated of investors, and no more than 5 percent of a person's portfolio should be placed there. Institutions that carry fiduciary responsibilities for their investors are not supposed to invest in such low-quality paper. That's reason enough for us to avoid them.

Are bonds a hedge against inflation?

Basically, no. One of the disadvantages of investing in fixed-income securities (bonds) is that they offer no protection against inflation. Although you may earn 9 percent on your investment, if inflation is 10 percent (we don't wish it!), you would actually lose money on your investment in terms of purchasing power.

SUMMARY

Historically, bonds were a conservative investment for widows, orphans, and investors who wanted *modest* returns with small risk. The late 1970s saw an end to this thinking. Wildly fluctuating interest rates made it imperative for all investors to learn more about bonds before investing.

Bonds can still be conservative investments for many investors, but the rules of the game have changed greatly. New products in the form of zero coupons, junk bonds, etc., have opened new vistas for us all and, for many, muddied the waters of once easy investing. More and more people are realizing that their portfolios need fixed-income securities to one degree or another, no matter what their age or financial situation. Again, we recommend some cautions *before* you invest:

- Stay on top of the general prediction of interest rate directions. The underlying value of your bonds will react in the opposite manner.
- Know the rating of the issuer before you buy. Never buy a bond rated less than BBB/Baa unless you're willing to take additional risk.
- Check the ratings of your bonds periodically. Ratings are not carved in granite. They will be lowered if the issuer falls on hard times.
- Keep your bonds at the firm where you bought them when possible instead of taking possession of the certificates. If bonds are called, you'll be the *first* and not the last to know.
- Remember that short-term bonds face less interest rate risk than long-term bonds.
- Know all call dates before you put your money down. This is particularly important if you plan to buy bonds at a premium (more than face value).

FURTHER INFORMATION
BOOKS

The Handbook of Bond and Money Markets, by David M. Darst (McGraw-Hill)

Buying Municipal Bonds: The Common Sense Guide to Tax Free Personal Investing by John Andrew (The Free Press)

Zero Coupon Bond Investments by Donald R. Nichols (Dow Jones-Irwin)

Fixed Income Portfolio Strategies Frank J. Fabozzi (Probus Publishing)

PAMPHLETS

*Investing for Income: A Complete
   Guide to Bonds and Other Income Investments*
A. G. Edwards and Sons
Corporate and Marketing Communications Dept.
One North Jefferson
St. Louis, Missouri 63103
(12 pp.; free)

NEWSLETTERS

Donoghue's Moneyletter
P.O. Box 540
Holliston, Massachusetts 01746

Income Investor Perspectives
Uniplan, Inc.
3907 N. Green Bay Avenue
Milwaukee, Wisconsin 53206

Lynch Municipal Bond Advisory
Lenox Hill Station
P.O. Box 1086
New York, New York 10021
(212) 249-9595

*Robert Kinsman's Low-Risk Growth
   Letter*
70 Mitchell Blvd.
San Raphael, California 94903

Value Line Options and Convertibles
Value Line Inc.
711 Third Avenue
New York, New York 10017

5

Investing with
Uncle Sam

> Affairs of state are operated so that one generation pays the
> debts of the last generation by issuing bonds payable by the
> next generation.   DR. LAURENCE J. PETER

Like it or not, it takes billions of dollars to keep the U.S. government
running every year, and every year we come up short. To help Uncle Sam
meet his budget needs, government paper is offered to investors, allowing
the government to raise money and investors to make money.

The Treasury Department, under the Public Debt Act of 1942, has the
authority to determine how much money and what types of securities (obligations) are needed to meet the budget requirements of our country. The
Treasury Department is responsible for financing the budget deficit, an awe-
some job. To accomplish this task, the department issues bills, notes, bonds,
and mortgage-backed securities to the public.

The big attraction to government securities lies in the fact that Uncle Sam
backs these offerings with the full faith and credit of the government. In
other words, Uncle Sam promises the investor that no matter what happens,
his money will be returned, along with any interest due. If the government
has to print more paper money to accomplish this, it will, even if the newly
printed money isn't worth anything!

No matter what your feelings about the government may be, the securities
issued by Uncle Sam are considered the safest investment you can make.
There is no rating of government securities as there is with the bonds of
corporations and municipalities. None is needed. The almost unlimited taxation power promises you a return of your principal and interest. That's
why there are so many Americans and foreigners alike who buy government
obligations. That is also the reason why government investments offer a

lower rate of return to an investor. Remember that the absence of risk means a smaller reward. To compensate for these lower rates, many government securities are taxable only on the federal level.

There is a place for *every* investor in the government securities market. The following questions and answers will help us all become more knowledgeable about investing with Uncle Sam.

What is a Treasury bill?

A Treasury bill is a short-term security with maturity dates of three months, six months, nine months, or one year. T-bills are issued in denominations of $10,000, and unlike Treasury notes and bonds, they pay no interest along the way. They are similar to zero coupon bonds because you buy them at a price less than their $10,000 face value (a discount) and receive at maturity the full $10,000. Using an example, you might pay $9800 for a nine-month T-bill. At maturity you would be paid $10,000— your original investment of $9800 plus the $200 in interest that the T-bill generated.

Why doesn't a $10,000 Treasury bill cost $10,000?

Because T-bills are short-term investments only existing from a period of three months to a little less than a year, it would become a bookkeeping nightmare for the Treasury if it had to issue checks to investors for all the different maturities. Instead, the Treasury calculates how much interest will be due the investor at maturity, subtracts the amount from $10,000, and requires only the balance as an investment.

Where can I buy Treasury bills?

Treasury bills can be purchased directly from a Federal Reserve bank, many brokerage firms, and many local banks.

How do I decide whether to buy a three-month, six-month, nine-month, or one-year T-bill?

Two factors should dictate what length T-bill you buy: 1) interest rates, and 2) when you will need your money. If interest rates are moving upward (or there is a possibility that they will move upward in the near term), a smart investor will buy the shortest maturity T-bills. If interest rates seem to be inching down, then a longer maturity makes more sense. Secondly, if you think you will be using the money you are currently investing in Treasury bills six months down the road, it would make no sense to buy a nine-month or one-year T-bill and tie up your funds.

How am I taxed on a Treasury bill?

The interest you receive from the Treasury bill is taxed as ordinary income. You are only federally taxed. T-bills are generally exempt from state and local taxes.

Will I receive a certificate of ownership if I buy a Treasury bill?

No, you won't. T-bills are offered in book-entry form only. That means that banks that are members of the Federal Reserve system hold the securities in the Fed accounts. All record keeping is computerized.

Why would someone invest in a Treasury bill?

A person looking for a short-term parking place for some money or a *very* conservative investor wishing 100 percent safety might be well served using a T-bill. You have complete safety of principal, a favorable tax treatment, and liquidity, because Treasury bills are continuously traded.

How do Treasury notes differ from T-bills?

First of all, Treasury notes pay interest semiannually. Secondly, Treasury notes are intermediate-term securities. They take over where T-bills leave off. The life of a Treasury note can be from two to ten years.

In what denominations are Treasury notes issued?

As a rule, in denominations of $1000. They're far more affordable for many investors.

Does the government set the interest rate when it issues Treasury notes?

No, it doesn't. That's why the financial news often talks about a Treasury auction taking place. The government lets the marketplace determine the rate of interest. When the government issues new securities, the large dealers and *large* investors make competitive bids for the securities. (This is also known as a Dutch auction.) Bidders offer prices for the securities, and the highest bid wins.

What are the tax consequences of a Treasury note?

As with a Treasury bill, you are generally exempt from state and local taxes.

Where can I buy Treasury notes?

As with T-bills, they are available directly from a Federal Reserve bank, some local banks, and some brokerage firms.

How does a Treasury bond differ from T-bills and notes?

Treasury bonds may be issued with any maturity date, but they are most often long-term maturities of ten to thirty years. Treasury bonds can be issued in denominations of $1000, but they usually trade in $10,000 denominations, like T-bills. These bonds pay interest to investors every six months, just like Treasury notes.

How can I buy a Treasury bond?

Treasury bonds are available from a Federal Reserve bank or from some local banks and brokerage firms.

Some corporate and municipal bonds can be called before they are due. Does the Treasury have the right to call its bonds, too?

Some Treasury bonds may be called three to five years before their maturity dates. But as an investor, you would be made aware of this call date before you bought. The government would also have to give you four months' prior notice before calling the bond.

I want to borrow some money and use my government securities as collateral for the loan. Is this possible?

Yes. Treasury bills, notes, and bonds can all be used as collateral, and anytime you can collateralize a loan you're saving yourself money. Of course we caution you to borrow wisely. Those Treasury securities could become the bank's property if you miss loan payments!

I want to invest in Treasury securities, but I don't know whether to buy bills, notes, or bonds. What do you recommend?

We recommend that you take a look at interest rates and do some reading to find out what the majority of experts think interest rates will be doing in the future. If interest rates seem likely to fall, longer-term notes and bonds will lock in higher rates for a longer period of time. On the other hand, if interest rates seem poised to rise, short-term T-bills will not tie you into lower rates for a long time. The key to smart bond buying, whether corporate, municipal or government, is to keep in mind that long-term bonds are more subject to price fluctuations due to interest rate changes than short-term bonds. If interest rates were to go up sharply and you wanted to sell a Treasury bond before maturity, you might find yourself selling it for less than you paid.

Can I sell my Treasury securities before they mature?

Yes, you can. To help keep an open market in government securities, the Federal Reserve system allows certain banks and brokerage firms to buy and sell Treasury securities directly through the New York Fed's securities department, commonly called the Desk. By contacting one of these firms or banks, you can sell your Treasury securities before maturity.

I check the government bond prices in the financial section of my newspaper before I buy, just to see what the market looks like. But the prices I see there are always better than what I end up getting. How come?

This is a complaint many people have, so don't feel like the Lone Ranger! Government bonds are always quoted in round lots just the way stocks are. However, a stock round lot consists of 100 shares while a government bond round lot consists of $1 million worth of bonds! If you have $1 million available to invest in government bonds, we're sure you'll get the price you see in the paper! If not, you'll pay a little bit more and get a little less yield.

I own a Treasury bond that's about to mature. How do I cash it in at maturity?

There are two ways to go about cashing in a matured Treasury bond. You can take the security to a commercial bank, which will submit it to the Federal Reserve bank for you. The Federal Reserve bank then credits the bank's account and the bank credits yours. You may be charged a fee by the bank for this service. A second method is to send your area's Federal Reserve branch a letter and the security requesting payment. At maturity, the Federal Reserve branch will send you a check for the full face amount. We recommend, however, that you forgo the mails and find a local institution that you can deal with face to face.

What's a U.S. savings bond?

A savings bond is a contract with the U.S. government that shows you have loaned money to the government, which it promises to repay with accrued interest or semiannual interest checks.

Where can I buy U.S. savings bonds?

They can be purchased both in person or by mail from most banks and savings institutions.

What is a Series EE savings bond?

Like a zero coupon bond, a Series EE savings bond is bought at a deep discount from face value. In fact, you pay exactly half the face amount. For example, a $100 savings bond would cost you $50. Interest accrues at a stipulated rate for the life of the bond. You receive the accrued interest when you cash in the bond or when it matures.

How does the government determine the interest rate of a savings bond?

Savings bond interest is calculated twice a year. May first and November first, by taking 85 percent of the five-year Treasury note rate at that time.

Does that mean that a savings bond adjusts the rate it pays twice a year?

It sure does, and that's one of the benefits of buying U.S. saving bonds. If interest rates go up after you've purchased a savings bond, your rate will go up, too. You're not locked in.

But suppose interest rates went down substantially?

You're protected in that case as well. If you buy a bond today and hold it for at least five years, the government guarantees that you will receive no less than 6 percent at this writing, even if interest rates go down to 4 percent. If you bought savings bonds between November 1, 1982, and November 1, 1986, you're in even better shape because the government promises to pay you no less than 7.5 percent if you hold them for five years or more. You really can't lose!

What's the interest rate on older bonds?
Series E and EE issued after October 1947 earn interest at the market-based rate.

What is a Series HH bond?
Series HH bonds are issued and redeemed at face value and pay interest semiannually, just like a corporate bond.

Do the interest rates paid by Series HH bonds fluctuate?
No, they don't. The interest rate is fixed at the time you acquire the bonds.

Where can I buy Series HH bonds?
Series HH bonds can't be purchased outright. They can be acquired only by exchanging Series E or Series EE for them.

How long do Series HH bonds earn interest?
Series HH bonds earn interest for ten years.

I have a lot of savings bonds that I bought over a number of years. I'd like to know what they're worth now. Where can I find this out?
The Bureau of Public Debt, 200 Third Street, Parkersburg, West Virginia 26101, has free copies of simplified redemption tables for $25 Series E and $50 EE bonds. This department will also help you locate a *lost* savings bond.

Can I sell or redeem my savings bonds at any time?
Savings bonds cannot be sold to another investor, but they can be redeemed for their current cash value anytime after six months from the date of issuance.

Is there a limit to the number of Series EE bonds I can buy?
Yes, there is. An issue price of $15,000 ($30,000 face amount) per person per year is the limit. You can double the limit by buying bonds and registering two people as co-owners.

What will it cost me to buy U.S. savings bonds?
There is no fee to buy or to redeem bonds. The Treasury Department reimburses banks for handling the transactions.

I had $5000 in savings bonds that I can't find. I've torn the house apart and I don't know where they are. Is there anything I can do or am I out all this money?
It will be very helpful if you have kept a record of the bonds' issue dates and serial numbers in a separate and safe place. If not, it will take some

time, but your bonds will be replaced without cost to you. You'll have to fill out form PD 1048. These forms are available from some local banks, your nearest Federal Reserve bank, or the Bureau of Public Debt.

Do I have to bring anything with me to cash in my savings bonds?

Yes, you do. The Treasury Department requires a paying agent to ask for one of three types of identification:

1. *Customer identification*: if you are a customer who has had an account for at least six months.
2. *Personal identification*: by persons known to the paying agent who can satisfactorily identify the person cashing in the bond.
3. *Documentary identification*: a driver's license or employee card with a photo, etc. will be accepted.

I'm a new bride and I have some savings bonds that I bought while I was single. The bonds are registered in my maiden name. Do I have to get all these bonds changed to show my married name?

No, you don't. When you want to cash those bonds, just sign both your maiden and married names on the bonds, and they will be redeemed with no trouble. Don't forget to bring along some personal identification, too.

Can I use my savings bonds as collateral for a loan?

Because savings bonds are registered securities, they can't be transferred, negotiated, pledged as collateral, or sold to someone else.

If I buy U.S. savings bonds, how will I be taxed?

Interest on both the Series EE and HH bonds is exempt from state and local tax but not federal income tax. But another great feature of savings bonds is that you can defer the taxes until you redeem them or they mature. If at maturity you exchange those E or EE bonds for Series HH bonds, federal income tax may again be deferred.

Who should buy U.S. savings bonds?

Anybody who doesn't need current income from an investment should consider U.S. savings bonds. Their tax deferred nature and favorable tax treatment upon maturity, not to mention their safety, make them extremely good investments.

Would you recommend U.S. EE Savings bonds to fund a child's education?

Most definitely! U.S. EE Savings bonds are one of the least risky and easiest to understand investments for a college education. But listen to this great news: As of this past January (1990) when these bonds are cashed in at maturity and the proceeds are used for higher education, those proceeds are tax-free from federal taxes (they have always been exempt from city and state taxes). Tax free . . . you heard it right!

Are these new U.S. "EE Education" bonds similar to the "old" EE Savings bonds in that the annual interest rate is adjusted twice yearly on April 1 and November 1 and that Uncle Sam guarantees payment of interest and principle?
Yes.

What is the annual rate of return on the U.S. EE Education bonds?
If you hold them a minimum of 5 years, you are guaranteed an annual rate of 6% per year although it could be more if interest rates are higher than 6% when the bonds adjust (on April 1 and November 1).

Are there any restrictions that I should know about with U.S. EE Education bonds?
Yes, there are a number of restrictions. Among them:

* Bonds must be issued in either one parent's name or both parent's names.
* Purchaser must be at least 24 years of age.
* Single taxpayers with incomes between $40,000 and $55,000 and married couples filing joint returns with incomes of $60,000 and $90,000 will be able to exclude some but not all of the interest from federal taxes.
* Room and board are not eligible expenses to be paid with savings bond proceeds.

Where can I learn *more* about Education bonds?
This "new" investment is *well* worth the effort to learn more. Write for a free copy of:

> "U.S. Savings Bonds: Now Tax-Free for Education"
> Office of Public Affairs
> U.S. Savings Bond Division
> Washington, D.C. 20226

How can I find out what the updated rate of interest on a savings bond is?
The U.S. Treasury Department offers investors a toll-free number to call for rates and other savings bond questions. Just dial 1-800 U.S. BONDS for rate updates.

I hear about Ginnie Maes all the time. What are they?
Ginnie Mae or GNMA (pronounced the same way) stands for Government National Mortgage Association. Ginnie Maes are mortgage-backed securities.

Is Ginnie Mae the same thing as Fannie Mae?
No, it's not. GNMA is a wholly government owned corporation that was established in 1968, when Fannie Mae (FNMA, or Federal National Mortgage Association) left its status as a government-owned corporation to become a public company.

What are the differences between FNMAs and GNMAs?
There are a number of differences.

FNMA	GNMA
• not guaranteed by the U.S. government	• guaranteed by the U.S. government
• minimum $50,000 purchase	• minimum $25,000 purchase
• public corporation	• government-owned

I've heard GNMAs referred to as pass-through securities. What does that mean?
Roughly translated, a pass-through security *passes* income from debtors (home-mortgage payers) through intermediaries to the investors. Mortgage-backed securities, like GNMAs, are the most common forms of pass-through securities. Principal and interest payments from homeowners pass from the banks or savings and loans, where the mortgages originated, through a government agency to the investors.

What does a GNMA consist of?
A GNMA consists of pools of FHA (Federal Housing Administration)- and VA (Veterans' Administration)-guaranteed mortgages.

How does a GNMA work?
The process begins when someone buys a home and finances it with a mortgage issued by an FHA-or VA-approved lender. The banker then places this mortgage in a pool and gets the guarantee of the Government National Mortgage Association for timely payment of principal and interest. The pooled mortgages are held by a custodian, often the trust department of a bank. All mortgages in the pool will be the same type, i.e., same type of house, same interest rate, and a thirty-year life.

If GNMAs are made up of thirty year mortgages, how come they never seem to last for thirty years?
Most home mortgages and GNMA certificates have a stated maturity of thirty years, but because mortgages are prepaid or refinanced before they expire, the actual maturity of GNMAs is usually around twelve or thirteen years. GNMA yields, therefore, are calculated on this assumption.

How is the price of a GNMA set?

The current market value of a GNMA will depend upon the amount of principal remaining to be paid. The more principal that remains, the more valuable the GNMA certificate. For this reason we strongly urge a would-be GNMA buyer to learn more about the GNMA *factor,* which is an eight digit decimal amount that tells the broker and the investor how much principal has not yet been repaid.

I buy GNMA certificates because I like their safety and their yield. But I've always wondered why GNMA yields are compared to corporate bond yields when my broker quotes them to me.

GNMA yields are quoted with an equivalent corporate bond yield next to them in order to provide a fair and accurate comparison for the investor. Because GNMAs make twelve payments a year rather than the twice-a-year payments of corporate bonds, adjustments are made to take into account compounding if monthly payments are reinvested. The equivalent corporate yield indicates how much more return you would have to receive from a corporate bond to net the same amount of money.

How do GNMA yields compare to other investments?

GNMA yields offer safety and competitive yields. GNMAs generally yield ½ to 2½ percent higher than long-term Treasury bonds.

What does my monthly GNMA check include?

GNMA checks, issued on the fifteenth of each month, include both interest and returned principal, as well as any prepayments that occurred the previous month.

Are there any dangers in investing in GNMAs?

We won't say it's a danger, but the biggest mistake some investors make is not paying attention to the monthly statement. Because each month brings a return of principal and a possible return of more principal due to early prepayments, a careless investor might spend the principal as well as the interest without taking notice. More than one investor has found the principal "missing" when a GNMA matures!

Are some GNMAs better than others?

GNMAs are backed by the full faith and credit of the U.S. government. For this reason, there are no good and bad GNMAs. No other entity markets a GNMA.

How are GNMAs taxed?

The interest received from GNMAs is subject to federal and local taxes. Your return of principal is not taxed if the original purchase price equaled 100 percent of the remaining principal balance in the mortgage pool. But don't forget that if you sell a GNMA before its term is over, you may realize a capital gain or loss.

Who should invest in GNMAs?

GNMAs are good investments for income-oriented investors looking for safety, competitive yields, and liquidity.

Are there any dangers in liquidating (selling) my GNMA certificate before it matures?

As with any bond, selling a GNMA before maturity may bring you more, less, or the exact same amount that you paid for it. Because GNMAs are valued in accordance with mortgage interest rates, if interest rates go up, the value of your GNMA will fall; and if rates go down, the value of your GNMA will rise.

I like the idea of investing in GNMAs, but I don't have the minimum purchase price of $25,000 available. Do I have any alternative?

There is a less expensive alternative to "straight" GNMA participation. You can buy a GNMA *fund* for as little as $250, with some funds. For an in-depth discussion of GNMA funds, see pages 100–102.

SUMMARY

Measuring risk and reward is the key to successful investing. By investing with Uncle Sam, you are able to minimize this risk and yet maintain a reasonable reward. Government securities offer a great deal of liquidity, with safety and moderate returns. They also offer, in many cases, tax benefits for the investor.

There are few cautions to mention to an investor in government paper, unlike some other investment alternatives, but as always, we stress education before you dive into the water!

- Take the time to learn how to read quotes. They're a little more complicated than stock quotes, but they tell the whole story.
- Simply because Uncle Sam guarantees an investment doesn't necessarily make it right for every investor.
- Interest rate movement affects the market value of government securities in the same way as it affects corporate and municipal bonds. Long-term government bonds and Series HH bonds are subject to more interest rate risk than short-term Treasury notes and bills.
- Some governmental agency issues are *not* backed by Uncle Sam.
- Don't look for a lot of help from brokers with government securities purchases. They don't make a lot of money from the transaction, so generally they don't do a lot of homework on government issues.

- There is a wealth of information available about government securities. Take the time to read it before you invest.

U.S. government securities can be a wonderful investment for many people. Look into their advantages!

FURTHER INFORMATION

Consumer Information Center
P.O. Box 100
Pueblo, Colorado 81002
The Savings Bond Question &
Answer Book
Publication 451V (50¢)

Bureau of Public Debt
200 Third Street
Parkersburg, West Virginia 26101
Redemption Tables for U.S. Savings
Bonds
(PD 3600—free)

Federal Reserve Bank of Atlanta
104 Marietta Street, N.W.
Atlanta, Georgia 30301
(404) 521-8653

Federal Reserve Bank of Boston
600 Atlantic Avenue
Boston, Massachusetts 02106
(617) 973-3800

Federal Reserve Bank of Chicago
230 South LaSalle Street
Chicago, Illinois 60690
(312) 322-5369

Federal Reserve Bank of Cleveland
1455 East Sixth Street
Cleveland, Ohio 44101
(216) 579-2490

Federal Reserve Bank of Dallas
400 South Akard Street
Dallas, Texas 75222
(214) 651-6111

Federal Reserve Bank of Kansas City
925 Grand Avenue
Kansas City, Missouri 64198
(816) 881-2862

Federal Reserve Bank of Minneapolis
250 Marquette Avenue
Minneapolis, Minnesota 55480
(612) 340-2075

Federal Reserve Bank of New York
33 Liberty Street
New York, New York 10045
(212) 720-6619

Federal Reserve Bank of Philadelphia
100 North Sixth Street
Philadelphia, Pennsylvania 19106
(215) 574-6675

Federal Reserve Bank of Richmond
701 East Byrd Street
Richmond, Virginia 23219
(804) 697-8372

Federal Reserve Bank of St. Louis
411 Locust Street
St. Louis, Missouri 63102
(314) 444-8506

Federal Reserve Bank of San
Francisco
101 Market Street
San Francisco, California 94105
(415) 974-2330

Office of Public Affairs
U.S. Savings Bond Division
Dept. of the Treasury
Washington, D.C. 20226

BOOKS

The Treasury Bond Basics
Burghardt, Lane and Papa
Probus Publishing

Fed Watching and Interest Rate
  Projections
David M. Jones
N.Y. Institute of Finance

Professionals' Guide to the U.S.
  Government Securities Market
George M. Bollenbacher
N.Y. Institute of Finance

6

Mutual Funds

The [mutual fund] choices before you are overwhelming. Available or in the works are a junk-bond fund for nonresident aliens; a fund for employees of religious groups and cemetery companies; a fund that buys only shares of companies in Ohio; and a fund for Muslims.   FORBES magazine

Americans have "discovered" mutual funds and have invested over one trillion billion in them, more than the present total amount of personal savings in banks and savings and loans. The total number of dollars invested in funds today has increased eighteen times since 1976.

While Americans have been pouring money into mutual funds, the funds themselves have been proliferating like rabbits. In the past ten years, the number of mutual funds available to investors has grown four times over. At last count, there were 2740 funds registered with the Securities and Exchange Commission. Does that make your job of choosing a fund easy? Don't bet your life on it!

No matter what your investment goals, it's possible today to find a fund or a number of funds that will meet your goals. Whether you want safe income or very aggressive growth, there are lots of funds that will offer you what you're looking for . . . and more. The question is: When presented with 150 funds all offering the same thing, how do you choose? There are no simple answers to this problem. But in this chapter we will set you on the right course for success.

The biggest problem we've encountered on radio, television and in seminars is the lack of knowledge of many mutual fund investors. All mutual funds are not created equal, yet people often rush into these investments without understanding them. In fact, many people who have already invested in one don't know what a mutual fund *is*. The rush on mutual funds has created a philosophy of investing that might be hazardous to your wealth.

89

Many people are investing in mutual funds, not because they understand them and have done their homework, but because all their friends are investing. Let's try to clear up some of the misconceptions and learn the facts about these potentially useful, potentially dangerous funds.

What is a mutual fund?

A mutual fund is a professionally managed, diversified portfolio of securities. The fund continually issues shares to investors. These are redeemable on any business day at the current net asset value. All owners of the fund participate in the gains and losses of the fund.

Whenever I hear someone talk about a mutual fund, the term *net asset value* seems to come up. What is that?

Net asset value is what each share of the fund is worth at the end of the day. The fund manager arrives at this figure by subtracting the liabilities from the total assets of the portfolio and dividing this figure by the number of shares outstanding. This is calculated once a day, based on the closing market price for every security in the fund's portfolio.

How does a mutual fund work?

When you buy shares of a mutual fund, the portfolio manager pools your money with the money of all the other investors to buy and sell securities for the group. By placing money in a mutual fund, rather than in individual stocks and/or bonds, you become part of a multimillion-dollar organization. This gives you more clout in the marketplace and an edge over the small, individual investor. You also receive professional management, reduced brokerage fees, and a greater diversification than most small investors can afford.

I've heard mutual funds referred to as open-end companies. What does that mean?

It means that the fund doesn't operate with a fixed number of shares, but it issues new shares to accommodate investors whenever necessary.

Do I make money in a mutual fund only if the price of the shares rises?

Not at all. Portfolio managers periodically sell securities for capital gains. Most mutual funds pay capital gains to their investors at least once a year, and if the fund invests in bonds or dividend-paying stocks, dividends are paid to investors also at least once a year. An investor in a successful mutual fund can make money in three different ways: share price appreciation (paper profit); dividends; and capital gains distributions on stocks or bonds actually sold at a profit.

I assume that not all the stocks or bonds sold by the portfolio manager are sold at a profit. How does this affect a capital gains distribution?

Unfortunately, you assume correctly. The capital gains distribution is a net figure, paid once a year if the portfolio manger has sold more stocks or bonds at a profit than at a loss.

How long should I tie up my money in a mutual fund investment?

Mutual funds, excluding money market funds, should not be treated as short-term investments. In most cases, an investor is best served by staying with a fund for five years or more.

My mutual fund is always sending me dividend checks that I don't need. I'd rather reinvest this money, but the checks are never large enough to meet the fund's minimum investment requirement to purchase new shares. What can I do?

A fund handles dividend and capital gains distributions according to the instructions of the investor. When you first bought shares in the fund, either you told them to send you the check or it was assumed you wanted the check sent. Go back to the fund, if you bought it yourself, or go back to the broker, if you bought it through a broker, and have the fund notified that you prefer to have all dividends and capital gains reinvested. The fund managers will be happy to comply.

Wouldn't it be better and more efficient to go directly to the fund whether or not you bought it through a broker initially?

Have you ever tried to call a mutual fund company? Some companies' telephone lines are almost constantly busy. If you bought a mutual fund through a broker, you paid a hefty commission for his or her service. Use it!

How can I buy mutual fund shares?

Fund shares can be purchased directly from the fund over the phone or through the mail. You can also buy mutual funds through a full-service broker, discount broker, financial planner, and some banks and insurance companies.

What does it cost me to buy mutual fund shares?

The price varies from *no cost* to you all the way *up to 9 percent*. In fact, the question you raise is one of the most hotly contested in the mutual fund industry today! The battle lines have been drawn with the no-load funds on one side and the load funds on the other. We sometimes think the poor investor is caught in the middle with gun barrels focused on him or her from every angle!

What's the difference between a load fund and a no-load fund?

The load is an up-front sales commission that is deducted from your initial investment in the fund. For example, if you invested $10,000 in a fund with an 8.5 percent load, $850 would immediately be deducted from your purchase. Of your $10,000 investment, only $9150 would actually be available to purchase shares. On the other hand, a no-load fund charges no *initial* sales commission. That means the same $10,000 investment in a no-load fund would purchase $10,000 worth of shares. Every investable dollar goes to work immediately.

Then why would *anybody* buy a load fund?

Thanks for asking the burning question of the century! A *load fund* makes sense for people who don't understand mutual funds, feel uncomfortable with the lingo, and like to have help in making investment decisions, for which they *should* pay a commission because they're buying help. A *no-load fund* makes sense for people who are comfortable making their own decisions, have some knowledge about mutual funds, and have the ability to deal with the fund firsthand if an error crops up. In our opinion, there's no one hard and fast rule for everybody. We strongly believe that mutual funds have a place in almost everyone's portfolio. If an investor fears the do-it-yourself approach of no-load fund investing, there is absolutely nothing wrong in buying a load fund through a broker. It should also be noted that during the October 19, 1987, crash of the stock market, and for several days thereafter, investors in no-load mutual funds had a much harder time trying to get through on overworked phone lines to sell their fund shares.

It doesn't seem to me that a load fund gives you any more help in decision making than a no-load fund. Am I wrong?

The funds, load or no-load, don't give you any help at all, but a good financial adviser will. The financial adviser will help you choose a fund, receives copies of your monthly or quarterly statements to review, and will recommend when to hold and when to sell. Some investors need this help.

I like the idea of no-load fund investing, but a friend recently told me that not all funds listed as no-load are what they seem to be. Is she right?

She sure is. The biggest mistake an investor can make is to assume that no-load means no cost. Remember that there isn't a mutual fund in existence that manages your money for nothing! No-load means no *initial* sales charge. *Initial* is the key word. *All* funds charge management fees, and some no-load funds may also charge redemption fees or an annual assessment against assets of the funds.

Are all management fees the same, or do some funds charge more than others?

Some funds *are* more expensive than others. Assessments against a fund's assets, besides management fees, may include accounting fees, marketing fees and printing costs, and the cost of mailing reports to shareholders. These costs range from .3 percent to 5 percent of *your* investment in the fund. The funds usually lump together all these assessments in the prospectus as a percentage of net assets and call it the *expense ratio*.

What is the expense ratio?

The average expense ratio is $1 per $100 of assets (1 percent). Always check Part B of the prospectus, the statement of additional information. This will spell out that particular fund's expense ratio.

Aren't management fees and assessments still cheaper than an up-front commission?

Maybe and maybe not. Don't forget, we said the *average* expense ratio is $1 per $100 of assets. Many load and no-load funds charge more, and many charge less. The fact is that over a ten year period, an 8.5 percent load fund with an expense ratio of $1 per $100 (1 percent) will cost you *less* than a no-load fund with an expense ratio of $2 per $100 (2 percent). Try to avoid any fund, load or no-load, that has an expense ratio of $1.50 (1.5 percent) or more.

Isn't the commission charge for investing in a load mutual fund deductible on my taxes as a miscellaneous expense (cost of earning money)?

No. Commission charges for buying mutual funds are not tax deductible.

A broker called me yesterday and said I could buy a no-load fund through him. He called it a 12b-1 plan. Should I do it?

In our opinion, no. The 12b-1 funds get their names from the Securities and Exchange Commission's rule 12b-1, which permits funds to levy certain fees for commissions to brokers and advertising costs. About 40 percent of all existing funds use 12b-1 fees. The 12b-1 funds sold by brokers generally have deferred sales charges that an investor ends up paying if he doesn't stay with the fund for the specified number of years. In just about every case, 12b-1 funds have higher expense ratios than most load and true no-load funds, and in a couple of instances, the 12b-1 fees aren't even included in the fund's expense ratio. We feel 12b-1s are too expensive for investors.

If I buy a load fund and choose to reinvest my dividends and capital gains, will these be reinvested with or without a sales charge?

In most cases, the funds will not charge you to reinvest. But there are a few funds that do charge. We take exception to these few funds that continue to hit investors again and again. If you plan to buy a load fund and reinvest dividends and capital gains, first ask the broker or financial planner how the fund handles reinvestment and then read the prospectus *yourself* to be sure you received the correct answer. Some funds within the Franklin, IDS, Massachusetts Financial, and Lord Abbott groups do charge you a commission to reinvest. To put it bluntly, that stinks!

Discount brokers are now selling no-load mutual funds. What do you think of buying through a discount broker?

Discount brokers will charge you a transaction charge to buy a no-load fund, but it is a very small price to pay when compared with the 4 to 8.5

percent that a full-service broker will charge. Discount brokers, like Charles Schwab, handle over two hundred no-load mutual funds. For a small fee, they'll do the telephoning for you.

My brother insists that no-load funds outperform load funds every time. He keeps telling me I'm crazy to buy load funds. Is he right?

No, he isn't. Constant studies have failed to show that no-load funds perform better than load funds. On the other hand, these same studies haven't shown that load funds perform better, either. Remember, though, that to match the performance of a no-load fund, a load fund has to do substantially better to overcome the front-end charges you pay.

I've finally managed to save $2000 and I'd like to invest in a mutual fund, but with so many choices, I don't know which way to go. Do you have any suggestions?

You'll find the right fund for yourself by using a process of elimination. The best suggestion we can give you to start off with is to decide what kind of investor you are; i.e., can you take a lot of risk, just a little, or something in between? Next you must decide whether you want growth, income, or a combination of the two. By carefully thinking this out before you begin analyzing the funds, you'll be able to skip a great number of them. For example, if you decide that you're looking for growth with minimal risk, then you can eliminate all aggressive growth funds as well as bond funds and funds that invest in a combination of stocks and bonds. Understanding your goals and how much risk you are willing to assume are the first steps to smart investing.

How can I tell whether a fund is an aggressive growth fund, bond fund, or something else?

Read the prospectus. Under the section labeled "Objective of the Fund" you will find what type it is.

After I decide what my objectives are and how much risk I can take, how do I pick the best fund? Do I go for the hottest performer of the year?

More often than not, this year's hot fund becomes next year's cold potato. A fund's short-term performance is rarely a reliable indicator of long-term performance. We strongly urge would-be mutual fund investors to study the five- to ten-year track record of a fund whenever possible. Successful mutual fund investing comes from *consistency* of performance. Howard Ruff summed it up best when he said, "In a stiff wind, even turkeys fly." When the market is strong, even the worst-run fund should achieve some success. But the victory belongs to the fund manager who can perform even in bad times, when the market moves against him.

Does the size of a fund's assets influence how well it will perform? In other words, is lean and mean better than fat and maybe sluggish?

Some experts do feel a smaller fund can move in and out of positions more easily and, thus, gain better performance. But one only has to take a look at the Fidelity Magellan Fund's record over the past ten years to argue the point! Size has never really concerned us when we analyze a fund. Track record is most important. But here are some points to consider:

LARGE FUND	SMALL FUND
• broader diversification (safety in numbers)	• can quickly buy or sell a position
• volume discounts on brokerage costs (lower costs)	• fewer holdings may benefit fund if only one takes off
• large quantities of stock may bring down price before fund is totally out of a position	• greater flexibility
	• less diversification may cause greater volatility

I've done a lot of homework on mutual funds and I've finally narrowed down the choice to five. Now what?

We don't want to frighten you, but now the *real* work begins! Get the prospectuses, annual and quarterly reports, and start reading! Pay particular attention to Part B of the prospectus, which spells out the fees and charges. If your attention starts to wane as you read, just remind yourself that your hard-earned dollars will be riding with your choice. We'll list some of the questions you should keep in mind while you read this material:

- What's the fund's objective—growth or income, preservation of capital? Make sure the answer matches your needs.
- If it's a stock fund, does it stay fully invested in bad times or does it sell and go to cash or fixed income investments? A fund that stays fully invested at all times is far more aggressive and volatile.
- Does the fund look for undervalued stocks, stocks with growing earnings patterns, or a combination? Steadily rising earnings in stocks should give more safety than undervalued situations.
- With bond funds, what is the average maturity of bonds in the portfolio? Short-term bonds are less subject to interest rate risk than are long-term bonds.
- Does the fund swap long-term bonds for shorter maturities when interest rates start rising? A yes should indicate less risk of principal.
- Does the fund contain bonds currently priced above face value? An early call by the issuers could result in a loss of principal.

Is there anything else I should pay attention to when analyzing mutual funds?

Yes, there is. Take a look at the fund's year-by-year share price changes, which you'll find in the prospectus, and compare that to other similar types of funds. Also see if positive share price changes were due to one or two lucky years or *consistent* growth. If the fund has been around long enough, find out how it performed in the "bad" years for stocks—1977, 1981, and 1984. Were they *worse* years for the fund? Lastly, make sure that the portfolio manager currently running the fund is the same one who accomplished past glories.

I hate the thought of having to do all this reading and analyzing myself. Are there any books or newsletters that analyze mutual funds for investors?

Every September, *Forbes* magazine runs its annual mutual fund survey. It grades fund performance and shows expense rations and other important information. *Money* magazine and *Changing Times* also do their own analyses during the year. All of these surveys are very helpful in choosing funds.

I followed all your suggestions and I still have three funds that are in the running. I wish I had enough money to invest in the three! But I can afford only one. What should I do?

When you can't weed out any further, go with the fund that has the lowest internal expenses and the one that trades less actively. Less trading means lower costs and, hopefully, more money for investors.

How can I check out a portfolio manager?

You can try calling the fund and asking how long the portfolio manager has been in charge of the fund. But don't be surprised if they won't tell you. Many funds don't want to encourage investors to invest with a person who may not be with them in the future. They like to have the fund stand on its own merits and not the merits of the portfolio manager. If the fund won't answer your question, the *Mutual Fund Sourcebook* will. This book is published every November and lists the name of the funds' managers and how long they've run a particular fund as well as other pertinent information. You can find this book in some major libraries or by contacting the publisher, at 53 West Jackson Blvd., Suite 1661, Chicago, Illinois 60604. The cost of the book is $49.50.

My neighbor invests in mutual funds all the time. When I mentioned that I'd like to start investing, he told me I shouldn't put in a lump sum. He recommended that I dollar cost average instead. Can you explain what he means?

Happily. Dollar cost averaging is a strategy by which you invest a fixed amount in a fund at regular intervals instead of all at once. For example, instead of placing $5000 in a particular fund all at once, you would invest $250 every month for twenty months. The thinking behind this strategy is that your investment ends up buying fewer shares when prices are high and more when prices are low. Over a full market cycle, which means about five years, you should have accumulated shares at below-average prices. It can be a very good way to invest. Ask anyone who put all of his or her money into a stock fund just before the market started on a downward run!

Aren't mutual funds only for sissies?

That's a rumor started by stockbrokers, many of whom make a wonderful living when you buy and sell individual stocks or bonds on a regular basis. Many brokers don't like to see their clients invest in funds because of the long-term nature of fund investing. Once you've tied up $25,000 in a mutual fund, it might be years before that broker can use that portion of your portfolio again. Mutual funds are for smarties, not sissies. They offer wide diversification, professional management, and safety that an individual stock or bond purchase will never provide.

What does the term *growth fund* really mean?

Growth funds buy and sell stocks. Their primary aim is to increase the value of the fund's stock portfolio.

Are there different kinds of growth funds?

Growth funds can be divided into two classifications: long-term growth funds, for steady increases in share value, and maximum or aggressive capital-gains funds, which take greater risks to achieve greater profits.

Are long-term growth funds less risky than maximum capital gains funds?

Generally speaking, yes. The stocks that make up a maximum capital gains growth fund are usually more sensitive to market movements and tend to react more violently when the market drops. On the other side of the coin, they can appreciate much more quickly in a good market.

How come when the Dow Jones Industrial Average goes up substantially in a day, my growth fund doesn't always follow? Am I in a badly run fund?

Not necessarily. Unless the fund you're invested in is buying the thirty stocks that make up the Dow, don't expect it to follow a run-up in the Industrial Average. If you want your fund to mirror a major market indicator like the Dow or the Standard & Poor's 500, you'll have to be sure that you've invested in an *index fund*.

What is an index fund?

An index fund invests in many or all of the stocks in a major indicator in order to keep up with the direction of the market. Buying an index fund can be a smart strategy if you're looking to minimize risk, but it won't necessarily be as sensational a performer as other stock funds in bull markets.

What's an income fund?

An income fund invests for the most part in bonds rather than stocks, although some income funds do try to achieve capital appreciation as a secondary goal by purchasing convertible securities and stocks that pay high dividends, too. The primary goal of an income fund is to pay regular dividends.

Are income funds only a smart investment for retirees?

Not at all. Income funds are most especially suited to a retiree's needs, but growth investors should also look into income funds to help diversify their portfolios and to lessen risk from very aggressive investments.

How often do bond funds pay dividends? I'm retired and would like a check more often than every six months.

Because the primary objective of such a fund is income, most of them pay dividends every month. If you don't need the monthly income, you can always reinvest the dividends.

I don't really feel comfortable buying individual bonds. Would you recommend municipal and corporate bond funds as a way for me to participate?

Yes. We strongly recommend that most investors avoid purchasing individual stocks or bonds. We are *not* saying that if you have a large portfolio and the necessary time, understanding, and experience to make educated investments you shouldn't do so, but most people don't qualify.

Why do you both believe so strongly in mutual funds?

The past few years have shown dramatic changes and fluctuations in both the stock and bond markets. Computerized trading, huge mutual funds, and a wider use of options have made it virtually impossible for the small investor to follow a self-made conservative course. A fifty-point swing in the Dow Jones Industrial Average creates a roller-coaster ride that is too much to handle for conservative investors. Instead of fighting the big guys, a battle we are sure to lose, we can buy mutual fund shares and become one of them.

I always see advertisements for bond funds that talk about the fund's current yield. What is a mutual fund's definition of current yield?

Current yield is the annual interest paid on a bond divided by the current market price.

I'm considering two bond funds. Both have a good reputation. One fund has a higher yield, and the other is selling at a lower price, which would bring me more shares. Which fund should I choose?

Neither, if those are your methods for choosing a bond fund. The biggest mistake an investor can make is to choose a fund based solely on its current yield. The key to a successful bond fund is its *total return.*

What's the difference between current yield and total return?

With some funds, it's the difference between meaningful profits and loss of principal! For example, a fund may advertise that its return was 24 percent for the past twelve months. There are no bonds available paying 24 percent, so how can the fund advertise this? Because it has totaled up both the income from dividends and the market appreciation of the bonds in the portfolio (the growth of the principal amount). Don't confuse this with yield. Most of the 24 percent came from market appreciation. The actual *yield* may have been only 3 or 4 percent. Now, suppose that the next year the bond market drops 10 percent. As it drops, it takes the fund down with it the same 10 percent. The fund may still have a current yield of 3 percent, but the fund's total return would now be −7 percent. We bet you won't see any ads about total return that year! Think of current yield as grains of wheat and total return as a wheat field. Total return increases not only the number of grains but the size of the field. More field means more grains. Losses diminish the size of both the field and the crop. Harvest the grains, but don't cut back the size of the field. If you buy bond funds only for yield, that's exactly what you'll do.

Besides total return and current yield, is there anything else I should check before I buy a bond fund?

As with any mutual fund, take a look at past years' performances. One good year doesn't necessarily make a good fund. As we suggested in an earlier question, pick up a copy of the *Forbes Annual Mutual Fund Survey* or *Changing Times* and *Money* magazines' annual survey of mutual funds for further help. All three magazines track bond funds as well as stock funds for performance and fees.

Some bond funds are called high yield and high income funds. What are your thoughts on these kinds of funds?

There's no free lunch! High yield funds generally invest in below-investment-grade bonds, also called junk bonds. These bonds pay a higher yield because they are more risky. High income funds enhance a fund's yield by using sophisticated strategies, which also bring higher risks to the investor. If you're a conservative investor at heart, you would be better off avoiding high yield and high income funds.

Could you explain the hedging techniques used by the high income funds? Why do these techniques make the funds more risky?

To increase the yield of these bond funds, portfolio managers often sell options and futures on the bonds in their portfolio. This means that for a fixed period of time, the person who paid for the option has the right to buy certain bonds in the portfolio at a present price, no matter how high the bond's price may go. If the bond's price remains the same or drops, the fund keeps the option money (called an option premium) and sells another option on the bond. This increases the cash flow in the fund and gives the investor a greater yield. The risk comes with the possibility that the bond *will* appreciate in price. If this happens, the portfolio manager must sell the bond at the lower pre-set price, which loses a paper profit for fund investors and also removes a higher yielding bond from the portfolio. If the portfolio manager miscaluclates the direction of interest rates, it can cost a high income fund investor money.

I've been doing some reading about bond funds and now I'm really confused. Some funds advertise short-term bonds while others have long-term bonds. What does that mean to me as an investor?

Long-term bonds are more susceptible to interest rate risk than short-term bonds. Interest rate fluctuations cause the value of a bond to rise or fall. The value of a bond moves in the opposite direction of interest rates (interest rates up, bond prices down, and vice versa). Imagine a yardstick in your outstretched hand. As you move your hand up and down, the part of the yardstick closest to your hand hardly moves. But the farther out you go on the yardstick, the more swing there is. So it is with long-term and short-term bonds. Long-term bond funds have a higher yield because they are more susceptible to interest rate risk. Once again, the greater the risk, the greater the return.

How can I check the maturities of bonds in the fund if it doesn't say whether it's a short-term or long-term bond portfolio?

The prospectus will tell you what the average maturity of the portfolio is. If you're buying the fund through a broker or financial planner, ask. He or she *should* know.

How much money should a fund manger have at his or her disposal in order to maintain proper diversification within the bond fund?

A fund needs at least $100 million to really do the job with complete diversification and safety.

How many different bonds should be in a bond fund portfolio?

There should be at least thirty-six different issues, and no more than 10 percent should be issued by companies in the same industry.

What is a government securities fund, and what should I be aware of before I invest?

A government securities fund is a bond fund made up of Treasury bills, notes, bonds, and possibly GNMAs and, therefore, subject to the same scrutiny as any bond fund. An investor must always keep the direction of interest rates in mind. If the portfolio is made up of long-term bonds and rates suddenly shoot upward, you can expect, in most cases, a loss of principal.

My broker told me that everything in the government securities fund is guaranteed by the U.S. government. How could I lose some principal? I thought that was guaranteed, too.

That may be the biggest misconception about government securities funds. The underlying portfolio of government paper is guaranteed for timely payment of principal and interest by Uncle Sam. Unfortunately, Uncle Sam *doesn't* guarantee that the fund will make money. There isn't even a guarantee that the dividends will remain the same, or continue at all, for that matter. Never forget, the securities *are* guaranteed, but your fund investment *isn't*.

I saw an ad for a government securities fund that is paying over 2 percent more than the current T-bill and thirty-year Treasury bond rates. How can this be?

There are two different ways that advertised yields for government securities funds can be higher than current rates. Many government securities portfolios were put together before a drop in rates. Portfolio managers were able to purchase Treasury bonds with higher yields and lock them into a portfolio, which then went on sale to the public. Thus, a higher yield is available to investors. But the funds that are advertising substantially higher yields than current rates may also be using very sophisticated hedging techniques, which we discussed in an earlier question, to enhance an already higher yield. A thorough reading of the prospectus will tell you why a fund has a particular yield.

I'm considering two government securities funds and I don't know why one is paying 9.5 percent while the other is paying 11.5 percent. They both invest in the same type of government securities, according to the prospectus.

Once again, we suggest you read further in the prospectus. The higher-paying fund, composed of the same securities, is most likely using hedging techniques to increase its yield and your risk.

I am a very conservative investor. Would you recommend that I avoid investing in a government securities fund that uses enhancement techniques?

If you're as conservative as you say you are, then by all means go with the fund that *doesn't* employ sophisticated strategies. Even with a government securities fund, you can't forget the rule "the greater the reward, the greater the risk."

Are the securities in a GNMA fund guaranteed by the U.S. government?

Yes, they are. GNMA funds are portfolios made up of government-backed pools of VA and FHA mortgages. But just like a government securities fund, your principal and dividends *aren't* guaranteed.

I bought a GNMA fund in September 1985. By March 1986, the net asset value was going down on what seemed like on a daily basis. I got nervous and sold. It had done so well until then. What happened?

You became a casualty of the push by many VA and FHA mortgage holders to refinance their homes when mortgage rates began falling to a new low. As mortgages were refinanced, old pools of GNMAs were paid off and principal was returned to the GNMA fund portfolio manager, who then had to go out into the marketplace and purchase new GNMA certificates that didn't have the same high coupon rates as before. This caused an overall drop in the value of GNMA-fund shares and sent a lot of nervous investors, such as yourself, scurrying to the sidelines. GNMA funds flourish when interest rates remain flat.

Did I make a mistake selling my GNMA-fund shares when I did?

The textbook answer is yes. Mutual funds should be bought and kept for the *long haul*. However, the human side says that if you found it difficult sleeping at night because you were worried about the investments, then you did the right thing.

If interest rates start a rapid rise upward in the future, what will happen to my GNMA fund and government-securities fund?

Because the market value of bonds and GNMAs decreases when interest rates increase, a sudden upward move in interest rates would cause a loss of principal, but it shouldn't be as severe as the drop in the market value of individual bonds and individual GNMAs. The funds' managers should sell large amounts of long-term bonds and GNMAs from their portfolios and reinvest in the money market and Treasury bills. The short-term positions don't react as much to interest rate moves. But because life isn't perfect, it would be nearly impossible for any fund manager to anticipate a sudden move accurately enough to remove all the troublemakers from the portfolio, and so you would see some decline in share price.

I've heard about something called a target fund. What is that?

Target funds buy bonds that all mature in the same year. The purpose is to give a long-term investor predictable income or a fairly precise idea of what the investment will be worth at a specific date. There are currently only a couple of mutual fund families that have target funds.

You mention total return funds all the time. What are they?

Total return funds combine the best of growth and income. These funds invest in the growth potential of common stocks as well as the income and safety of corporate and government bonds. Their goal is to provide an investor with long-term growth and small fluctuations from day to day. There are two types of total return funds: growth and income funds and balanced funds. A growth and income fund invests mostly in high-dividend stocks and convertible securities that pay fixed income like bonds but that can be exchanged for common stock. Balanced funds generally invest in stocks for growth and bonds for income.

How can I determine which funds are total return funds?

A few of the funds have the *total return* right in their names. However, to find most total return funds you will have to read the prospectus.

I find myself reading lots of ads nowadays that offer sector funds for investors. What exactly are sector funds?

Sector funds are portfolios that concentrate on investing in the stocks of a *single* industry, such as drugs, health care, manufacturing, etc. These highly specialized funds tend to undergo wide swings in share value because they aim at extremely high capital appreciation in a very narrow field. If you invest in a technology stock fund and the overall industry begins to lag, there's nowhere to hide! Unless you're an experienced investor, we really don't recommend sector investing. Mutual funds exist basically to give you some safety through wide diversification. Sector funds defeat this purpose.

I'm convinced that utility stocks will do well in the next few years. I know you're not great fans of sector funds, but I'd like to invest in a utility fund anyway. How much of my portfolio should be in this area?

Many experts recommend that you put no more than 20 percent of your portfolio into sector investments. Being more conservative than many, we feel 10 to 15 percent is a safer margin.

What about investing overseas? Are international funds also considered sector funds?

Yes, they are. Many people invest in international funds to take advantage of a favorable rate of exchange when the dollar weakens or when the U.S. markets turn bearish. Those who invested in international funds in 1986 reaped great rewards. We like to see a portion of a growth portfolio invested overseas, but we recommend that you do it in a global fund rather than an international fund.

What's the difference between a global fund and an international fund?

International funds invest solely in foreign securities. Global funds invest in *both* the U.S. and overseas. Because a global fund widely diversifies its portfolio among different countries, it tends to be the safest way to invest. Although 1986 was an exception to the rule, historically, global funds have outperformed international funds.

What do you think about investing in a single country or regional fund?

We think these funds are appropriate only for investors who like to take big chances. Because these portfolios focus in so narrowly on stocks of one country or one region, they rise and fall faster than many investors can move to lock in profits or avoid losses. If you consider yourself a conservative investor, we strongly recommend that you avoid these funds.

The financial planner with whom I'm currently working has suggested that I invest in a precious metals or gold fund to hedge my portfolio against inflation. Is this a smart idea?

Gold and other precious metals have been an excellent hedge against inflation in the past. In 1979, when we were experiencing rampant double-digit inflation, gold hit an all-time high of $850 an ounce, and precious metals stocks and funds earned huge returns for investors. However, inflation is currently under control and precious metals are underperforming almost every other kind of investment. If you are young and have many years to go before retirement, we see nothing wrong with a small investment in a precious metals fund; but no more than 5 percent of your portfolio. If, however, you are nearing retirement or already retired, don't bother. In our opinions, an investment in precious metals will need a lot of time to bear fruit.

I'm only thirty-two years old, so I think hedging my portfolio with a precious metals fund will be a good idea. Please give me some points to be aware of before I choose a fund.

Our first piece of advice is: *Buy no-load!* It's one of the few times we'll stress this. Precious metals funds generally need inflation to perform well. With no inflation of any import currently in sight, don't pay an up-front commission on something that has a better chance of going down right now than going up. At least give yourself a shot at success by seeing all your investment working for you right at the beginning. Secondly, and this is also the only time you'll hear us say this, don't be too concerned about the fund's past performance. With precious metals, past performance doesn't count a whole lot toward future return. Lastly, make sure that the fund is fully diversified among North American, Australian, and, if your social conscience isn't too active, South African stocks. To keep your risk under some control, great diversification is needed. If you find South African stocks too distasteful, there are funds that diversify well in North America and Australia without buying South African companies.

I'm starting to hear more about closed end funds. Are these mutual funds, or are they something different?

A closed end fund relies on professional management and diversification for the investor, but unlike an open end mutual fund, it has a *fixed* number of shares. These trade just like stocks on stock exchanges and over the counter. You must use a broker to buy closed end shares, and you will pay a commission. To our knowledge, there is no such thing as a no-load closed end fund.

Why do some portfolio managers choose to run a closed end fund rather than a mutual fund?

Mutual fund shares can be redeemed at any time, so if he or she is fully invested, a mutual fund manger may have to liquidate enough shares to pay the person cashing out. That could cost the manager and the fund money. A closed end manager can stay fully invested at all times if he or she so chooses because, as with stocks, a buyer must be found for those shares before a person can sell.

How do I choose a closed end fund wisely?

Just as you would with an open end mutual fund, make sure the portfolio fits your investment goals. The closed end fund should also have a solid track record of net asset value growth, just as you would look for in an open end fund.

How can I get a good buy on a closed end fund?

A closed end fund can be a bargain when it is selling at a discount to its net asset value. *The Wall Street Journal* publishes discounts and premiums on Mondays for closed end *stock* funds under the heading of "Publicly Traded Funds," and on Wednesdays it does the same for closed end *bond* funds. The best time to buy a closed end fund is when it's trading at a wider discount than usual. Performance data for many closed end funds can be found in *The Weisenberger Investment Companies Service* and *The Value Line Investment Survey*. Both books are available at most large public libraries.

Is a closed end fund a better performer than an open end mutual fund?

Closed end funds are not generally compared to open end funds, because it's rather like comparing apples to oranges. Our good friend Ken Weber, who tracks open end funds very successfully in his newsletter *Weber's Fund Advisor*, however, is very vocal about his personal dislike of closed end funds. Ken considers investing in an open end fund similar to being in a boat on the ocean. The investor is constantly rocked by investment waves. Closed end fund investing, however, is like being on a waterbed in a boat on the ocean. A closed end fund reacts not only to how well the portfolio manager is doing or not doing, but also to how well the public *perceives* the manager is doing. That could mean double trouble for an investor.

How often should I check the net asset value of my mutual fund?

Unlike a single stock, which you might want to look at every day, mutual fund shares for long-term growth and growth and income funds only need to be looked at quarterly. Too many investors live and die by the daily price changes in their mutual fund shares and inevitably feel the urge to sell when they might be better off sitting tight or even buying more shares. For sector fund investors, however, we recommend you check those prices every day.

I had no trouble picking a mutual fund to *buy*, but trying to decide when to *sell* it is driving me crazy! Help!

Deciding when to sell a fund is often more difficult than choosing a fund. Our emotions always seem to get in the way once our money is committed. In order to find the right time to sell, it is wise to check frequently the fund you own with other similar funds and with your goals, if your goals have changed. Here's a list of events that would suggest you consider selling your mutual fund shares:

- *A change in your financial situation:* brought on by nearing retirement, loss of your job, need to pay for your child's college education, etc.
- *A change in the fund:* it may have grown too large, increased its fees, lost a successful manager, or changed its objectives.
- *A continued poor performance record:* determined by comparing its record with other funds of the same type.
- *A market shift:* whether you invest in a stock or bond mutual fund or combination of the two, funds tend to rise or fall with the general market's strengths or weaknesses. A bear stock or bond market may suggest a time to sell shares.

I contacted a mutual fund company and told them to sell my shares. The person on the other end of the phone told me that my money wouldn't be released for a few days because it would adversely affect the fund if my shares were sold that day. Is that legal?

It could very well be legal. The Securities and Exchange Commission allows funds up to seven days to pay you your money. In some funds' prospectuses, it is stated that the fund reserves the right to withhold immediate payment if such payment would adversely affect the fund. In other words, if a very deep drop in the market triggered a flood of sell orders from investors, a fund that stated the aforementioned warning in its prospectus might wait for a few days to cash out your shares. Sector funds often have this provision in their prospectus and they've frequently been known to hold up payment to shareholders for a few days. However, the Investment Company Act of 1940 stipulates that an investor must receive his or her funds within seven days.

I want to sell my fund shares. I really need the money as soon as possible. What's the fastest way to get it?

The quickest way to get your money is to ask the fund to wire it through the Federal Reserve's electronic transfer system directly to your bank account. That should give you use of your money within two days. But also be aware that using this electronic transfer system isn't free—it could cost you up to $20 to do it.

I'm about to liquidate my position in a mutual fund, but I'm confused by the tax consequences. How do I treat the capital gains and dividends that were reinvested?

Don't feel bad about the tax confusion you're going through. Mutual fund taxation can be a killer! However, as to *reinvested* capital gains and dividends, you've paid taxes on them in the year they were made. So there's no need to pay taxes again! Subtract from your gain, if you have a gain, the value of shares that were purchased through a reinvestment program. You can forget about them.

I'm planning to sell a portion of shares I own in a mutual fund. The first shares cost much less than the shares I bought later. How will the IRS tax me when I sell?

The first rule of any mutual fund sale is: If you make a profit when you sell shares, you'll be taxed on that profit! Now, let's go on from there, assuming you have a profit. If you haven't saved all your statements from the fund, which identify the different prices at which you bought shares, then the IRS will more than likely choose to believe that you are selling the first shares you bought rather than the last. This first-in first-out tax treatment could create bigger paper profits than what you actually received, and cost you more taxes.

I've kept all my statements of purchase from the fund, thank goodness. How do I get the IRS to consider this partial sale of shares as a sale of the most expensive shares?

There are two ways to go about it, depending upon the fund's growth record:

- *Last in, first out:* Use this strategy with a fund that has had a steady rise in share value. Inform the IRS that you are selling the last shares you bought. In this way you can postpone paying taxes on shares that have a lower cost and a bigger gain.
- *Identifiable cost:* Use this strategy with a fund that has share prices that have fluctuated up and down. Tell the fund to sell the shares for which you paid the most. By your telling them the date of purchase and the price, they'll be able to do what you ask. Also ask the fund for a written statement that proves these shares were the ones you sold, just in case Uncle Sam asks for an audit.

I invested in a mutual fund with a lump sum. Now I want to sell. Is there some way I can avoid paying too much money in taxes?

A lump sum purchase or a sale of all your shares at once will add up to a bigger tax bite, no matter what you do. There is nowhere to hide. You will have to add up what you paid for the shares and subtract that from the proceeds received from the sale. Once again, we remind you to subtract from the gain any shares purchased by dividend and capital gain reinvestment because you already paid the taxes on those shares in the year they were purchased.

If I buy shares in a mutual fund, am I insured if the mutual fund company goes out of business?

Federal law requires all mutual funds to carry insurance to protect investors against losses due to fraud. However, there is no insurance to protect you if your fund goes down because of bad investment decisions. Funds that advertise insured municipal bonds or government-backed securities mean that the *individual securities* are insured or backed by the government. They do *not* mean that the fund performance is insured. Take comfort in the fact that, to our knowledge, no fund has ever gone out of business in the history of the industry, although some funds have failed to come back after heavy losses from falling markets, coupled with bad investment choices.

SUMMARY

Mutual funds have come into their own. Once considered an investment fit only for the uneducated or the small investor, they have now become a major force to be reckoned with, allowing people to band together and stand their ground side by side with the big guys, i.e., the institutions whose buying and selling en masse has dominated the financial marketplace.

People have discovered that mutual funds allow them to deal not only with the ups and downs of the stock market but also with more conservative investment strategies, such as bonds and government securities.

Entire portfolios are now built on mutual fund investments from real estate to precious metals, from international investing to limited sectors of the U.S. economy.

All investments, even professionally managed portfolios, have certain rules for success:

- Read the prospectus *before* you invest.
- Be sure the fund's objective matches your own.
- Total return is more important than current yield.
- Insured or government-backed portfolios don't ensure or guarantee performance for the investor.
- Excessive management fees can be as costly as an up-front sales charge.
- Track record plays an important part in choosing a well-managed fund. The "hot" performer of one year may not make the grade in following years.

Properly chosen and monitored, mutual funds can be your most successful investment vehicle.

FURTHER INFORMATION
ORGANIZATION

Investment Company Institute
1600 M Street, N.W.
Suite 600
Washington, D.C.
(202) 293–7700

The Mutual Fund Fact Book (yearly
$9.95)
The 1990 Guide to Mutual Funds
(yearly $5.00)

MAGAZINES

Forbes annual mutual-fund survey
(September issue)

Changing Times annual mutual-fund
survey (October issue)

Money semiannual mutual fund
survey (spring and fall)

DIRECTORIES

*Handbook for No-Load Fund
Investors*
The No-Load Fund Investor, Inc.
P.O. Box 283
Hastings-on-Hudson, New York
10706

Mutual-Fund Sourcebook
53 N. Jackson Blvd.
Chicago, Illinois 60604

*Weisenberger Investment Companies
Service*
Warren, Gorham & Lamont
1633 Broadway
New York, New York 10019

NEWSLETTERS

*Jay Schabacker's Mutual Fund
Investing*
Phillips Publishing, Inc.
7811 Montrose Road
Potomac, Maryland 20854

Sector Funds Newsletter
P.O. Box 1210
Escondido, California 92025

Weber's Fund Advisor
Ken Weber, Inc.
P.O. Box 3490
New Hyde Park, New York 11040

No-Load Fund Investor
The No-Load Fund Investor, Inc.
P.O. Box 283
Hastings-on-Hudson, New York
10706

The Mutual Fund Letter
Investment Information Services
205 W. Wacker Drive
Chicago, Illinois 60606

CDA Mutual Fund Report
CDA Investment Technologies
11501 Georgia Avenue
Silver Spring, Maryland 20902

BOOKS

*Mutual Funds—How to Invest With
the Pros*
Kurt Brouwer
Wiley & Sons, Inc.

7

Insurance

Bud Abbott and Lou Costello once took out a $100,000 insurance policy with Lloyds of London that required payment if any of their audience died of laughter. That's probably the first and only time insurance and humor have ever been lumped together!

For as long as we can remember, the thought, much less the mention, of insurance has sent shivers through most of us. A salesman's foot in the door, hard-sell tactics, and a big hand out for premium checks are just some of the pictures that come to mind.

We all realize that *protection*, insurance's prime goal, is a noble reason for going through the sometimes tedious process of actually dealing with the insurance company and its salesperson, but taking that big first step can be frightening and confusing. The proliferation of many new and different kinds of insurance policies, as well as the proliferation of the many different types of companies (banks, brokerage firms, etc.) offering these varied alternatives, has further confused and put at arm's length many potential insurance buyers.

In this chapter we'll discuss three important types of insurance designed to protect those we love from the financial problems of death, traumatic injury, and health problems—namely, life, disability, and health insurance.

Insurance is a most important financial planning tool. Are you ready for some painless insurance information? Let's dive in!

What is insurance?

Insurance is a system that reimburses individuals and companies in the event of loss. The insurer makes profits by investing the premiums (payments) it receives. This transfers the risk from an individual or company to a larger group, which is more able to pay for losses.

What is the difference between cash value insurance and term insurance?

These are two very distinct and different types of life insurance.

Cash value (whole life, for example) is the amount the insurance company will return to a policyholder upon cancellation of the policy. Often, the insured can borrow against the cash value in the policy at better than market rates.

Term insurance is cheaper than cash value or whole life insurance, because the owner of the policy only pays for death protection. No cash value is built up. Term insurance becomes more expensive as the policyholder grows older, because he or she is statistically more likely to die.

Why should I buy life insurance? My wife has money in the bank and a job to support herself.

Well, she'll have a lot to pay for—as would you—if you were to die first. Who's going to:

- pay funeral costs, pay medical bills if you were sick prior to your death, and pay probate estate fees?
- finish paying for your home, auto, etc.?
- pay for child care on one salary?
- pay for any necessary job training to advance her in the work force?
- pay for your children's college educations?

Any more questions?

We've just gotten married and want to start off on the right foot insurance-wise. Any suggestions?

Sure. First investigate the merits (and low cost) of term insurance, which has no cash buildup but will give you the biggest bang for your insurance buck.

Once and for all, would you please give me an understandable explanation of term insurance?

Let's give it a try. Term is the simplest kind of insurance. You insure your life for a fixed period (one year, five years, or more) and pay an annual premium. No cash value buildup—death benefit only.

How is the annual premium determined on a term policy?

It's determined by your age at the time of purchase. The older you get, the more the policy costs.

What types of term policies are available?

You may purchase level term or declining, decreasing, or reducing term.

What is level term insurance?

Level term is a type of policy where the amount of coverage, the face amount, remains fixed at the same amount for the policy's life.

Are declining, decreasing, and reducing term insurance different kinds of policies, or are they the same thing?

They are the same thing. This is a type of policy where the face amount periodically drops according to a fixed schedule over ten, fifteen, twenty, or more years. You receive more protection during the early years, when, for most families, the children are small and the expenses are high.

Suppose we would like to use insurance as an investment instead of just for death protection?

If permanent cash value life insurance is more to your liking, look into a modified life policy. This is an insurance policy in which the premiums (payments) start relatively low and increase during the following years as your income builds. This policy will give you cash buildup as well as death protection.

How does a person decide whether to buy a term policy or a cash value policy?

That's a good question and a tough one! If death protection is your major need and you feel comfortable with your ability to save money and invest it prudently, you may very well be better off with the cheaper insurance, term. If you are less concerned about death protection and find the investment feature of insurance—either at your direction or at the insurance company's—and the forced-saving concept of premium payments attractive, then cash value insurance is for you.

Some cash value policies do offer some attractive investment alternatives, as well as the opportunity to borrow from the policy on a tax-free basis or below the going market interest rates. Take the time to investigate the flexibility of some of these policies.

Do I really need an insurance agent when I can buy a policy through my bank or financial adviser?

Everyone, it seems, is in the insurance business, and everyone is an insurance expert. Hardly! Although insurance expertise is available in a number of places, it's important that you find out the level of expertise of the financial professional with whom you are considering working. Our preference? Work with an *insurance* agent who has a minimum of five years' experience and is certified as a chartered life underwriter (CLU).

Why do I have to buy life insurance? My company carries it for me.

Often the amount of life-insurance coverage offered by a company is relatively small ($25,000 to $50,000). These policies are basically designed to supplement other coverage. Company coverage is great to have, but it's usually not enough.

What are the most common mistakes people make when they buy insurance?

Jim Hunt, the director of the National Insurance Consumer Organization, has come up with a *great* checklist of consumer mistakes.

- *Mistake 1:* to buy life insurance when you have no dependents. If you're single, you don't need life insurance.
- *Mistake 2:* to buy mail-order insurance. Often it's a bad bargain.
- *Mistake 3:* to put money into an insurance policy that builds up cash value without having established an IRA account. You're better off with a term policy unless you plan on holding that cash-value policy for at least ten years.
- *Mistake 4:* to buy a cash value policy or *any* policy from a high-pressure salesperson. Agents make five to ten times more in commissions selling you a $100,000 cash value policy than a term policy for the same amount. Be alert to the hard sell.
- *Mistake 5:* to buy life insurance and not disability insurance. A long-term disability can be even worse financially for a family than can a death. If you're disabled, you not only lose income, you still incur living expenses. Only 30 percent of American workers have disability coverage at work.
- *Mistake 6:* to buy riders on your policy, such as accidental death benefits or additional purchase options. These are high-profit items that are best avoided.

I'm single, have a good job, and have no plans to get married in the near future. Do I really need insurance?

Unless you have a substantial asset to protect, such as a home, investment property, or the like, we see no reason to have any insurance at this stage in your life. It's also possible that you have a company benefit plan that is adequate for your needs.

My children are grown, I have a good job, and my wife and I have invested wisely. We have a very substantial portfolio of investments. Why should I buy life insurance?

Maybe you shouldn't buy *life* insurance if your investments will take care of your wife if you die. However, you should have disability coverage, because you're more likely to become disabled than to die before age sixty-five. We discuss disability insurance later in this chapter.

Am I better off investing my money wisely than buying insurance to protect my family?

For your family's protection, you should have some insurance while your investments grow. We recommend that you buy term insurance, the cheapest kind, and invest the rest.

I assume that selecting an insurance agent is an important step in getting my insurance act together. Can you give me some selection direction?

We'll try. You're right, it is a very important step. As with any other member of your personal financial planning team (lawyer, accountant, broker, etc.) you should pick an agent who:

- has had professional training in the insurance area, with a designation such as CLU (chartered life underwriter). This is a helpful guideline, although not *every* good agent has certification.
- has had at least five years of experience.
- will provide ongoing service to you, not sell a policy and disappear forever.
- will objectively review your needs on a regular basis and suggest courses of action.
- will meet with other members of your financial team (lawyer, CPA, etc.).
- makes you feel comfortable in terms of style and approach.

How can I find the names of several insurance agents to begin evaluating?

There are a few ways to begin. The best method is to ask your lawyer, CPA, and doctor for referrals.

I've finally admitted that I need insurance. I have an appointment with a life insurance salesman, and although I have done some homework, I really need a list of questions to ask. I want the best coverage for my family. A checklist, please!

Congratulations on stepping up to the insurance plate! Here are a few questions that you want answered *clearly* or you will *not* purchase a policy, right? Okay! (Some of these questions are specifically aimed at either term or cash value policies, but the basic idea here is *disclosure.*)

1. Is there a free look period with the company, during which you can cancel the policy without a surrender charge? This would be somewhat less important if you *really* did your homework before buying a policy. Unfortunately, many people don't.
2. What is the rate of return, and how is it calculated? The *key point* is, How much is my money going to earn? (cash value policies)
3. Is the rate you're quoting net or gross, i.e., before or after your company's expenses? (cash value policies)
4. A. M. Best rates the financial stability of insurance companies. How does it rate yours? (A or better means a financially sound insurance company.)
5. How is the death benefit handled? Some policies begin with a low death benefit that increases as your cash value builds, and others start

with a higher death benefit that *doesn't* grow as cash value builds. In the latter case, your death benefit actually will shrink if you borrow the interest built up in your policy. (cash value policies)

6. What are the borrowing provisions, interest rate to be charged, repayment schedule, fees, etc.? (cash value policies)

7. Are you able to surrender the policy without penalty if there is a major occurrence such as a precipitous drop in interest rates, i.e., a much lower return on your money than planned? (cash value policies)

How can I compare one insurance company's cash value policy with another's? There must be hundreds of choices!

There may be thousands! One telltale sign is the consistency of a company's dividend payments. If you're having trouble getting that answer from your agent, you may be dealing with the wrong company. Secondly, a company *must* be rated A or better by A. M. Best and Company, an insurance company rating service, or you shouldn't even *consider* that company.

Do some insurance companies pay dividends, and do they all pay the same amount?

Yes and no. Many insurance companies pay dividends, but they do vary from company to company. It's important to check a company's track record before buying its policy.

How can I check a company's dividend payment record?

Best's Review magazine, available at most major libraries, is a great source of many types of information relating to insurance companies, including dividend payment records. You can also ask your agent for a copy of the *Best*'s rating of the company he's recommending.

I've asked my insurance company for pertinent financial information because you always stress the importance of an insurer's financial stability. No luck so far. Do you have any suggestions?

You may (and in this case *should*) contact your state insurance department and ask for its help. It will give you assistance because *you're* paying the salaries of its employees!

Are there any special prices on term insurance?

- Women pay approximately 10 percent less for a term policy.
- Nonsmokers pay from 30 to 75 percent less for a term policy than smokers do.

Is there any advantage to purchasing an insurance policy from a large company versus a small one?

Our recommendation is to deal with a large insurance company that has been around many years and that has lots of money. However, some of the smaller companies are very stable, provide good service, and sell very attractive policies. To make the decision easier, check out the A. M. Best rating as well as the experience of the person with whom you will be dealing.

What about buying a policy from a lesser-known company that advertises cut-rate/discount policies? There seem to be some real bargains.

You get what you pay for!

My company offers free group term insurance. It seems like a good deal, but I've found that the better something looks, the more careful I should be. Your thoughts, please.

Good philosophy! The final decision to participate is, of course, yours. Here are some factors to weigh *before* making a final decision.

Advantages:
- It's usually available to group members without a medical examination.
- The ability to convert term group insurance to a whole life policy if you leave the group is sometimes offered.

Disadvantages:
- The amount of group life insurance available may not be enough for your needs.
- The insurance ends when you leave the group or retire, although more and more companies are continuing to include their retired employees in the plan in an amount equal to one quarter or one half their preretirement amount.

If it's free, how bad can that be? However, don't automatically assume that the coverage is enough for you and your family.

My company offers group term insurance at a reduced rate. Should I sign up?

Before you do anything, check that the benefits offered by your company's plan are what you need. If they are, then shop around before you sign up, to be sure that what the company offers is competitive.

I'm in middle management at my company. The company gives me $100,000 in life insurance, but I'm single and don't need that much. Are there tax consequences to receiving this amount of coverage?

Generally speaking, there may be tax consequences attached to the amount of insurance that you receive over $50,000 in face value. Check with your company's benefits department and your accountant.

How can I get the amount of my company life insurance coverage lowered?

It's likely that the amount of coverage you receive is stipulated by the company. There is probably a formula whereby members of management must receive a specific amount of insurance relative to that of other employees and other criteria. It's not likely that you will be able to change the amount.

My fraternal organization has offered all the members term insurance coverage. Is this a good deal? Will it be better than an individual policy?

Unlike buying directly from an insurance company to receive an individual policy, buying the insurance through an association or sponsored group covers you only through the seller's (insurance company's) master contract, which means if you leave the group, the coverage stops.

There are two things to make note of here:

- If you leave the group and the coverage stops, generally the coverage can be maintained only by converting the term policy into a cash value policy, which will mean higher premiums.
- Individual policy premiums can increase only up to a guaranteed maximum, but there's no such guarantee with association/group plans. With these, the issuer may raise the rate beyond what is normal for individual policies.

Who sells association insurance plans?

Many of these policies are offered by mail. Sellers of mail-order life insurance claim that their less expensive way of selling insurance allows them to pass along the savings to you. Your saving (or lack of it) depends upon your particular needs and your stick-to-itiveness in comparing mail-order and non-mail-order policies.

Do mail-order policies have certain restrictions?

Generally, they do.

- The policy may be offered only during limited enrollment periods.
- Generally speaking, the amount of insurance that you are able to buy is fairly modest.
- The full face value isn't paid for deaths that occur within at least the first two years that the policy is in force.
- The premiums are generally much higher, because a medical exam is not always required.

Would you recommend mail-order insurance?

It's worth checking into, but use it only as as supplement to your individual insurance plan, not as a foundation for family insurance.

My insurance agent has compared the term policies of several companies with the policy *his* company is offering. I'm afraid he (and the numbers) may lack objectivity. Is there a service that will make an objective comparison for me?

You bet. A frequent guest on our radio show is Milton Brown, president of Insurance Information, Inc. For $50, Milton's company will search for the five companies with the most favorable rates and best coverage you can get in term insurance. The company refunds your $50 if it can't save you at least $50 on your first year's premium after a thorough search. And the best news is that Insurance Information *does not* sell insurance!

> Insurance Information, Inc.
> 110 Breed's Hill Road
> Suite #4
> Hyannis, MA 02601
> (508) 790–2866
> (800) 472–5800 (outside Massachusetts)

I wish I'd heard about Insurance Information sooner. I already bought a term policy.

No problem. Insurance Information will also compare rates of your current policy with similar policies offered by other companies. It's never too late. A comparison now could still save you lots of dollars over the life of your policy.

Is there a similar service that will compare other types of insurance policies?

Yes. The National Insurance Consumer Organization will compare a wide variety of cash value and term insurance policies, including annuities. The charge is $25. For more information, contact:

> The National Insurance Consumer Organization
> 121 N. Payne Street
> Alexandria, Virginia 22314
> (703) 549–8050

I bought a term policy about ten years ago. It seems to me that the premiums of the newer policies are lower. Is that fact or fiction?

Generally, it's a fact. After checking, you might find that you can replace your older policy with a lower-priced new one, especially if you're a non-smoker.

What is meant by the convertible feature of term insurance?

This is an important benefit of term insurance. Under this provision the policy may be converted, for a higher premium, into a cash value (permanent) policy without your having to meet the medical standards at the time of conversion.

My insurance agent keeps stressing the importance of annual renewable term insurance. What is that?

Annual renewable term insurance is a policy that allows you to renew every year without undergoing an annual medical exam. Generally speaking, it may be in force to age sixty-five, seventy, or one hundred.

What do you think of annual renewable term insurance?

We like it *very* much. The ability to be able to depend on insurance from year to year even though a medical setback may occur is a major insurance plus. It's also a good value in the early years but gets very expensive as you grow older. Ask about reentry provisions, which allow you, as a policyholder, to take medical exams, usually every five years, to qualify for lower rates. That would keep the cost down a little.

Why would I buy a decreasing term policy?

This type of policy is most often purchased to protect a family's home from the unexpected death of the breadwinner. In an ideal situation, as you pay down your mortgage, the face value of your term policy declines as well. Properly constructed, as the home mortgage is paid off, the term policy lapses. It's mortgage protection. Of course, since most families face very high expenses when their children are college age, these policies may have to be rethought.

My mother wants to buy a life insurance policy for our new child, her first grandchild. Does that make sense?

We're more concerned that you and your husband have adequate insurance coverage so that your child will be taken care of if anything happens to *one of you*. If you're not properly covered, buying *you* life insurance would be a better gift! We recommend growth-oriented mutual funds, zero coupon bonds, or U.S. savings bonds as baby's first investment.

How much life insurance do I really need to support my family if I'm not around?

It's difficult to put a formula on the need factor because it varies according to age, life-style, etc. But a good general rule is that you should provide *six* times your annual wage in life insurance if you have a young family. In the case of an older couple whose family has grown and moved out, providing for long-term medical care becomes the major concern. We discuss this later in the chapter.

Where does an insurance company get the money to pay the $100,000 my family will receive when I die? My premiums won't total anywhere near that amount!

When you buy insurance, the premiums you pay are combined with those of all the other policyholders in the company. This forms a pool of funds from which all claims are paid. But the insurance company doesn't just sit on this money. The company invests it to make it grow.

Some of the new policies are being touted as investment vehicles. Is this a new twist?

A new twist, yes, but not the reason to buy life insurance. If you can make a few extra dollars from buying an insurance policy, great. But life insurance should be purchased for one *fundamental* reason: You buy to protect the people who depend on you for their support and who would need financial assistance if you died—*income protection*. There are other benefits to some types of insurance, such as tax-free withdrawal, but family protection is, in our opinion, the primary reason for insurance.

What is whole life insurance?

Whole life is a type of life insurance that offers death protection and also builds up cash value. The policy stays in force for the lifetime of the person insured or until it is canceled or it lapses. The policyholder generally pays the same annual premium for the entire life of the policy. The cash value earnings are tax deferred and can be borrowed against. Whole life insurance is also called ordinary life, permanent life, or straight life insurance.

Who should buy a whole life insurance policy?

The first consideration must be can you afford a large premium payment? Whole life policies should be looked at as a forced savings plan for those who may lack the discipline to save on their own. If you are considering whole life insurance, you must also be aware of the lack of liquidity in this type of investment. You should be able to do without the original cash placed in your policy for at least ten years.

How often are premiums paid on a whole life policy?

Premiums, in a fixed amount, can be paid monthly, quarterly, or annually.

I hear that the sales commission on a whole life policy is a big one. Is that true?

Yes. Your insurance agent pockets between 50 and 100 percent of the first year's premium, and that is subtracted from your invested dollars. With such hefty charges, it takes a year or two for many policies to get out of the red. We're not saying don't buy this type, but you must be aware of the expense.

How does the cost of a whole life policy compare with a term policy?

A term policy is much cheaper. For instance, a man in his mid-thirties wanting to purchase $200,000 of insurance could buy term insurance for less than $300 a year. The cost of whole life would be $2500 a year!

Why would *anyone* buy whole life rather than term after hearing the difference in premium cost?

Because there are several good points about whole life:

- Whole life premiums *never* change. The price of term insurance can increase every year.
- After ten years, the cash value of a whole life policy starts really building up. Term insurance doesn't accrue any cash value.
- A whole life policyholder can borrow against his policy's cash value at low interest rates. A term policyholder cannot borrow (no cash value).

I think I heard my insurance agent say something about an excess-interest whole life policy. Is there such an animal?

There sure is. An excess-interest whole life policy is one in which the death benefit is fixed and premium payments may be periodically changed by the company. After a number of years, when the cash value has sufficiently built up, premium payments may be reduced or eliminated altogether.

Who should look at an excess-interest whole life policy?

This type of policy might be particularly attractive to someone who is in his or her peak earning years now and would look forward to a cut or elimination of premium payments later in life, when income might be lower due to retirement.

Can I borrow against my whole life policy?

Yes, you can.

What rate of interest will I be charged if I borrow against my policy?

Approximately 4 or 5 percent. The face of the policy will tell you exactly what your company charges.

I've found a policy that pays higher dividends than my present nine year old policy. It looks awfully tempting. Should I switch?

We're sure it looks tempting, but don't forget one key factor. You've already paid the sales cost for the original policy with the premiums from the first year, and maybe more. You may have to pay that charge again if you switch. So don't be too hasty. Work the numbers *before* you make a move.

Are there any circumstances where it might make sense to switch policies?

Yes. But don't get the wrong idea. We're not saying switch or don't switch. We are giving you guidelines:

- If you need more protection than your existing whole life policy gives and want to minimize premium payments, consider borrowing against your whole life policy and buy some term insurance with the proceeds, or even make some conservative investments with the borrowed money.
- Maybe you currently own term insurance, but after doing your homework, you find another insurer who will give you the same coverage

for less money, along with comparable conversion and renewability guarantees. In this case, you should consider switching.

- You're a nonsmoker. New policies may reward you with lower premiums than some older policies, so consider switching.

My insurance agent has recommended that my husband and I switch insurance policies from an older one to a new hybrid type, with investment options and borrowing provisions. Should we be interested?

Interested, yes. However, very often you'll be better off holding on to what you already have.

- It's likely there's another sales commission involved with switching policies—very likely!
- You're older now, so expect higher premiums with a new policy.
- With the older policy, you're covered. A new policy brings the two year period of contestability, which is protection for the insurer. For various reasons, such as a preexisting ailment, the insurer may refuse to pay the benefit if something happens.
- Your present policy may have better terms relating to disability, settlement options, etc.

Take a real hard look before you do *any* switching!

I've found two whole life insurance policies that appear to have exactly the same provisions. I'm really having trouble comparing them any further. What can I do?

Here are the questions to ask to help choose the right one:

- What dividends are you likely to receive from each policy? (That will depend on the companies' investment expertise.)
- Ask the company what cash value is likely to be available from each policy.
- Find out the sum of the premiums you'll pay over the life of the policy. (Pick age sixty or sixty-five as the duration of the policy for the sake of comparison.)

What is variable whole life?

Variable whole life is a type of insurance that gives policyholders a chance to earn capital gains on their insurance investment. As a policyholder you can choose to invest in stock, bond, or money market accounts or allow the insurance company professional to make those decisions for you. The annual premium is a fixed one, but a portion of that premium is marked for the investment side of the product. As the policyholder you bear all risk of investment decisions, and the insurance company guarantees you a minimum death benefit that is not influenced by losses the investment portfolio may incur.

Who should buy variable whole life?

Variable whole life is for a person who wants/needs death protection but is willing to take some risk in order to possibly receive a larger death benefit and a higher cash value.

Is variable whole life more risky than straight whole life?

Yes, it is. Never forget one thing: The greater the potential reward, the greater the potential risk is.

What similarities does variable life share with straight whole life?

There are several similarities:

- Premiums are a fixed amount paid monthly, quarterly, or annually.
- Investment choices include stock, bond, and money market portfolios.
- You may get a policy loan at similar rates with both types of policies.

What about a rate of return comparison between straight whole life and variable life?

Straight whole life guarantees an amount that your accumulated premiums/earnings will be worth in the future. That's not the case with variable life. That rate of return fluctuates with investment performance, though a minimum death benefit is guaranteed.

I understand very little about insurance, although I know that it's important for my family's protection. I thought I was getting an education in insurance, and then someone mentioned universal life. What the heck is that?

Universal life, which was "born" in 1985, is a variation of whole life, with some important differences, including:

- *death benefit:* a fixed amount with whole life, but variable with universal life (UL). You can raise or lower the amount annually.
- *premiums:* a fixed amount with whole life, but with UL you can increase or reduce premiums and even skip a year if you so choose.
- *rate of return:* with whole life, a guaranteed cash value accumulation, but with UL there is usually around a 4 percent minimum floor rate of return; above that, there's a variable rate because rates change from day to day. The success of the insurance company's investment of your premiums may enhance your return.
- *access to cash value (loans):* with both whole life and universal life, you can borrow at rates of approximately 6 to 8 percent. With UL there is a $25 withdrawal fee.

Which is cheaper to buy, whole life or universal life?

Although cheaper shouldn't be the sole criterion for choosing one type of policy over another, universal life costs about one third less than a whole-life policy with the same death benefit. Universal life also provides more flexibility than whole life because it allows you to vary your premiums, coverage, and investment strategy.

I understand that a universe life insurer, unlike many whole life insurers, will inform me of the current rate of return and how much of my premium is being used for expenses.
That's right. It's another plus for universal life.

What is universal life II? Is that son of universal life?
Not exactly. Universal life II (UL II) is a policy for family protection that has both premium payment and investment flexibility. You can choose how your premiums are invested and you can increase or decrease the premium or skip an entire year altogether.

What are the death benefit provisions with UL II?
You choose an amount of coverage when you buy the policy. Coverage will increase if your investments prosper.

How about the rate of return on my cash value with universal life II?
There is *no* guaranteed rate of return. It varies with investment performance.

Can I borrow on my UL II policy?
Yes, you can and at *very* competitive rates.

My insurance agent tells me that I have an option with *his* universal life policy to pay exactly the same premium each year instead of different amounts. This might give me a higher yield because his company could plan on using a specific amount of money every year. What do you think?
That may be, but to give up the flexibility of paying larger or smaller premium payments is giving up one of the key pluses of a universal life policy. We recommend you don't do that!

I've done some investigating and found out that I can buy several times more life insurance with a term policy than I can with single premium life insurance. How come?
In order to be able to offer tax-free loans on policies, single premium life insurance companies offer the minimum of life insurance benefits. Once again, we stress that the attraction of being able to borrow money tax-free from built-up cash value (accumulated earnings) at low interest rates is the hook for single premium life insurance. It's *not* death protection.

What is single premium life insurance?
Single premium life insurance is a cash value policy that allows you to

make one lump sum premium payment and no more. You pay between $5000 and $1 million, and the death benefit remains a fixed amount.

With a single premium policy can I dictate how my premium is invested?
No, you can't.

Is the rate of return on cash value guaranteed?
A guaranteed floor rate of return, usually around 4 percent, is stipulated. Above that 4 percent, the return is variable, depending on the prevailing level of interest rates. The rate paid usually changes every two or three years.

Is it expensive to borrow against a single premium policy?
No. The cost ranges from 2 to 4 percent, and when you factor in your earnings from the policy, it may cost little, if *anything*, to borrow against it.

What happens if I have to cash in a single premium life insurance policy during the early years?
Grief! A single premium life policy is *not* a short-term investment. If you cash in early, the closing fee is subtracted from your lump sum premium, usually 9 percent in the first year and one percentage point less for every year after that. Since it takes *at least* seven years to accumulate enough cash for tax-free borrowing, an early termination cancels out the primary reason for buying the policy—tax-free money.

Single premium life insurance seems to be the hottest insurance policy on the market today. Is it primarily for death protection or investment?
Actually, it's neither. A single premium policy is bought primarily as a tax-advantaged investment rather than as an insurance vehicle. An attractive tax benefit is that you can borrow against the accumulated earnings at a net cost of zero.

What are the tax consequences when I cancel my single premium life insurance policy?
If you cancel the policy, income taxes are due on the accumulated earnings, and cashing in the policy within the first few years may mean an early surrender charge to the insurance company.

What is a single premium variable life policy?
It is similar to a single premium policy, but:

- You can choose how your premiums are invested—in stock, bond, or money market portfolios. You can also change your decision from time to time.

- The limited death benefit may increase if your investment decisions are good.

With a variable single premium policy is there any minimum guaranteed rate of return?

No. Once again, the rate fluctuates with investment performance.

Borrowing with this type of policy is advantageous too, isn't it?

Yes. As with a single premium policy, loans are generally free of charge on earnings and 2 to 4 percent on your lump sum amount. However, it takes around seven years' worth of accumulation for a sufficient amount of capital to have been built up to borrow.

Should I borrow against a variable single premium policy?

It doesn't make much sense to borrow against your policy when your cash is invested in the stock portfolio. You might miss the chance for a big gain. If you've borrowed from the stock portfolio, all the insurer will credit you with on borrowed money is a return equal to your loan interest. That might cost you dearly.

I have been deemed a higher-than-average risk because of unexplainable dizzy spells. Is it going to cost me more for life insurance?

Unfortunately, yes. Here's one of the perfect reasons to have a trustworthy, experienced insurance agent. In this instance, your agent must help you shop for the best rate, because underwriting standards vary greatly from company to company.

I've been paying higher life insurance premiums because I have had some mild epileptic fits in the past, but now I'm completely cured. Is there any chance that my premiums can be lowered?

If a person's health improves or there has been no evidence of disease for a period of time, then it is possible that his or her premium may be reduced.

How can I go about getting my premium charge reduced?

Call your insurance agent and have him go to bat for a lower premium. Having some documentation provided by your doctor will help the agent when your case is reviewed.

I was just filling out some forms to take out additional life insurance when I was informed that I need delicate heart surgery. Needless to say, I didn't bother finishing the application. Is there anything I can do?

There is insurance available called short-term surgical-survival insurance, which is paid to a beneficiary if the insured (you) dies within thirty days as a result of surgery.

How much surgical-survival insurance is available for someone facing heart surgery?

Up to a maximum of $500,000 is available.

Surgical-survival insurance must be awfully expensive, right?

The cost of this specialized insurance is a one-time premium of 1 to 5 percent of the face value of the policy. Call your insurance agent, and good luck!

My father has just passed away. Among his personal effects we found what appears to be the number of an insurance policy. How can we track down this phantom policy?

Check through your father's canceled checks and receipts. You may find evidence of payment to an insurance company. If not, don't give up. He may have been covered at his current or former place of employment. Check the company's personnel department. If both these courses of action fail, contact the Life Bureau of the Department of Insurance in any state in which your father lived. This office *may* have your father's policy listed under his name rather than under the policy number. Another source of help is the American Council of Life Insurance which offers a free search service. You may receive a lost policy questionnaire and further information by writing to the Council's Policy Search Department, 1001 Pennsylvania Avenue N.W., Washington, D.C. 20004. Enclose a stamped, self-addressed, business-size envelope.

My wife and I have been very faithful in making the monthly payments on our life insurance policy. Unfortunately, I don't think that we're going to make this month's payment. Will they cancel our policy?

If you fail to pay a premium by the due date, you will normally be given at least thirty days to make up the amount of the missed payment. It's possible that if you do *not* make the payment within that grace period, the policy may lapse.

I've been told that although my policy has lapsed because of nonpayment, it still may have value because of its nonforfeiture rights. Could you please explain what this means?

Nonforfeiture rights are certain rights and values that you can't lose (or forfeit) if your policy lapses. In order to protect any value in your policy if it lapses, it's important that you understand these rights.

Do term policies have nonforfeiture rights?

No, they usually don't.

Can you explain what a reinstatement right is?

Sure. If you're still in good health and can prove it, you can put a policy back in effect by paying the past due premiums. Most insurance companies allow you to reinstate a policy within five years of the lapse date.

My insurance agent always talks about a policy's surrender value. I'm not quite sure what that means. Could you help?

Of course. Surrender value allows you to cash in a policy if it lapses and get any cash value that has built up. Every cash value policy has a table in the policy that lists the cash value of the policy per $1000 of insurance at the anniversary date.

My policy has something called extended term value. What does that mean?

After a policy lapses, if you have not taken out the cash value, you can use that money to buy a fully paid-up policy with the same face value that will be good for a limited term.

In doing some homework before buying life insurance I've stumbled across the term "reduced paid-up value." What does it mean?

This is the amount of insurance the cash value in your policy will buy. It will remain in force for the remainder of your life even if you never make another premium payment. For example, on a typical $50,000 whole life policy, if the policy lapses after ten years, the accumulated cash value will buy about $15,000 in paid-up insurance. This $15,000 insurance remains in force for the rest of your life without further payment required. The exact amount of paid-up insurance you can buy is stipulated in your contract.

I let my life insurance policy lapse when I lost my job, because things got pretty tight. I'm now employed and back on my feet. I'd like to protect my family again with insurance. Can I get the old policy reinstated?

Probably. You can usually reinstate a lapsed policy within five years by paying the back premiums (plus interest) and by taking a new physical exam. You can elect to turn in the old policy for its cash value, if it's not term insurance, or convert it to a paid-up policy for a reduced amount. Whatever you decide to do, *don't* ignore the old policy. It may have some valuable benefits left in it.

What does a waiver-of-premium rider mean on an insurance policy?

A waiver-of-premium rider means that the insurance company will keep a policy in force with no further premiums due if you become disabled.

Should I buy a waiver-of-premium rider on my insurance policy?

In general, this *is* a waiver worth having. But we recommend you first check:

- how much the rider will cost
- how the company defines *totally* disabled
- if the waiver lasts for life or only until you recover or a specific number of years

- what the age cutoff is
- how long the waiting period is before the rider takes effect

Must my wife, as beneficiary, take the lump sum proceeds of my life insurance policy at my death?

No. There are several different payment options available. These include interest income; income for a specified period; income of a specified amount; and life income.

Could you explain what the different payment options mean?

- *Interest income:* The company holds the proceeds and pays out interest for a specified amount of time or for life, at a rate stated in the policy. With some policies, portions of principal may also be withdrawn along with interest.
- *Income for a specified period or of a specified amount:* This provides payouts of both principal and interest on a predetermined schedule and at a predetermined rate of interest.
- *Life income:* This option guarantees income for the life of the beneficiary, with amounts determined by the sex and age of the beneficiary at the time of the policyholder's death.

Under the life income option, what happens if the beneficiary lives longer than the company's mortality tables calculate?

What a great question! If you live longer than anticipated, you will continue to collect principal and interest.

And if I die earlier?

If you die sooner than expected, a substantial portion of the principal may be forfeited unless a specified number of payments was *guaranteed* when you elected this option.

My husband's insurance policy pays me monthly installments. My accountant tells me I can no longer receive interest tax-free on the unpaid amount. Is that correct?

It is. The Tax Reform Act of 1986 closed the door on that benefit.

Can I deduct from my federal taxes interest on my life insurance policy loan?

The permissible write-off of interest expense phases out from 1991 on.

I've been told that an endowment policy is a good way to ensure that there will be enough money for college education for our children. Is that right or wrong?

An endowment policy guarantees that a specific sum of money will be available on a specific date. In order to ensure that figure, however, you will pay higher premiums than you would with straight permanent insurance. Consequently, you will have higher cash values.

What happens if I die before the endowment policy is paid up?

As with any other insurance policy, if you should die before it's fully paid, your family would still receive the *full* face value.

Should I buy an endowment policy?

We don't think it's a good idea during inflationary times. With widely fluctuating interest rates, you would likely be better off with another form of investment.

What is credit life insurance? My local new car dealer is offering this type of insurance to go along with the note on my new car.

Credit life insurance is usually a decreasing term insurance policy. This policy would pay off the outstanding balance on your new car if you were to die before finishing the payments.

Does credit insurance make sense?

Credit insurance protection makes sense to many people. It *doesn't* make sense if:

- you're single, with no dependents to be concerned about.
- you have other forms of insurance to cover the debt.
- you're young (twenties or thirties), because there are other services at better rates.

Depending upon your age and health, you can generally buy long-term insurance in larger amounts for less money than a similar amount of credit life insurance.

I've decided to take a credit life insurance policy from my new car dealer to cover my car loan. Should I finance it as part of the loan or pay for it in cash?

No! Pay it off! If the credit insurance is added to the loan, you end up paying to insure not only the loan principal but also the insurance premium and all the finance charges. You'll end up insuring the insurance!

Since I can borrow against my insurance at 4 percent per year, I'm going to take some of the cash value and invest it in government securities at 6.5 percent. Am I missing something here?

No, that's pretty savvy thinking! There are usually no hidden charges and your policy probably calls for simple, not compound, interest. It is important that you pay the loan interest on an annual basis because if you don't, the company will subtract the amount due from your policy's cash value.

What does an accidental death rider really mean?

An accidental death rider, also called a double indemnity rider, pays your beneficiary double or triple the policy face amount if you die by accident rather than by illness.

Is an accidental death rider really worth the extra money?

No, not in our opinion. Does your family need *more* insurance if you die in an accident instead of from an illness? Not if you've planned properly. A better option is to take the money the rider would cost and buy additional term insurance if you feel you need additional coverage. The new policy will pay your beneficiary this extra money no matter *how* you die!

A rider that really seems to make sense to me is the one that does away with the need for a medical exam—guaranteed insurability. Do you agree?

It can be a *real* benefit if you ask the right questions and get good answers. Find out:

- the cost
- the age limit for buying additional coverage
- the minimum/maximum amounts you *must* purchase
- at what intervals additional purchases can be made

This provision, which guarantees the right to buy additional coverage without a medical exam, is most often available in whole life policies, seldom in term policies.

I'm eighty-seven years old and in very poor health. How long before my death must I transfer ownership of my policy to make the transfer valid?

The transfer of ownership must be done at least three years before the date of your death, otherwise the money is counted as a part of *your* estate no matter who owns the policy.

My wife is the beneficiary of my insurance policy. I'm afraid of the way in which the proceeds will be taxed after my death. Should I be concerned?

Not at all. The 100 percent marital deduction allows you to leave an unlimited amount of assets to your spouse. That means your death benefits will be tax-free.

Since my wife is deceased, I would like the proceeds of my insurance policy to pass to my son. How can I minimize the tax bite?

It gets tricky with a beneficiary other than your spouse. Your insurance company will provide you with a form that allows you to change the ownership of the policy, but you then must sign away all rights to it, such as the right to change beneficiary, borrow against it, or cash it in. This gift to your son must be *irrevocable* to receive favorable tax treatment.

Is income tax due on dividends from my life insurance policy?

No income tax is due on dividends paid on life-insurance policies whether you receive a check or have the dividends applied to the next premium. The thinking behind this is that dividends are considered a refund that reduces the cost of your policy, not as a part of your personal income.

Does it make any sense to purchase life insurance from the machines that I see in the airport?

No, no, no! First of all, the chances of *dying* in a plane crash are infinitesimal and many credit cards provide trip insurance at no charge to you anyway. The cost of these policies is so out of line with other insurances that you're wasting your money!

Today in the mail I received an offer that says I can't be turned down for this insurance policy, regardless of my health, if I return the application by a specific date. It looks great to me. What do you think?

Group life policies usually offered by mail often don't require proof of insurability. The Direct Marketing Insurance Council and most state insurance commissions have dictated that promises made in writing in *any* insurance advertisement or mail offering are legally binding. So, proceed with caution and notify your state insurance commission if the company's promises are *not* kept.

I understand that some insurance policies have a no-load provision. Could this possibly be true?

Yes. There are some insurance policies that don't carry sales commissions (no-load) or that have only low commissions. If you feel confident about what you're doing, this may be the way for you to go. But for some people, it makes more sense to pay a commission and have a personal agent to answer questions and clear up any problems.

Does no-load mean that there are *no* charges associated with the purchase of an insurance policy?

No *up-front* charges, yes! However, many such no-load/low-load policies have a surrender charge, the amount that you'll pay to give up the policy. This is usually between 7 and 8 percent of policy value after the first year. The charge gradually decreases to 0 percent after the eighth, ninth, or tenth year. There's no free lunch! Check all the charges.

Is there somewhere that I can find information on no-load insurance policies and where I can buy one in my area?

You should write or call: The Council of Life Insurance Consultants, 600 West Jackson, Chicago, Illinois 60606, (800) 533-0777, (312) 993-0355.

I just read that the average family of four will spend more than $10,000 a year on health insurance in the year 1990 and even more than that in following years. The only health insurance I have is through my company. What kinds of health insurance are available?

There are all sizes and shapes available. We'll give you a brief rundown of the different types:

- *Basic coverage:* covers hospitalization and medical benefits including surgery.
- *Major medical:* protection against long-term illness usually used to supplement the basic coverage.
- *Medi-gap:* provides older people with coverage where Medicare leaves off.
- *Disability income:* insurance protection that provides you with a percentage of your earnings if you are disabled through illness or injury and unable to work.
- *Hospital indemnity:* provides direct care benefits (at-home care) after you have been hospitalized. Usually sold by mail and on television.
- *Dread disease:* pays benefits for specific conditions.
- *Health maintenance organizations:* prepaid preventive and treatment services for a set price. It's not exactly insurance, but rather protection at a predetermined price.

My company offers life and medical insurance to me and my family. How can I tell if the coverage is enough?

Your company's plan should include provision for:

- basic protection for surgical, hospitalization, and medical benefits for all family members
- major medical covering you against long-term illness, designed to take over when the basic coverage stops
- a life insurance amount equal to six times your annual salary

Although not all companies provide free disability protection, if that is not offered through the company plan, get it!

What does the term *deductible* mean in my health insurance policy?

The deductible is the amount of medical expenses you must pay *before* the insurance company begins its reimbursement.

How much of a deductible should I have on my major medical policy?

The deductible can run from $100 to $2000 or more. The larger the deductible, the lower the cost of the policy. A rule of thumb is that the deductible should be an amount that you and your family can pay without severely affecting your household budget.

My doctor submitted a charge for an appendectomy that is far more than the insurance company will accept as a reasonable charge. What do I do?

Stand back and let the doctor and the insurance company duke it out! They usually will work out a reasonable compromise. If the problem continues, refer the matter to your lawyer.

My major medical policy has a coinsurance feature where I pay 20 percent of the total cost and my company pays the balance (80 percent). I've heard about a stop loss for this, but I don't know what that is.

A stop loss allows you to pay only up to a predetermined amount and no more after that. The insurance company will pay 100 percent over that amount. Read your contract to see if you have a stop loss provision. If you can't find *the clause* in your policy, go get one!

Some health insurance polices stipulate a maximum amount payable over a lifetime. How much should that be?

At least $250,000. Believe it or not, one serious major illness can eat that amount up very quickly. Don't forget the stop-loss provision.

I'm a small business owner with three employees. I want to be sure both my family and my employees are properly covered for medical emergencies, but the cost is not to be believed. What can I do?

Call the group department of several large insurance companies and ask about the group rate for your small number of employees. You should also ask about the possibility of combining you and your employees with other similar small companies to lower the group rate. A third way to proceed is to check with any local, state, and national associations affiliated with your line of business. They may be able to help.

Our son graduates from college this June and will be doing some traveling during the summer before he begins his first job in September. How can he get health insurance for that summer interim period?

Check with your insurance agent to see if your policy has a conversion privilege under which he can obtain individual coverage. Usually, it's possible if he does so within a specified period of time. If your policy lacks a conversion privilege, ask your agent about a short-term policy (usually 60 to 180 days). Ninety-day coverage for a person in the early twenties, with a $100 deductible, should cost approximately $150 to $200.

Wait until you hear this one! I found that I was pregnant just after my company switched group coverage. The old company says it's not responsible and the new company says, "Forget it, it was a preexisting condition!" I'm stuck in the middle. Do you have any suggestions?

Talk to your employer. There may be some provision to continuing coverage under the old policy of which you may not be aware. If you don't have any luck there, contact your state insurance department and find out if the state requires a successor group insurance plan that provides continuous coverage for sixty days while your company establishes a new health plan. But be aware that not all states insist on this. Good luck!

I'm getting nowhere in dealing with my insurance company about a medical claim for my daughter. I'm just about at my wits' end, so I'm asking you as a last resort.

Thanks for thinking of us! Insurance companies can be as inefficient as the worst government bureaucracy. Our friend Ben Lipson, the insurance columnist with the *Boston Globe* and president of his own firm, passes along these steps to follow when dealing with insurance claims:

1. Claims should be reported immediately.
2. Contact your insurance broker, give him the details, and let him *earn* his commission.
3. Get a claim number. Use it in all correspondence with the insurance company and your agent.
4. Make sure you always deal with the same person, and make note of his or her name, title, and phone extension.
5. If a problem arises with the person you're dealing with, contact the supervisor.
6. If you work, don't call on your lunch hour. Insurance companies take lunch breaks, too!
7. Don't let anyone bully you. If you have to undergo an interview, before agreeing to it, insist on having a copy of the questions and your answers or a duplicate of the tape if it's recorded.
8. If the company is going to dispute your claim, don't immediately run to your own lawyer. Ask the insurance company's law department to review the claim first.
9. If all else fails, contact your state insurance commission.

Stay calm and logical when dealing with the situation. Threats and emotional outbursts won't get you anywhere.

I see on television, from time to time, some celebrity pushing health insurance for *very* reasonable rates. In fact, some policies are downright cheap! Should I trust what I hear?

Be *very* cautious! Those hospital indemnity polices are designed to reimburse you for out-of-pocket health care costs and are paid to you directly. They are best used to *supplement* other coverage. They are helpful (not necessarily adequate) if you are otherwise uninsurable. These policies are restrictive in that they pay benefits *only* while you are in the hospital and generally only after you've been in the hospital for a specified number of days. If you or a family member has a history of long hospital stays, make sure you find a policy with immediate (no waiting period) or almost immediate payments. But those premiums will be higher. Often there is a long waiting period before full coverage begins, as long as two years. Some states are even considering banning some of these commercials because of misleading claims. We don't recommend these policies.

I'm considering major medical coverage. Whether I take an individual policy or get it through my employer, it isn't cheap! Do I really need it?

If you can afford only one type of insurance, major medical is *it*! It will cover you against the very steep cost of a major illness and protect you from financial disaster. A member of our family ran up a hospital bill of $48,000 in a three-week intensive care stay and yet, after the reimbursement from the insurance company, a grand total of $19.47 was due. You can't afford *not* to have major medical.

I've quit my job and will begin a new position in three or four months. I'm wondering whether I should be insured during that period.

Have you checked out hospital costs lately? You definitely need temporary health insurance. Several of the major insurance companies (Prudential, Aetna, Kemper, among others) offer this type of insurance, which generally runs from 90 to 180 days. However, it's not cheap.

Do temporary policies cover ongoing conditions that require a doctor's consultation?

No. Most policies don't cover a pre-existing condition that requires a doctor's consultation within one year of the policy purchase. That period may vary from company to company. If you or any member of your family has a chronic medical problem, it's smart to convert your old company's group insurance to an individual contract. Call Blue Cross, because you can obtain this coverage regardless of job status.

My husband has just lost his job because of layoffs at his company. Will our group health insurance lapse on his last day on the job?

Happily, no. Federal law protects your husband and you as long as he has not lost his job because of gross misconduct. Your group policy *must* stay in force for *up* to eighteen months *if* you are willing to make the premium payments yourself. This is a good idea, because an individual health policy is usually *much* more expensive. If you are employed, see whether your husband can be included in *your* coverage. Most companies allow this for little or no charge.

I can't even afford a temporary health insurance policy for me and my family. I'm in terrible financial shape. Help!

You'll be in worse shape if a medical calamity hits a family member. Check the cost of a partial policy that covers only hospitalization, where costs are the *most* dramatic. It will cost about half as much as the comprehensive temporary policy.

My husband and I are about to be divorced. I'm very concerned that I will lose the benefit of his company's group health-insurance program. Will I be left high and dry?

Not by your husband's company! Generally speaking, for companies of twenty employees or more, spouses can keep the temporary extension of health coverage for up to thirty-six months, for themselves and dependent children. It's called continuation coverage. You have sixty days to decide whether you want this extension, and you are covered during this time of decision, although you must pay the two monthly payments involved. Continuation coverage is also provided for spouses of employees who die while employed and even when a spouse becomes eligible for Medicare.

I am about to turn seventy years of age, and my company says that because I qualify for Medicare, it is terminating my health insurance coverage. Can it do that?

An emphatic *no*! Tell your benefits department to check relatively recent federal legislation that has prohibited this practice.

I am seventy-one years old and have worked for the same firm for forty-three years. My health insurance is very important to me, but with so many younger workers being hired, I'm afraid my benefits as an older worker will be affected. Is this possible?

It's illegal to discriminate in any manner because of age. A federal law prohibits employers from offering employees over sixty-five health benefits that differ in *any way* from what is offered younger employees.

Disability Insurance sounds like something that would be helpful to have but not really necessary. Do you agree?

Sorry, but we don't agree with you at all! You are more likely to be disabled than to die before the age of fifty-five. Plan for that possibility. Disability insurance is an absolute necessity.

My company provides a disability policy, known as a full-scale group policy. It will provide a portion of my salary if I'm disabled. What percentage of my full-time pay should my disability income be?

An adequate disability program should provide at least 60 percent of your current income when the disability benefit is added to funds that you will receive from Social Security.

What is the best buy in disability insurance?

The best way to save money is to keep the monthly benefit high and trade off the time period before benefits start. This is okay because most companies will still pay their employees for at least the first few months of disability. Buying a policy with a six-month elimination is much less expensive than an immediate benefit policy. For example, someone in the mid-thirties, in good health, could purchase a disability policy with a six-month elimination period for approximately $450 a year for each $1000 of monthly benefit desired. The older the individual, the higher the cost. A person in the late fifties would pay between $750 and $1000 a year for the same coverage. This is only a rough guideline. The premium will vary according to waiting period, cancelability, health of insured, etc.

I'm convinced, after listening to the two of you, that I need disability income protection. Give me some guidelines I should follow when selecting a policy.
There are five guidelines to follow:

1. *Get a noncancelable policy.* The company can't cancel the policy for medical conditions or the number of claims you submit, and it can't change the premium before your sixty-fifth birthday. A guaranteed renewable policy is not as good, because premiums may increase when the policy is renewed.
2. *Make sure benefits are payable over a long period.* The first choice is a lifetime policy; the second, coverage to age sixty-five. Any other type of policy leaves a big gap.
3. *The policy pays as long as you can't practice your own occupation.* "Own" occupation means the job you had before you were disabled.
4. *The insurance company pays its claims on time and in full.* Have your insurance broker confirm the company's track record in this area.
5. *Benefits should be subject to cost of living adjustments.* This may cost a few extra dollars, but it's worth the price.

I'm not able to work at my old job (home construction foreman), but I can do easier work, such as a cashier, where I can sit down most of the day. May I still collect my disability income check?
If your policy allows double-dipping, i.e., working at a less taxing job and earning less than your old job, then you're safe. But some policies stop paying disability payments if you do *any* work. So we recommend you check your policy before taking the job!

Are disability payments taxable?
If you purchased your own disability insurance and paid your own premiums, the benefits are *not* taxable. However, if the premiums are paid by your employer, the benefits are then taxable.

What is a residual disability policy?
It is income replacement insurance, and it makes a lot of sense for many people. If your disability allows you to work but in a job that, for example, brings in only 50 percent of your former salary, the insurance company will make up the 50 percent difference.

I understand that many insurance companies cap disability payments at $2000 to $3000 per month. If I am disabled, Social Security will pay

me about $1000 a month. Unfortunately, I need a total of $5000 to live comfortably. Do you have any solutions?

Sure. You can buy additional coverage with a special supplementary disability policy. Maybe your company will even pay for it!

I own my own business. Is 60 percent of my salary enough if I become disabled?

No, because if you're put out of commission, it's likely that the operation of your firm will suffer and there will be a need for cash flow to cover business overhead expenses.

Where can I get more information on disability insurance?

"What You Should Know About Disability Insurance" is available (free) by sending a SASE to:

> Health Insurance Association of America
> P.O. Box 41455
> Washington, D.C. 20018

I'm covered under Social Security for retirement benefits. Do I have disability coverage, too?

Yes, you are automatically covered. Under the Social Security program, you would receive a monthly benefit if you became disabled for an extended period. The benefits are evaluated as if you had retired at age sixty-five in the year the disability began.

Who qualifies for disability income under Social Security?

The Social Security Administration says that a worker is disabled if he or she has a physical or mental condition that prevents that person from doing any substantial, gainful work and is expected to last, or has lasted, for twelve months or is expected to result in death.

Among those eligible are insured, disabled workers under sixty-five and their families, as well as children of any age if they are disabled before age twenty-two. Disabled widows and widowers and, under some conditions, surviving spouses age fifty or older of workers who were insured with Social Security at the time of their death also qualify. You must have paid into the Social Security system for a minimum number of years, depending on the age at which you become disabled.

I applied for Social Security disability payments four months ago and I'm *still* waiting to find out if my application has been approved. I was told that there's a five-month waiting period before benefits start. Does this mean that I'll have to wait five more months *after* I'm notified that I've qualified?

Thankfully, no. The five-month waiting period starts from the time that you were disabled, no matter how long it takes for you to be notified of qualification.

I'm a widow who received a Social Security disability check every month. I'm considering marriage to a man with a pension. Will this affect the amount of my check?

No, it won't. Every worker, married or not, receives a benefit based on his or her own work record *if* it's higher than he or she would receive as a spouse.

I worked for the railroad and need some information relating to disability payments. Where do I write?

The address is:

> Information Service
> U.S. Railroad Retirement Board
> 844 North Rush Street
> Chicago, Illinois 60611
> (312) 751–4500

Are there sources of disability benefits other than from an individual policy or Social Security?

There are. It may very well take some digging, but check out:

- automobile insurance policies that include benefits for disability resulting from an auto accident
- a waiver-of-premium provision (previously discussed), whereby you owe no further premiums should you become disabled
- credit insurance, which includes the payoff of installment debt if you become disabled
- Worker's Compensation for a job-related disability
- Veteran's Administration's pension disability payments
- civil service disability benefits
- state welfare benefits
- group union disability payments

I'm a senior citizen on Medicare. I want to get some protection from medical expenses *not* covered in the Medicare program. Do you have any guidelines?

There are several things that you should be aware of before buying what is called a medi-gap policy:

- Is there a maximum per-day hospital payment above and beyond Medicare A?
- Will the policy pay the semiprivate rate?
- Does it give you a new benefit period or does it follow Medicare guidelines?

• Will the policy pick up the difference between Medicare reasonable costs and the amount that you actually pay?

For more information, contact:

American Association of Retired Persons
Health Advocacy
1909 K St., N.W.
Washington, DC 20049

and

Consumer Information Center
P.O. Box 100
Pueblo, Colorado 81002
"Guide to Health Insurance for People With Medicare"
Publication 512V
"Medicare & Prepayment Plans"
Publication 514V

and

your state insurance department

Is an annuity a form of insurance?

To a degree, yes. It is a contract between you and an insurance company that provides for a guaranteed life income.

Should everyone buy an annuity for retirement purposes?

Not necessarily. Before considering the purchase of an annuity, you should evaluate the effect of Social Security payments, retirement plans, income from other investments, and so on.

How do I evaluate the insurance company that's offering the annuity?

Just as with life insurance, the company should be rated A or better by A. M. Best and Company, an independent rating service company. Its findings are available at most major libraries.

Who should buy an annuity?

You should consider annuities if:

• you are in a tax bracket where a tax-deferred vehicle makes sense.
• you have additional dollars to put aside for retirement.
• lifetime income is your goal.

Are all annuities the same?

No. There are two basic types of annuities: a deferred annuity, which starts paying at a specific future date, and an immediate annuity, which pays as soon as you've paid the premium.

I've seen the initials "SPDA" and I know they refer to annuities, but I don't know what the initials stand for. Can you explain?

SPDA refers to a single premium deferred annuity. You make one lump sum premium payment and the annuity grows tax-deferred until you start receiving income.

Do I have to purchase an annuity with one lump sum? I don't have *that* much money.

Although many annuities are purchased with substantial sums, sometimes from an IRA or pension fund rollover, annuities can also be purchased through periodic installments.

I was told that if I invest in an annuity, the interest earned will compound tax-deferred. What does that mean?

Simply stated, all the interest paid into the annuity account accumulates tax-deferred for the life of the policy and is taxed only when you begin to received payments. Your initial contribution (principal), made with after-tax dollars, is not taxed again.

At retirement, I'm interested in making monthly withdrawals from my annuity. What will the tax consequences be at that time?

They will be very attractive for many retirees. The tax laws treat part of each payment during your lifetime as principal; you pay tax only on the part that is *interest*. That means that part of each payment is tax-free.

Don't annuities tie up your money until you retire?

Annuities are designed mainly to provide retirement income. Therefore, they make the most sense if held until age fifty-nine and a half. Money removed from an annuity prior to that age is taxed, and a 10 percent penalty is imposed on the funds for premature withdrawal. Annuities are *long-term* investments.

What type of payout can I expect?

Payouts can be fixed, with the same size checks for a designated period of time, or they can be variable, guaranteeing a minimum return but with payments fluctuating, depending upon the investment success of the portfolio.

What payout options are available in an annuity contract?

1. *Straight life:* payments for the duration of your life.
2. *Refund:* pays somewhat less than straight life because it guarantees payment of at least the annuity payments you made *regardless* of when you die. A refund for any balance is made to the beneficiary in a lump sum.

3. *Joint and survivor:* payments for as long as you or your designated survivor is alive.
4. *"Certain" period:* makes payments for life, with a guaranteed number of years.

What should I ask a saleperson before I buy an annuity?

We're happy to have you thinking about what to ask *before* you buy. Here's the list:

1. What is the current rate of interest being paid?
2. How is a rate change calculated?
3. How often does it change?
4. What's the minimum rate of interest guaranteed?
5. Are there any penalties for early liquidation, and what are they?
6. What are the costs and charges?
7. How much of the cash value can be taken as a loan, and how long must the annuity be in place before a loan can be made?
8. Is there a bailout option that allows you to cash in the annuity without penalty if the rate of interest falls below a specified percentage?

What kind of penalties do I pay if I liquidate an annuity and walk away from it?

Some companies will charge a penalty of 6 or 7 percent of principal withdrawn for liquidating a contract, no matter how long it's been in place! Others have graduated penalties, i.e., a 7 percent penalty during the first year, 6 percent during the second, and 5 percent during the third. Our choice would be a graduated schedule annuity.

How is a loan against an annuity treated by the IRS?

The IRS treats a loan against an annuity as a withdrawal; consequently, you may very well be subject to both a tax and a 10 percent penalty.

The state in which I live requires $25,000–$50,000 auto insurance coverage. Is this enough?

Emphatically, no! Your coverage should be a minimum of 100/300/50; i.e., the policy would pay up to $100,000 for a single injury, but no more than $300,000 for all injuries in any one accident, and up to $50,000 in property damage.

I just received the bill for next year's auto insurance and almost died! Is there any way that I can save a few dollars without sacrificing my coverage?

1. If your car is more than five years old, consider dropping your collision and comprehensive coverage. After five years, most American cars are worth no more than one third their original value.
2. Shop insurance companies for their "forgiveness" quotient. Some companies will raise your premium by 30 percent if you file a claim in excess of $400. Some will increase your premium if you get more than one ticket for speeding or another moving violation.

3. By increasing your deductible from $100 to $500, no matter what your car's age, you may be able to cut your premium by 35 percent. Similar savings are possible in comprehensive coverage.
4. When you shop for a new car, be sure to check the differences in collision and comprehensive insurance premiums applied to different makes and models. Allstate, for example, offers 25 to 60 percent discounts for cars that are least likely to be stolen and the cheapest to repair. On the other side of the coin, cars that are frequently stolen and cars that are expensive to repair generally carry higher insurance rates.

Which cars are the best from an insurance point of view?

The autos that do offer better insurance rates are Chevrolet Impala, Mercury Marquis, Dodge Diplomat, and Oldsmobile Omega, among others. According to a recent survey, the makes that are stolen most often and/or are costly to repair are Chevy Corvette, Mazda RX7, Cadillac Eldorado, BMW, Porsche, and Saab, among others.

I did something last week while on vacation that may not have been too smart. I paid $9 a day ($63 for the week) for collision-damage insurance on a rental car. Was that foolish?

Computed on a $9-a-day charge, the collision insurance that you purchased from the rental car company would cost you $3200 a year! Before you rent a car next time, check with your insurance agent to find out if your policy on your personal car covers damage to a rental.

My personal car insurance doesn't cover a rental car. Is there anything else I can so to avoid the rental car company's expensive insurance rate?

Possible coverage may be found in the credit card you use to rent the car. Check with your credit card company.

Are there any other insurance items I should check before I rent a car?

There are three things you should know before you pay a rental car company for insurance: the dollar limit to which your personal auto policy covers rental car damage; if your policy covers damage that occurs to a parked rental car with no knowledge of who did it; and how much deductible you have.

What is an umbrella policy?

This is a type of insurance that takes over where your auto and home insurance coverage ends. If you have substantial assets that could be seized by a court to pay off a judgment that exceeds your auto coverage, by all means get yourself an umbrella policy.

I'm about to purchase a new car. The dealership has offered me an extended-service warranty for $750. Is that a good bet?

Extended-service warranties make the most sense for makes of cars that have been on the market for less than three years and especially for models with turbochargers, overdrives, front-wheel drives with automatic transmissions, or computerized digital dashboards. But, remember:

- Extended-service warranties are expensive. They can cost from $250 to $2500. The more expensive the car, the more expensive the contract.
- The more parts specifically mentioned as being covered, the better.
- The deductible on these contracts can range from $25 to $100 or more. The lower the deductible, the better.
- It's safer to buy this kind of contract from the car manufacturer or a large insurance company instead of the dealer. If the dealer goes out of business, you're out of business, too. The contract may be valid only at the dealership where it was issued.
- If the contract provides for rental car payments in the event of a breakdown, make sure that you will be reimbursed for the *entire* time that your car is in the shop, not just for the time it takes for repairs. It may take only a few hours to repair your car, but it might sit in the shop for a week if the right parts aren't in stock.

SUMMARY

Insurance can be a powerful tool for your overall financial plan—if it's properly utilized, but remember:

- Its prime purpose is to protect you and your family from unforeseen financial or personal disaster.
- Carefully compare the various types of policies before you buy.
- Determine how much *you* need and how much *you* can afford. Don't let the agent dictate to you.
- Don't deal with any insurance company rated less than an A by A. M. Best and Company.
- Be *well* aware what your health insurance policy does or doesn't cover. Don't bump into unpleasant surprises when you can least afford them.
- Never fudge the truth on an insurance application. You're asking for big trouble.
- Try to find an insurance salesperson who can service both your life and health insurance needs.
- Consider *disability* insurance. At almost any point in your life you are more likely to be disabled than to die!
- Make sure that your insurance company is licensed in your state so that any problems can be referred to your state insurance department.
- Annuities are valid investments for retirement income, but do your homework before you buy.
- Review your insurance coverage *on a regular basis*. This should happen at least every three years. Needs and circumstances change due to births, job changes, sickness, college expenses, among other things.

Although insurance is often the butt of many jokes, it is an important part of your financial life and health. Poor planning or, worse, totally avoiding insurance may place the joke squarely on you.

FURTHER INFORMATION
BOOKS

Best Insurance Reports
(independent ratings service of
   insurance companies; available
   from your local library)

*Life Insurance: A Consumer's
   Handbook*
Joseph M. Belth
Indiana University Press (1985)

Consumer Information Center
P.O. Box 100
Pueblo, Colorado 81002

"A Consumer's Guide to Life
   Insurance"
Publication 467V (50¢)

"The Consumer's Guide to Long-
   Term Care Insurance"
Publication 435V (50¢)

"Health Care and Finances: A Guide
   for Adult Children and Their
   Parents"
Publication 437V (50¢)

*How to Collect on Your Insurance
   Claim*
Benjamin Lipson
Simon and Schuster

Taking the Bite Out of Life Insurance
James H. Hunt
National Insurance Consumer
   Organization
121 N. Payne Street
Alexandria, Virginia 22314

8

Benefits: IRAs, Keoghs, and 401(k)s

Opened IRA, was immediately told I'd done it at the wrong
place. Moved IRA to a new place, was immediately told it
was the wrong new place. . . . All I have more of at the end
of each year are ways to feel stupid about the same $2000.

CATHY

Many Americans are confused by individual retirement accounts (IRAs),
Keogh plans, 401(k)s, and other benefit plans. We realize there are a number of different vehicles designed to provide for our retirement. These plans
shelter money from taxes until it is withdrawn later in life, when most likely
we'll be in a lower tax bracket. But it's hard for us to know what's right
for our own situation. Not since the Social Security system was established
more than fifty years ago have benefit plans had such a profound effect on
a broad base of Americans.

Whether we are self-employed or working for someone else, it's important to build a strong financial base for our golden years—especially if Uncle
Sam will help us contribute with tax-deferred dollars.

By 1990, more than half a *trillion* dollars will have flowed into IRA
accounts alone, even with the restrictions exacted by the Tax Reform Act
of 1986. Contributing $2000 per year for twenty years will not get your
name on the *Forbes* magazine list of the richest people in America, but
there may be over $55,000 in your IRA account to help defray the costs of
retirement.

In this chapter we will take a look at a variety of benefit investments,
their tax implications, and why one or more of these plans deserve your
immediate attention. We're about to discuss our own personal tax shelter.

What is an IRA?

IRA stands for individual retirement account. This is a personal retire-

147

ment fund set up by an employed person, permitting contributions of up to $2000 a year. Interest earned on this money is not taxed until it is withdrawn at age fifty-nine and a half or older. You must begin to withdraw by age seventy and a half.

Is it true that since the Tax Reform of 1986, IRAs are just a thing of the past?

That's a bad rumor. Millions of Americans still qualify for tax deductible contributions. Even if you no longer qualify for tax deductible *contributions*, interest and dividends *are still tax-deferred.*

Where can I open an IRA?

You can open an IRA account with any IRA-approved custodian or trustee, such as a bank, brokerage firm, mutual fund company, or insurance company.

Does it make sense to borrow the money to invest in an IRA? I'm a little short of cash this year, but I don't want to miss this once-a-year opportunity?

It doesn't make sense since the Tax Reform Act of 1986 began phasing out interest deductions on personal loans. Without the interest deduction it has become too costly.

May I borrow against my home to fund my IRA?

Yes. A home equity loan is a permissible source of money for IRA funding. The interest you'll pay on this loan is deductible from income within certain borrowing limits. See Chapter 11 for a full discussion of home equity loans.

I'm fifty-five and not covered by any type of pension plan. Is it too late for me to start an IRA?

No, no, no! Although we wish you had made contributions in years past, there's no time like now to begin. There's still plenty of time for your money to grow. If you start immediately and contribute $2000 a year until age seventy ($30,000 in contributions), at an average return of 9 percent a year, possible through a mix of investments, you will have well in excess of $60,000 by age seventy. Is that enough incentive?

I'm very confused by the latest IRA rules. One friend says my husband and I make too much money and another friend says it doesn't matter how much money we make—we can still contribute tax-deductible money to our IRAs. Can you tell us who's right?

Sweet and simple, here it is:

- If neither you or your husband is covered by any type of pension or profit-sharing arrangement or Keogh plan, you may both contribute to

IRAs and take a tax deduction on the contribution, *no matter how much money you make.*

- Even though you or your husband has pension coverage at work, as long as your joint income is below $40,000, you can make IRA contributions with tax-deductible money.
- If you have a pension at work and make between $40,000 and $50,000 a year, you may make partially deductible IRA contributions.
- With a salary over $50,000 and a pension at work, no tax-deductible contribution is allowed, but you can still contribute and the *earnings* will grow tax-deferred until withdrawal.

I'm married, filing jointly, and my husband is covered by a pension plan. Our joint income is $45,000 a year. How much can we put into our IRAs and still have it tax-deductible?

One thousand dollars. Over 40,000, your ability to deduct phases out at the rate of $200 for every $1000 more you earn. In this case, the extra $5000 in earnings means you lose $1000 in IRA deductibility. By the time you reach $50,000, you have no deductibility.

How do tax deductions for IRA accounts apply to single filers?

If you are single and *not* covered by a pension plan, you can still contribute tax-deductible funds to an IRA *no matter how much money you make.* If you *are* covered by a pension plan and make less than $25,000 a year, your contributions are completely deductible. If you make between $25,000 and $35,000, the deductibility of your contributions phases out at $200 per thousand over $25,000, as with a joint filer.

Should I open an IRA account even though the contribution is no longer deductible?

Even with the restrictions, we believe that an individual retirement account is still one of your best personal tax shelters. For many people it's a forced savings plan, and the earnings on the contribution remain tax-deferred until withdrawal.

Should I try to contribute even if I can't afford the maximum $2000 annual contribution?

Absolutely. Many people can't put aside $2000 every year, but even a smaller amount will grow considerably over the years.

Together, my husband and I earn $61,500. My husband is covered at work by a pension plan, but I'm not. Can I deduct my IRA contributions on my taxes?

Unfortunately, no. An IRA is not deductible for a noncovered spouse if joint income exceeds $50,000 per year.

I have a $10,000 balance in my IRA account, of which my 1990 contribution of $2000 is non-deductible. How do I calculate any taxes due on withdrawals when I turn sixty next year?

The answer is a little complicated. Since 20 percent of your IRA is non-deductible ($2000 of a $10,000 account equals 20 percent), you will pay taxes on 80 percent of any money you withdraw from your IRA. For example, if you withdraw $2000 next year, tax will be due on $1600.

Are IRA administrative fees tax-deductible?

Yes, if you itemize. Remember to pay all fees by check, separate from the IRA contribution, both as evidence of payment and to make sure that you are able to put the *maximum* capital to work, without deducting the fee.

Is there any penalty for switching money from one IRA to another?

Usually, no. You can switch your money from one IRA to another as long as you personally don't take possession of the funds. The money must pass from one IRA custodian to another. This allows you to fine-tune your IRA funds as investment climates change.

My company provides pension plan coverage for me, but it's really a small amount, must less than the $2000 IRA payment that I could otherwise deduct. Another problem is that I make over the allowable limit for deductibility of my IRA contribution. Is there anything I can do?

No, there isn't. Because you make more than the allowable salary for deducting IRA contributions, you cannot elect to leave the company pension plan in order to restore IRA deductions.

I know that I have until April 15 of the following year to make my IRA contribution. If I file an extension of the tax deadline, can I make my IRA contribution after the April 15 deadline too?

No. You must make your IRA investment for a given calendar year no later than April 15 of the following year. Extensions do not apply to IRAs.

Does the 10 percent early withdrawal penalty on an IRA account apply to me if I take early retirement?

If you are fifty-five years of age or older, the 10 percent penalty imposed by the IRS for early withdrawals does not apply. However, don't forget that retired or not, you may begin taking money from your IRA at age fifty-nine and a half without penalty.

My mother keeps stressing the importance of making my IRA contribution during the first few days of January rather than waiting until the end of the year, when I usually do it. Does it really matter when I put in my money?

Mother knows best! It makes a big difference when you make your IRA contributions. The more days that your IRA money is compounding tax-deferred, the more money you'll have later, when you need it. For example:

Assuming an 8 percent per year yield on an IRA investment, a $2000 contribution made at the beginning of each year by a person aged forty would be worth approximately $157,000 at age sixty-five. The same $2000 investment made by the same forty-year-old at the end of each year would be worth approximately $146,000. Wouldn't that extra $11,000 come in handy at age sixty-five? Enough said!

May I open more than one IRA account during the course of the year?

Yes, and this fact confuses a lot of people. You may open as many as you like (although it might be expensive in fees, and a lot of work) as long as your contribution doesn't exceed your total allowable contribution.

I work part-time as a department store salesperson and I'm not covered by a pension plan. How much can I contribute to an IRA working part-time?

You can contribute up to 100 percent of your part-time wages or $2000, whichever is *less*. In fact, some people work part-time just to fund an IRA!

Are certificates of deposit a suitable investment for an IRA?

If you have five years or less to retirement and, therefore, safety is really important, CDs make a lot of sense.

I have put CDs in my IRA because I don't want to take any chances, but I always find that if I could deposit more than $2000 every year, I could get a better rate. Is there any way I can cash in on a better CD rate without overfunding my IRA?

Here's a little trick to consider. As you've discovered, generally speaking, the larger the CD purchase is, the higher the yield. Put this year's contribution into a five-year CD, next year's into a four-year, the following into a three-year, etc. In the fifth year, all your CDs will come due at the same time and you can then reinvest the entire lump sum into one CD paying a higher rate because you will have five years' worth of IRA investments and interest to use. However, if you believe that interest rates will be rising before the five-year CD matures, you will be increasing your yield slightly now and losing the opportunity for a higher yield next year. Before using this strategy, ask yourself, Am I gaining a little now with the possibility of losing a lot later?

Part of my IRA at my bank is invested in a certificate of deposit. Since I made that investment, interest rates have gone up. Is there any way I can take that CD out and reinvest it without penalty?

You can't touch that CD without incurring a penalty. Here's another idea, though, to take some of the sting out of your situation: Have the bank withdraw the accumulated interest and place it in a new CD with the higher yield. There's no penalty as long as you don't touch the principal. You can even instruct your banker to deposit future interest from your old CD in the new IRA account.

Would you please give me some idea of the risk factor attached to various investment alternatives for my IRA?

Sure, but remember one important fact: the closer you are to retirement, the more conservative your retirement investments should be.

Low/No risk
- Treasury bills, notes, and bonds
- certificates of deposit
- AAA rated corporate bonds
- annuities
- money market funds

Medium risk
- blue chip stocks
- stock mutual funds
- corporate bond funds
- real estate investment trusts
- GNMA securities
- U.S. liberty silver and gold coins
- zero coupon convertible bonds
- nonleveraged real estate limited partnerships

High risk
- junk bonds (rated BB/Ba or less)

My cousin suggests that I totally avoid taxes by buying a municipal bond for my IRA. What are your thoughts?

We disagree, simply because you are turning a tax free investment (the municipal bond) into a taxable one, since IRA funds are taxed when you withdraw them. It just doesn't make sense!

I'm looking for an aggressive IRA investment for my money. What do you think about limited partnerships?

They can certainly by an aggressive investment, but we do not like them as IRA investments. Unless you can find a limited partnership (LP) that doesn't have the heavy up-front commissions that usually come with them, we don't believe enough of your initial investment goes to work for you. See pages 246–247 for more limited partnership information.

My wife and I don't qualify for deductible IRA contributions, so we've decided not to make any more contributions. Would you recommend a long-term (no-fuss) investment strategy for the funds we've already accumulated?

Sure, but don't forget the forced savings concept of even nondeductible

IRA contributions. Enough badgering! A most conservative strategy is to have the IRA custodian consolidate all the funds into both money market and CDs. If you'd like to be more aggressive, consider putting part of your funds in a stock mutual fund.

Since my wife and I make too much money (not such a bad problem, I guess) to be able to contribute deductible dollars to our IRA accounts, my broker suggests that we consider either an annuity or a single premium whole life policy as an alternative. What do you think?

Clearly, there are some advantages to using these products in developing a retirement program. For instance, by investing in and annuity or single premium life insurance, earnings are tax deferred and there is no $2000 limit to the amount of money that you can invest. (Be sure to read Chapter 7, which explains these alternatives in detail.) We still like the forced savings aspect of both deductible and nondeductible IRAs, however. In your particular case, it makes sense to consider other investments in conjunction with an IRA.

My husband and I are both in our early forties. We've invested our IRA money ($21,000) into certificates of deposit. I think that we should be investing more for growth than income. My husband disagrees. What are your thoughts?

We *strongly* agree with you. At your age, you can afford more risk than a couple only five years from retirement. You should consider a growth mutual fund offered by a family of funds that will allow you to switch between funds as your investment objectives change.

Are gold and silver coins permissible in an IRA account?

Yes. Beginning in 1987, U.S. gold and silver coins were added to the list of acceptable IRA investments. Collectibles other than these specific types of coins are not allowed.

What IRA investments are acceptable?

Acceptable IRA investments include: certificates of deposit, zero coupon securities, mutual funds, unit investment trusts, limited partnerships, stocks, corporate bonds, U.S. government securities, money market funds, options (when traded in a self-directed IRA), and U.S. gold and silver coins.

My daughter works at McDonald's on the weekends while she's going to high school. Can she open an IRA, if I can get her out of the clothes stores?

She certainly is able to open an IRA and get started building up her investment portfolio, but since she's in such a low tax bracket, she won't get much tax benefit from an IRA contribution. It beats watching her spend every nickel she earns in a store, but a regular savings account would be just as beneficial.

My wife and I each earn less than the maximum income allowed to open a deductible IRA and we're not covered by a pension plan at work. To make things easier, can we open a joint IRA account?

No. As the name implies (*individual* retirement account), IRAs are for individuals. You'll have to open two IRA accounts, one for each of you.

My husband is disabled and cannot work. He does, however, receive disability payments. Can he set up an IRA?

Unfortunately, no. Disability payments do *not* qualify as earned income. If you work, you can open up a spousal IRA, which will allow you to put aside up to $2250 a year.

Please define a spousal IRA.

This is an IRA set up for one-income couples. Annual contributions can total $2250 rather than one IRA account with a maximum of $2000. This $2250 can be split in any fashion between the two spouses as long as no more than $2000 is allocated to either spouse.

I am sixty-eight and earn no wages because I'm retired. I receive pension and Social Security benefits. My wife is fifty-six and earns $11,000 per year. Can she put $2000 in my IRA?

No, she can't. She can contribute $2250 into a combination of her IRA and a spousal IRA for you.

How should my wife split the $2250 between the two IRA accounts?

We recommend that she place a full $2000 in her own IRA and the $250 in the spousal. In that way, the larger amount can earn more years of tax-deferred interest, because your wife has longer to go before she's seventy and a half, when the mandatory withdrawal will begin.

Several years ago, my husband set up a spousal IRA because I don't work. My work is taking care of six children! We are now divorcing. What happens to my portion of the IRA?

Your benefits remain your benefits. Like a pension, your husband's IRA is marital property subject to distribution in a divorce. In other words, you must negotiate how much of the IRA you will receive. Any IRA funds transferred to you won't be taxable to you even if you're under fifty-nine and a half. However, after it's transferred, all IRA rules will then apply.

For the purpose of IRA calculations, what is considered earned income?

Wages/salaries, tips, alimony, bonuses, self-employment income, income to a retired person for work in progress, professional fees, and accounts receivable as of your retirement date are all considered earned income.

Do rental income and interest and dividends qualify as earned income?

Sorry, but the answer is no.

How about income earned from sources outside the U.S.?
Good try, but no soap! This is not permissible earned income for IRA purposes.

What is a self-directed IRA?
A self-directed IRA is an account that allows you to manage your own investments.

My broker has offered me a self-directed IRA. I'm not particularly astute at investing, so I'm not sure that this makes sense for me.
Self-directed IRAs offer you a wide range of opportunities, such as stocks, bonds, options, real estate, etc. You will pay a start-up fee and an annual maintenance fee, plus brokerage commissions, every time you buy and sell individual products. In your case, we suggest that you stick to mutual funds, money market funds, and CDs until you feel more comfortable with your level of investment expertise.

To whom does a self-directed IRA make the most sense?
If you have investment experience over a broad base of alternatives and a primary objective of maximum capital gain, then a self-directed IRA is worth considering.

How much should it cost to set up a self-directed IRA?
Generally speaking, the initial setup fee ranges from $25 to $50. Annual custodian and trustee fees will run another $20 to $50, depending on the activity in your account. Some companies also charge a termination fee when you close the account. You can see that unless you're going to be earning a substantial amount of money, the fees can eat up your profits.

Is my IRA protected if my bank or brokerage firm goes out of business?
Your bank, if a member of the BIF or SAIF, insures each account up to $100,000. Many brokerage firms offer SIPC insurance (Securities Investment Protection Corporation) in amounts well in excess of $100,000 cash and $500,000 in securities. Check whether your broker does.

Can creditors seize my IRA account?
Yes. Your IRA funds can be seized if a creditor gets a judgment against you. An IRA has no special protection in cases of bankruptcy, either. And we have more bad news! For any deductible IRA contributions you made in the past, you pay income tax on the money withdrawn by your creditors, plus a 10 percent early withdrawal penalty if you're under age fifty-nine and a half. Thank, Uncle Sam!

What happens to my IRA funds when I pass away?
Upon your death, the funds in your IRA go to your named beneficiary.

Does my beneficiary get the money in one lump sum?

Either the funds can be taken in a lump sum or they can be withdrawn over a period of no more than sixty months. The exception to this is if you have already begun taking periodic distributions, which your beneficiary may then continue.

Are my IRA funds included in my estate for estate tax purposes?

Yes, and your beneficiary will have to pay ordinary income tax on the funds as received, unless the beneficiary is a spouse. Spouses may choose to roll over an inherited IRA into their own IRA account and continue tax-deferred growth.

My husband has just passed away with $44,000 in his IRA account. May I roll his IRA money into my own IRA account?

Yes. The rollover of a deceased spouse's IRA money is permissible even though you have made maximum contributions in your account. In this case, the annual contribution ceiling does not apply.

My wife has just passed away. I'm the beneficiary of her IRA. She had not yet begun to take mandatory withdrawals from the account. What are my options concerning how I receive her IRA money?

You have basically two choices:

1. You can roll over the contents of your wife's IRA account into your own. If you do this, however, you will not be able to take money out of it without incurring the 10 percent early withdrawal penalty until the year in which *your wife* would have turned fifty-nine and a half. You will also have to start taking distributions from the account no later than April 1 of the year following the one in which your wife would have turned seventy and a half. You have five years to decide whether to choose the tax free rollover.
2. You can take immediate possession of the funds and pay ordinary income tax on the amount.

My sixteen-year-old daughter has just inherited her grandfather's IRA funds. May she roll over those funds into an IRA account that she opens for this purpose and defer taxes until she begins taking money out?

It's a good idea, but unfortunately, the Tax Reform Act of 1986 closed that loophole. She may not roll over the funds even if she already has an IRA. Tax-deferred rollovers are available only to a spouse. Your daughter must report the entire amount as income.

What are the ramifications of my thirteen-year-old son's inheriting his grandmother's IRA account?

The entire amount is taxed as income to the child. In your son's case, because he is under fourteen, only the first $1000 is taxed at his lower income-tax rate; the balance is taxed at the parents' rate.

Can you please explain what an IRA rollover really is?

An IRA rollover occurs when you cash in an IRA account and take the responsibility for getting those funds into a new IRA. You have sixty days in which to do it. Rollovers can be used with any size IRA account. If you decided to move a $2000 contribution from one bank CD to another, paying a higher yield, you may opt to do it yourself through a rollover rather than having the bank transfer it.

How does an IRA rollover differ from an IRA transfer?

Both are ways to move an IRA, but in direct transfer, the individual does not take possession of the funds. You instruct the current IRA sponsor to transfer the account without ever touching the money yourself. This also carries a sixty-day time limit and can be used with any size IRA account.

Is there anything I should know before I try an IRA transfer?

Be sure that you know how long the transfer will take. Ask! Because both rollovers *and* transfers must be accomplished within sixty days, don't just assume that the custodians involved in a transfer will comply. Accidents do happen. Also find out how much it will cost (any exit fees or setup fees) before you transfer the account.

If I decide to use a rollover instead of a transfer, what would happen if I didn't get the new account open within the sixty-day time limit?

If you miss the sixty-day deadline, you forfeit your right to a rollover, and the IRS treats it as a withdrawal. The full amount is taxable, and if you are under fifty-nine and a half years of age, you must also pay a 10 percent penalty. This also holds true with IRA transfers.

When I went to roll over my IRA, the check I received was short 10 percent of the total amount. Why?

Sponsors of IRA accounts are instructed to withhold 10 percent of the funds and sent it to the IRS unless instructed not to by the person making the rollover. You must tell the sponsor not to withhold the 10 percent before you roll over the account.

How often may I roll over my IRA account?

Only one rollover is permitted in any twelve-month period.

It appears that I will be ordered by the judge overseeing my divorce to turn over all my IRA assets to my wife as part of the divorce settlement. Will I have to pay a 10 percent early withdrawal fee?

No. The law allows for a tax free transfer of all or part of your IRA to your former spouse under a divorce decree or written separation agreement. Your ex-spouse may then let the IRA assets compound tax-deferred until she reaches the mandatory withdrawal age of seventy and a half years of age.

I'm furious! I have repeatedly requested that my IRA custodian (my bank) transfer my IRA funds to another account, but no success. I can't even get a phone call returned or a letter. Help!

Transfers from banks, savings and loans, and credit unions should take a maximum of three weeks. Brokerage firms, insurance companies, and mutual-fund companies take up to sixty days. If no help is forthcoming, then you will be forced to go to an appropriate regulatory agency for help.

- For a brokerage firm or mutual fund company:

> Securities and Exchange Commission
> 450 5th Street, N.W.
> Washington, D.C. 20551

- For a nationally chartered bank, contact the consumer-complaint specialist at the office of the Comptroller of the Currency, (202) 447-1600.
- For a state-chartered bank and a member of the Federal Reserve system, complain to:

> Division of Consumer and Community Affairs
> Federal Reserve Board
> 20th and C Streets, N.W.
> Washington, D.C. 20551

- For a federal credit union, look in the phone book under "U.S. Government" listings for the nearest regional office of the National Credit Union Administration.
- For a state chartered credit union, contact your state banking or credit union department.

Please help me out with this most unusual and unfortunate circumstance. Six months ago, in an attempt to get a considerably higher yield on my IRA CD account, I rolled over my IRA account to another bank. I have just learned that my bank has failed! What happens to my IRA account now?

There's good news and bad news in this situation. First the good news: If your bank was a member of BIF or SAIF, you are protected in your IRA account for up to $100,000.

Now, here comes the bad news: Once the money from the BIF and SAIF is in your hands, the IRS says that constitutes either a premature distribution, if you're under fifty-nine and a half, or a rollover. Because you took advantage of a rollover just six months ago and you are allowed to roll over IRA funds only once in any twelve-month period, the IRS may continue to treat the bank failure as another rollover and thus assess the same penalty as a premature distribution.

Can I fight this ridiculous decision by the IRS?
Yes, you can. Write and explain the circumstances and ask for a private letter ruling on your situation.

> The Internal Revenue Service
> 1111 Constitution Avenue, N.W.
> Washington, D.C. 20224

I'm sixty-four years old and about to retire. I have money in a 401(k) plan. Can I roll over that money into my existing IRA account?
Yes. You can roll over a 401(k) lump-sum payment into an IRA within sixty days after you receive it if it is *at least* 50 percent of your balance.

Things are pretty tight for us and if we roll over our lump-sum distribution into an IRA, we can't use the money now. Is there another strategy that would allow us to get our hands on the cash *now* and not get killed by taxes?
You can use these strategies only *once* with a lump-sum distribution:

1. If you were fifty-nine and a half or older as of January 1, 1987, you can opt to use five-year income averaging, which means you would pay an immediate tax on the lump sum and the cash would be all yours, as if you had no other income over the five-year period. For example, if you received a $50,000 lump-sum distribution, your tax would be calculated each year, over the next five years, for one fifth or $10,000 per year of the lump-sum distribution.
2. If you were fifty years of age or older as of January 1, 1986, you can use the strategy we described in the above paragraph using the tax rates in effect *the year the payment was received* or use ten-year averaging (dividing the lump sum into ten $5000 distributions) using 1986 tax rates.

A person who was in a 50 percent tax bracket in 1986 will most likely opt for strategy number one, now being in a lower tax bracket. But consult your accountant before using either strategy.

What happens if I accidentally contribute too much to my IRA?
Contributions that exceed the limit are subject to a 6 percent excise tax. This tax applies to the excess amount contributed in the year it was contributed and each year thereafter, as long as the excess remains in the account. The best thing to do is to remove the funds on or before the due date of your tax return. No excise tax will be charged, but the interest earned on the excess funds must be distributed and taken as ordinary income.

If I withdraw funds from my IRA before the age of fifty-nine and a half, will the IRS place the 10 percent early withdrawal penalty on the entire amount withdrawn?

No. The penalty applies only to withdrawals of deductible contributions and earnings—in other words, contributions you took off your income tax. The part of your withdrawal that was nondeductible will not be subject to the penalty.

Did I hear right? Someone told me that I can avoid the 10 percent early-withdrawal penalty if I take a series of payments.

You did hear right. If funds are withdrawn in a series of payments made over your life expectancy or the joint life expectancy of you and your beneficiary, you can avoid the 10 percent penalty.

I can't believe what my broker just told me! He said that I can actually take money out of my IRA without penalty. Is this true?

It is true that you can withdraw funds from your IRA for any purpose as long as you do it only once a year and replace the borrowed money within sixty days. If you keep it longer than that, you will pay a penalty for withdrawal.

When must I begin taking distributions from my IRA account?

You must begin receiving distributions by April 1 of the year *following* the year in which you reach the age of seventy and a half.

Is there any specific way that the distributions must be made?

Distributions must be set up in such a way that the funds will be distributed over your lifetime or the expected lifetimes of you and your beneficiary. You can annually recalculate these life expectancies for distribution purposes. You can also choose to have the funds paid out in one lump sum.

What does the IRS consider a lifetime?

Here are the IRS life-expectancy tables for IRAs:

WITHDRAWALS at age:		WITHDRAWAL PERIOD (years)
MEN	WOMEN	
65	70	15.0
70	75	12.1
75	80	9.6
80	85	7.5
85	90	5.7
90	95	4.2
95	100	3.1

Don't forget: The rules under the Tax Reform Act of 1986 allow you to refigure your life expectancy *every* year. This generally lengthens the withdrawal period. Under the old rules, when you began taking withdrawals, you had to figure life expectancy and take money out at an even rate over that period.

Are there any exceptions to the proration rates for withdrawals from an IRA?

Yes. Both deductible and nondeductible IRA contributions can be withdrawn by April 15 of the year following the year the contribution was made with no proration or penalty. But there will be a penalty on any earnings.

What are the consequences if I don't take the distributions required by law?

A 50 percent excise tax *may* be imposed on the amount by which the distribution fails to equal the amount that should have been withdrawn that year! However, the IRS commissioner may waive the penalty for appropriate cause.

I'm about to turn fifty-nine and a half, so I won't have to pay any penalty for an IRA withdrawal. However, I understand that some banks have penalties for withdrawing IRA CD funds before the CD matures. Will the bank waive the penalty fees after I turn fifty-nine and a half?

Banks are allowed to waive penalty fees for their customers over fifty-nine and a half, but *they are not required to do so*. We suggest you check your bank's policy before you invest in a CD there.

What is a Keogh plan?

This is a tax-deferred pension account (similar in some ways to an IRA) for use by employees of unincorporated businesses or for people who are self-employed, either full time or part-time. A Keogh plan differs from an IRA because it allows you to contribute 25 percent of earned income up to a maximum of $30,000, a far greater contribution. There's no reason not to have both if you qualify.

Why do I need a Keogh plan?

For those who qualify, a Keogh plan is one of the most attractive methods of accumulating funds for retirement because tax-deductible annual contributions accumulate tax-deferred until retirement.

I'm a computer salesman during the week. On the weekends, I independently consult with small businesses. Would these weekend wages allow me to contribute to a Keogh plan?

Absolutely. The consulting fees that you charge qualify because they are self-employment income from personal services.

Who else would qualify for a Keogh plan?

A partial list of other Keogh qualifiers includes:

- free-lancers
- corporate directors who receive directors' fees
- part-time or full-time consultants
- employees with sideline businesses
- housewives who run service businesses from their homes, such as typing, computer work, telephone solicitations, etc.

How much money can I contribute to a Keogh plan?

That depends upon your particular plan. There are three types. The first two are defined contribution plans:

1. A profit sharing plan, in which the annual percentage contribution varies.
2. A money purchase plan, which has a fixed percentage contributed every year.
3. A defined benefit plan, in which you decide how much income you want at retirement and make annual contributions calculated to reach that goal.

Where can I open a Keogh account?

You can open a Keogh account at many banks, brokerage firms, insurance companies, and mutual fund companies.

Is there a minimum amount I must contribute in order to open a Keogh account?

Although there is no minimum set by the IRS, many institutions establish their own minimum opening balances, which can range from $250 to $1500.

How much will it cost me to open a Keogh?

Start-up and annual management fees range from nothing to $100.

Can I open a Keogh account by myself, or do I need help?

You can go to any institution to open the Keogh yourself, but we recommend that you spend a few dollars and get a lawyer's help to make sure that your Keogh plan is properly set up.

Can I contribute more with a money purchase Keogh than with a profit-sharing option?

Yes. That's why, for many people, a money purchase Keogh makes more sense. You can contribute up to 25 percent of your net income, up to $30,000.

Are there any drawbacks to a money purchase Keogh plan?

There is one drawback. When you open a money purchase Keogh, you are *promising* to contribute a fixed percentage for each succeeding year, even if your business is losing money.

Is there any way to take advantage of the money purchase Keogh without being stuck with promised payments?

There may be. Some financial institutions are now offering combination plans of the money purchase and profit-sharing Keoghs, to give you the best of both.

What is a defined benefit Keogh plan?

This type of plan lets you target a retirement income equal to an average of your earnings in your three consecutive highest paid years, up to a maximum of $102,582 per year. You then fund according to your current income, how many working years are left before retirement, and your life expectancy, among other factors.

Once I establish a defined benefit Keogh, must I make contributions each year even if I don't have any earned income?

Generally, yes.

When does a defined benefit Keogh make the most sense?

The best time is when you have relatively few years left before retirement. If you are forty-five years of age or older, you can make a larger annual contribution to a deferred benefit Keogh than you could to a money purchase or profit sharing Keogh.

How much will my lawyer charge me to set up a defined benefit plan?

As they say, "It ain't cheap!" Generally, this will cost you from $500 to $1500 for the setup. Your accounting fees (including certification) will run from $500 to $1000 per year.

I know that a defined benefit Keogh allows me to contribute enough to withdraw $90,000 per year if I retire at age sixty-two or older. But I want to retire at fifty-five. Can I still invest enough to take out $90,000 a year?

No. At age fifty-five you are permitted to draw a maximum of $75,000 per year from a defined benefit Keogh.

Which of the three Keogh choices gives me, as the business owner, the most flexibility when my sales figures vary from year to year?

The profit-sharing option gives you the *most* flexibility because you are able to vary your contribution from year to year or make no contribution at all.

Are there any drawbacks to a profit-sharing Keogh?

The one drawback is that the maximum deductible contribution is only 15 percent of your net earned income, up to $30,000. But that's still a lot higher than an IRA contribution!

When do I have to begin making withdrawals from my Keogh plan?

The same restrictions apply to Keoghs as to your IRA account, and the minimum withdrawal is based on the same IRS life expectancy tables (see page 160).

What are the best investments to put in my Keogh account?

This is a tough question to answer without knowing a lot more about your specific situation. The proper investments will depend on how much time you have until retirement and whether your Keogh is your sole source of retirement income. If you have other retirement income, you can afford to be more aggressive with your Keogh. But generally, we recommend relatively conservative investments such as CDs, high-grade bond funds, and blue-chip stock mutual funds.

Can I wait until April 15 of the following year to set up a Keogh as I can with my IRA?

No exactly. A Keogh must be *set up* and *funded* by December 31 of the year the deduction is claimed, although you can meet this requirement by funding it with only $25 or $50. You then will have until April 15 of the following year to complete the funding, and even until August 15 if you get an extension for filing your return.

I know that I have to start withdrawing funds from my Keogh by the time I'm seventy and a half. But what are my options concerning how I take the payments?

You can take the payments in installments or in one lump sum.

May I income average a lump-sum withdrawal on my tax returns?

If your plan has been in effect for five years or more, you may five-year income average the lump-sum distribution.

Does it make sense to take a lump-sum distribution at age fifty-nine and a half or thereabouts and then continue to make contributions to build my retirement fund while I'm still self-employed?

It might, but it's so complicated that we recommend you consult your accountant to make sure that this would be a wise strategy for you.

Is it only earned income that qualifies for contributions to a Keogh plan?

Yes. See page 154 for the definition.

May I have a Keogh plan and an IRA?

Yes. If you qualify for both, you may simultaneously contribute to both types of accounts.

Which is better, an IRA or a Keogh plan?

Both plans are designed to help you build retirement security through contributions that accumulate tax-deferred until withdrawn, but Keogh plans have some definite advantages. Among them:

- deductible contributions no matter what your income
- higher contribution limits
- You may continue to contribute even *after* you turn seventy and a half, although you must begin making withdrawals at that age.
- You may name anyone as trustee, even yourself.
- Some Keoghs allow additional voluntary deductions. Although they are not tax deductible, they still accumulate tax-deferred.

Get out there and earn some self-employed income!

I've been self-employed as a photographer for several years and I established a Keogh plan for this reason. Now I just accepted a full-time position, with no likelihood of extra time for self-employed income. What happens to my Keogh plan?

You simply leave your plan in place accumulating tax-deferred until you are ready for retirement. If you withdraw any funds before fifty-nine and a half, you'll have to pay the penalties.

I'm a participant in my employer's Keogh plan. May I also set up my own Keogh plan with some fees that I receive from a sideline activity?

Smart thinking. You sure can!

Am I obliged to include my employees in my Keogh plan?

You must include those employees who work for you full-time, are at least twenty-one years of age, and have been with the company for at least one year.

Can I contribute more than the tax-deductible amount to my Keogh plan?

Yes. You may make an additional nondeductible contribution, up to 6 percent of your self-employed income *after* subtracting your deductible Keogh contribution.

What is a 401(k) plan?

This is a retirement plan that, like an IRA or Keogh, allows you to make deductible contributions that will grow tax-deferred until you withdraw them. Unlike with an IRA or Keogh plan, your employer generally will match your contributions.

My employer has offered me an opportunity to contribute to a 401(k) plan. Should I do it?

Yes, by all means contribute because your employer will generally match 25 to 100 percent of the investment you make! Typically, you can transfer a portion of your salary, up to 10 percent at most firms, into an investment fund.

I'm about to retire and I've built up a substantial amount in my 401(k) plan. May I use the ten-year forward averaging strategy to minimize the taxes due when I receive the funds?

We recommend that you consult your accountant to discuss your particular circumstances.

What is the most I can contribute to my 401(k) plan?

You may contribute $7979 this year. That does not take into account what your employer may put into the plan on your behalf, up to a total of $30,000.

I've just been hired as a teacher by our local high school and therefore I qualify for its 403(b) retirement plan. That's what I was told, but I don't know what a 403(b) plan is! Can you explain?

A 403(b) plan is a retirement savings plan for eligible employees of public schools and certain nonprofit organizations.

Is it a good idea to participate in the offer of a 403(b) plan?

Yes, it is. These 403(b) plans invest your money in a tax-sheltered annuity (TSA), and your contributions, usually through a salary reduction plan, are excluded from your gross income. Taxes are not due on this investment until after you retire and begin withdrawing from the plan.

Are there any pitfalls in a tax sheltered annuity?

We will give you one word of caution: Investments in many 403(b) programs are limited to annuities that sometimes have heavy sales charges and low guaranteed rates. If the plan you are offered is not competitive with sales charges and rates of return, we'd say that you shouldn't invest.

How much may I contribute to a 403(b) plan?

You may contribute up to $9500 of your annual gross income, and you have a choice of investment vehicles provided by your plan.

If I change jobs, may I transfer an existing TSA to another employer's TSA?

Yes, or you may roll over the TSA into an IRA if you change jobs and no TSA is available.

How can I minimize the tax bite when I take money out of my 403(b)?

You can opt for a *one-time* five-year forward averaging, but this is available only after you reach age fifty-nine and a half. This is another instance, though, where a smart money manager like you will want to discuss withdrawal options with an accountant.

I am told by my accountant that a SEP (simplified employee plan) is less paper work than a Keogh. Is he correct?

Yes, a SEP is considerably easier to set up than a Keogh plan. This is a pension plan in which both the employer and the employee contribute to an individual retirement account (IRA). It allows you to deduct roughly 15 percent of your self-employment income or $30,000, whichever amount is smaller.

Where can I open a SEP plan?

You can open one at the same kinds of financial institutions that handle IRAs. In fact, very often you will use the same form.

Is a SEP better than a Keogh plan?

A SEP is different, not necessarily better.

- SEPs are generally less expensive to set up than Keoghs.
- You may set up and contribute to an SEP as late as April 15 and take a deduction for the previous year. Keoghs must be set up and at least partially funded by December 31 of the year that you're claiming a deduction.
- However, if you take your SEP money in a lump sum, you may not use ten-year forward averaging to reduce your taxes as you may with a Keogh plan.
- SEP maximum contributions are potentially smaller than a Keogh's— 15 percent to a maximum of $30,000, as opposed to the Keogh's 25 percent to a maximum of $30,000.

I understand that a maximum of $30,000 may be put in my SEP plan every year. How much of that $30,000 may I, as the employee, contribute?

You may contribute over $7,000, and the rest would be your employer's contribution. This amount changes from year to year.

Can a very large company have a SEP plan?

No. SEP wage-deferral plans are available only to companies of twenty-five or fewer employees and only if at least half the employees participate in the plan.

SUMMARY

The array of retirement plans available today is confusing. IRA, Keogh, SEP, 401(k), 403(b)—the list seems to grow with every year. And if things aren't tough enough, the Tax Reform Act of 1986 changed the rules in the middle of the game! The sad fact today is that many Americans think that certain retirement options are no longer open to them when in fact they are, in one form or another.

We all need to review the sources available for retirement savings to ensure happy and comfortable golden years. The rules may have changed, but the alternatives are still all there and very much available.

Remember:

- An individual retirement account may *still* be your best personal tax shelter even though your contribution may not be deductible.
- Check if your company has a 401(k) plan. It's a great chance to have your contributions matched by your employer.
- The IRS has preserved some attractive lump-sum and rollover tax strategies for withdrawing money from various benefit plans.
- You may open both a Keogh *and* an IRA if you have self-employment income.
- You may borrow money from your IRA as long as it is returned to your IRA account within sixty days.
- If you can't cope with the paper work and funding demands of a Keogh plan, investigate simplified employee plans (SEPs).

It isn't as difficult as it may sound to understand the various benefit plan alternatives. These important financial-planning vehicles will be the basis for a comfortable retirement.

FURTHER INFORMATION
BOOKS

The IRA Book
Center for the Study of Services
806 15th Street, N.W.
Washington, D.C. 20005

An Updated IRA Owner's Guide
Fidelity Investments
82 Devonshire Street
P.O. Box 832
Boston, Massachusetts 02103
(800) 544–0202
(free)

The Real Estate IRA
John J. Scavuzzo
Dodd, Mead & Company

Self-Directed IRAs for the Active Investor
Peter D. Heerwagen
Probus Publishing

The Assessment of 401(k) Plans
Commerce Clearing House
4025 W. Peterson Avenue
Chicago, Illinois 60646
(312) 583–8500

Employee Benefits Programs
Ernest & J.E. Griffes
Dow Jones–Irwin

9

A Secure Retirement

The thing I should wish to obtain from money would be leisure with security. BERTRAND RUSSELL

Back in 1985, the Teacher's Insurance and Annuity Association ran a survey
among retirees to find out if they were satisfied with their retirement. It was
discovered that the people who were most satisfied had done the most preparation for retirement. We think that says a lot!

Don't roll your eyes, but here we go again! To enjoy the retirement you
want takes planning, just like everything else we talk about. Careful planning for retirement will allow you to *choose* your life style instead of having
to settle for one. The earlier you start to plan, the better your chances will
be for living well on your retirement income.

Preparing for retirement has become more important than ever before for
the simple reason that Americans are living longer. You have the chance
now of living nearly as long after you leave work as you lived before going
to work! However, this doesn't mean that we should fear retirement. There
are more investment vehicles available today than ever before to help us
plan wisely. Individual retirement accounts, Keogh plans, 401(k)s, etc.,
weren't around in previous generations, nor were there as many corporate
pension and savings plans in previous years.

To add to the good news of retirement, many people even have an opportunity to choose *when* they want to leave their job. Many more corporations offer attractive packages to older employees looking for an earlier
retirement. With so many inducements to pack up and move on, proper
planning has become the most important facet of a smart retirement.

The best time to begin planning for your retirement is as you begin to

169

work. Unfortunately, too many young people starting out in their first job don't think that retirement will come as soon as it does. Since we can't seem to impress young people to start planning for their golden years early on, at least we can comfortably say, It's never too late to start.

At first glance, this chapter may seen to be geared for only those readers who are fifty and older; but look again. Thoughts and suggestions on securing a comfortable retirement are mandatory reading for everyone.

Important retirement considerations such as investments for IRAs and Keogh plans, lump-sum vs. rollover strategies, the $125,000 once-in-a-lifetime capital gains exclusion, and others are covered in other chapters of this book as part of larger subjects, but you'll find the lifeblood of retirement planning here.

So let's begin.

If I want to begin planning for a secure retirement, what's the first step to take?

At any age, the first step is to calculate how much income will be necessary to live in retirement with the same degree of comfort you have experienced while working. Get an estimate of what your Social Security benefits will be, as well as any pension benefits that may apply. Once you have an estimate of those figures in hand, it will be easier to determine how much savings and investment return will be needed to meet your personal goals.

Is there a rule-of-thumb figure that I should know about in determining how much of my current salary will be needed to live in the same way when I retire?

Yes, there is. We estimate you will need 65 to 75 percent of your salary to maintain the same standard of living in retirement. So for example, if your take-home salary is currently $4000 a month, or $48,000 a year, you will need between $31,200 and $36,000 a year, or $2600 to $3000 a month. The higher your salary before retirement, the lower percentage you will need—because, your tax bite will be greatly reduced. The lower your current salary, the higher percentage of current income—because, more than likely, your tax liabilities will remain pretty much the same.

I'm still in my mid-thirties. Isn't it too early for me to be able to figure out Social Security and pension benefits?

Admittedly, trying to come up with cash-flow predictions for your sixties and seventies is hard to answer precisely while you're still in your thirties. But as imperfect as the numbers are at your stage in life, they will still give you something to aim for. You can readjust figures as you get closer to retirement.

I'm going to retire in three years, at age sixty-two. I've run some numbers to determine how much I'll need in income when I retire, and I

really think I'll need every bit of my current salary. How can I accomplish that?

Why do you feel the need to duplicate your current income? Very few people can duplicate current income, and very few need to do this. There are certain expenses that will disappear completely once you stop working and other expenses that will lessen. For example, work-related expenses (clothing, food, transportation, etc.) won't exist anymore, and that may have accounted for 5 percent of your household budget. If your children are grown, you can cut back on life insurance and your tax bill will more than likely drop. At least half of your Social Security income will be tax-free, and there are exemptions that will begin for you when you reach age sixty-five.

I know that when I retire there will be a number of costs that I currently budget into my take-home pay that disappear, but are there any other costs that might crop up that I should count into my calculations?

There are. If you don't figure into the equation some reasonable amount of inflation, you could run into trouble ten years down the road. Goods and services aren't necessarily going to stay at present prices to help you out. That doesn't mean you should expect the worst regarding inflation. The good news here is that inflationary pressures on retirement income are generally only one half to two thirds as bad as the national rate. Medical bills may also increase. As we get older, we do seem to develop more creaks and pains! Good insurance will dilute some of this cost, but it pays to consider higher medical costs. Entertainment expenses may also rise. Many working people have company expense accounts used for fine dining. Once retired, you'll pay for that yourself. If you've been accustomed to a company car, frequent traveler benefits, and group insurance at lower rates, you may now be paying for these perks yourself.

Is there anything else besides money that should be taken into account when planning for retirement?

We don't mean to sound morbid, but you have to also take into consideration your life expectancy potential. Too many senior citizens start out beautifully in retirement only to outlive their projected needs. The fact of life is that most people cannot go through retirement solely on the interest generated by savings without dipping into the principal from time to time. Plan on living longer than expected and you'll err on the side of good sense.

My parents seem to have more than enough money for retirement, and yet I think they deprive themselves of certain pleasures by not spending money on trips or good restaurants. Could I be right?

Your parents are just one of many couples in retirement who fear running short of cash or not leaving enough of an estate for their heirs. They should not fear spending some of their principal once in a whole as long as it doesn't affect their annual income. Parents should not feel compelled to leave a fortune to their children. Let the children build their own estates. Proper retirement planning exists to provide money for retired people to do the things they didn't have time to do when they worked.

I'm way too young to worry about retirement, but I'd like to get an early start anyway. How much money should I start saving each year while I'm in my late twenties to help me reach a more secure retirement?

We applaud your good thinking! If you can manage to save 10 percent of your pretax income every year until retirement, you will have a worry-free retirement.

I know that it's hard to generalize, but what types of investments are the best to make *after* **I retire?**

Generally speaking, *conservative investments* are the words by which to live. You can't afford to lose a major portion of your nest egg, because it's taken you your entire adult life to amass that amount of money and in retirement it becomes difficult to replace losses. Suitable investments for many retired people include:

- bond and blue-chip-stock mutual funds
- government securities (Treasury bills, notes, and bonds)
- certificates of deposit
- corporate/tax-free bonds
- selected utility and preferred stocks

I want to check out a company's pension plan before I accept a job offer. Do you have a list of items I should ask about?

We do. It's a smart move to find out all about a pension before you accept the job. Here are the points to check and *compare* with other plans:

- what benefits you can expect
- at what age you can expect the benefits
- the type of survivor benefits your spouse will receive when you die
- if the pension is reduced by your Social Security benefits
- the amount you can or must contribute
- how long you have to be enrolled in the plan to be vested

The answers to these points have no hard and fast rules. Everybody must evaluate the answers by applying them to his or her own retirement needs and desires.

Please resolve an argument my wife and I have been having. I say that changing jobs every so often won't hurt the amount of money coming from a pension as long as I stay at each job long enough to be at least partially vested. My wife disagrees. Who wins?

Hands down, your wife is the winner! The more often you change jobs, the smaller your pension will probably be. A person who works for the same firm for forty years will more than likely get twice the pension as someone who switches every ten years and manages to receive four payoffs from four different companies. There may be four of them, but they will undoubtedly be smaller and end up costing that person dearly.

I've heard a few horror stories recently from people who suddenly discovered that their company pension plans were in a very shaky position. How can I find out how secure my pension plan is?

A great way to judge the condition of your company's pension plan is to watch for certain signs, such as:

- *a wide variety of extra or fringe benefits*: This generally means a progressive company with an impressive retirement plan.
- *company-organized retirement-planning seminars*: A company that offers this service to its employees is usually quite proud of the benefits it's offering.
- *a dental plan*: A company offering this usually has a good pension plan.

But, don't forget, these are only signals. Make an appointment to sit down with the benefits officer, and do some reading and research of your own.

I'm trying to decide if my company pension plan will be adequate for my retirement. How can I be sure?

There are a couple of points to consider:

1. Will your pension plan keep up with inflation? Assume that it won't.
2. The benefits you receive are not necessarily tax-free. Your contributions are tax-free, but everything above the money you contributed is taxable income. After taxes, will the payout be enough?

I did some homework concerning my company's pension plan and benefits. The problem I had was that I couldn't understand what really was being said with all the formulas and fancy language. What can I do?

There is a booklet available that helps define the language and show you simply how benefits are calculated. You may be very surprised by some of the things this booklet has to say. It is worth the 50¢ cost.

> "What You Should Know About the Pension Law"
> Consumer Information Center
> P.O. Box 100
> Pueblo, Colorado 81002

Am I supposed to receive some written information about a company's pension plan when I start working? So far I haven't seen anything!

There are five separate documents that must be provided by your employer regarding the company's pension plan:

1. *The summary plan description*: This is an introduction to the pension plan. You might find it in the employee benefits book. This tells you how soon you'll be vested, at what age you are entitled to a full pension, how to calculate benefits, eligibility requirements, and how time for vesting is counted. Updated reports of this should be distributed from time to time.
2. *The summary annual report*: By law, this must be distributed once a year. It looks like a balance sheet and is helpful in determining how well the plan is doing.
3. *The plan document*: This is a more detailed undertaking of the plan description and is available upon request.
4. *Personalized employee benefit statement*: Many employers provide this document, which will show you your accrued benefits and give you an estimate of what you will receive at retirement.
5. *Form 5500*: Also available upon request, this is your pension plan's tax return. It can show you in great detail how healthy your retirement plan is.

My husband is just approaching retirement. Unfortunately, we are getting a divorce, and because he never wanted me to work, I don't have a pension plan of my own. Do I have any rights to his pension benefits?

Likely, you do. The Retirement Equity Act of 1984 specifically recognizes that a pension can be considered marital property. Make sure that your husband's pension plan is included in your divorce negotiations.

A good part of my retirement plans center on my Social Security benefits. How safe is Social Security?

There have been scores of articles written about this subject and it has become a hotly debated topic in many quarters. In our opinion, from now through the first part of the next century, Social Security should encounter no problems even if it stays exactly as it is structured right now. However, we also believe that changes will be made in the system periodically to ensure that Social Security remains in place for the twenty-first century workers.

What benefits does Social Security offer me?

Social security offers you:

- retirement income
- payments if you are disabled at any age
- payments to your family if you die
- Medicare

Can my Social Security benefits be taxed?

Since 1984, Social Security benefits have been subject to income tax if the sum of a person's adjusted gross income, nontaxable interest, and half the Social Security benefits totals more than the base amount allowed. For an individual filing singly, the amount is $25,000 and for a couple filing jointly, it is $32,000.

If my adjusted gross income is more than the allowable base amount, how are my benefits taxed?

The amount of Social Security benefits subject to income tax is the *lesser* of two alternatives: one half of a year's benefits or one half the excess of the person's combined income over the base amount.

I'm on Social Security, and my wife and I file jointly. Our adjusted gross income is about $34,000 and I receive around $8000 a year in Social Security benefits. Can you give me a real example of what you just mentioned?

Of course. Since you file jointly, you are allowed a base of $32,000 a year. The excess of your combined income therefore is $2000 ($34,000 − $32,000 = $2000). One half the excess income is $1000. That is the least amount of the two methods of calculations and allowable as your tax liability under the IRS ruling.

When I make the decision to retire, should I wait until my company notifies the Social Security office?

Not at all. You can apply for benefits up to three months before you begin retirement. In fact, we recommend that you do notify your local Social Security office three months in advance so that you can receive your first check on time.

I've been thinking of moving abroad when I retire. Can I still collect Social Security if I live outside the U.S.?

You can collect Social Security retirement, disability, and survivors benefits if you live in a foreign country no matter how long you remain there. There are some restrictions that might apply and there are some countries to which checks cannot be sent. Ask your local Social Security office for all the details.

I did a tour in the armed forces before beginning my career. Does time in the service count when calculating my Social Security?

Basic pay that you received while on active duty or active duty for training in 1957 or later counts toward your Social Security calculation and should be recorded in your earnings record.

I've heard something about a Social Security delayed retirement credit. What is that?

The delayed retirement credit can mean a larger benefit payment. This credit adds 3 percent to your benefit for each year (or one quarter of 1 percent per month) that a person did not get benefits because of continuing work after age sixty-five. This payment will eventually be increased until it reaches 8 percent.

How does Social Security calculate what my benefits will be?
The amount you will collect if you retire at sixty-five or are disabled at any age is calculated on the basis of your average earnings under Social Security over a period of years.

Is it possible for me to get both my own retirement benefits as a woman and my husband's benefits based on his work?
No, you can't. But you can receive the higher of the two benefits.

I was married for twelve and a half years before divorcing my husband. He has remarried, but I have not. Am I still entitled to any Social Security benefits, or does his new wife get all the money?
Effective January 1979, divorced wives ages sixty-two or older are eligible for Social Security benefits on their former spouse's earnings record if they were married for at least ten years and have *not* remarried. In your case, you (and his new wife) will receive a benefit of 50 percent of your ex-husband's retirement benefit.

Can I collect on my ex-husband's Social Security benefits after age sixty-two even if he hasn't retired?
Since the beginning of 1985, it has become possible to collect an ex-spouse's Social Security benefit even if the spouse has not yet retired, as long as you are sixty-two or older and were married for at least ten years. The current wife does not have the same benefit. She must wait until her husband has retired to begin collecting.

I'm a woman who has never worked outside the house. Can I collect Social Security benefits?
You can collect benefits based on your husband's work record. If you wait until age sixty-five, you will receive 50 percent of his benefit. You may begin collecting at age sixty-two, but you will receive only 37½ percent of his benefit.

Does a wife's Social Security checks reduce what her husband is entitled to?
No. The wife's checks are in addition to checks her husband receives. His benefits are not reduced. If your husband dies, your checks will stop and you can begin to receive checks for the amount your husband was receiving, if it is larger.

When I applied for Social Security, I assumed that because I always earned the maximum amount covered by Social Security, I would definitely get the highest benefits shown on the chart. I didn't! How come?

You made a common mistake. So many people assume that because they always earned the maximum, they will also receive the maximum Social Security benefits. The fact is that the maximum amount of covered earnings was much lower in past years. Because benefits are figured on the basis of *average* earnings, the lower maximum allowed in past years were figured in with your higher ones from recent years, thus leaving you with less than you anticipated.

If I work past the age of sixty-five and don't take my Social Security benefits, do I still have to pay Social Security taxes on my earnings?

Yes. You must still pay full Social Security taxes on money you are earning through work.

I'm not a great fan of the Social Security system. Can I get out of paying in to Social Security if I don't want to participate?

You *must* contribute unless you fit into one of the following categories:

- a worker permanently employed outside the U.S. for a foreign company, government, or international organization
- a rabbi, priest, or minister who has chosen not to pay
- a railroad worker
- one who is able to live exclusively off an inheritance, capital gains, dividends, or real estate rental income, unless you are a real estate broker

If you have any other questions about Social Security, be sure to contact your local Social Security office. You may also write for an excellent publication entitled *Social Security . . . How It Works for You*, available free from:

> The Consumer Information Center
> P.O. Box 100
> Pueblo, Colorado 81002

What exactly will Medicare give me?

Medicare is really two programs: a hospital insurance plan and a medical insurance plan. The hospital insurance plan will pay for most of the cost of hospitalization and certain related care you might receive upon leaving the hospital. The medical insurance side pays for a large part of your doctor's bills and other medical expenses not covered by the hospital plan.

I'm sixty-five and still working. I'd like to continue working for at least three more years. Can I still get Medicare benefits while I work?

You sure can. You do not have to retire to begin Medicare insurance protection. But you will have to file an application in order for your Medicare to start.

If I continue working at sixty-five, when should I apply for Medicare benefits?

Notify your local Social Security office three months before your sixty-fifth birthday, so that Medicare coverage will begin on time.

I'm going to take your advice and apply for Social Security benefits and Medicare three months before I plan to retire. What documents do I need when I go to my local office?

When you apply, be sure you have:

- your Social Security card or a record of your number
- proof of your age
- a copy of your marriage certificate, if you're applying for wife's, widow's, or widower's benefits
- their birth certificates, if you're applying for your children
- your W-2—the annual statement of earnings your employer provides— for the last two years; or if you're self-employed, your last two federal tax returns

I was told that I should check my earnings record with Social Security once in a while. Do you agree?

Emphatically, yes! Every three years you should ask the Social Security Administration to send you a statement of earnings so that you can check it for errors. You can get form SSA 7004 (Request for Statement of Earnings) from your local Social Security office or by calling 1-800-234-5SSA and then mail it to:

P.O. Box 57
Baltimore, Maryland 21203

I don't think there's any real benefit for a wife to build up her own Social Security protection.

Then unfortunately, you think *wrong*! If a woman builds up her own record, she won't have to wait until her husband retires to get her benefits. She can take her own as early as age sixty-two whether or not her husband is taking benefits. Without her own account, she would have to wait until her husband begins taking his benefits.

I can't decide whether to retire at age sixty-two or sixty-five. What do you suggest?

We suggest you sit down with a counselor at your local Social Security office and see what the numbers have to say! By retiring at sixty-two, you will receive 80 percent of the total benefit available. If it looks good or not is something only you can decide. The longer you live, the more important *full* benefits are. At age sixty-three you receive 86.6 percent of the full (age sixty-five) benefit; and at sixty-four, you'll receive 93.3 percent. There are dozens (maybe hundreds) of important Social Security considerations. We recommend that you visit your local Social security office and get a copy of the publication *Your Social Security.*

Is there a phone number at the Social Security Administration I may call for general information?
Yes. 1-800-2345-SSA

I am 63 years old. How will my social security check be affected if I earn *more than* $6840 in 1990?
For social security recipients between 62 and 65, you are penalized $1.00 of benefits for every $2.00 you earn over $6840 per year. Recipients between 65 and 69 will be penalized $1.00 in benefits for every $3.00 earned over the annual limit.

If you are:	In 1990:
under 65	$6840
65–69	$9360
70 or older	No limit

My husband and I are about to retire. We're wondering whether we should sell our home. What are your thoughts?
Whether you're retiring or not, from a strictly good financial point of view, if your house is worth about as much as it's ever going to be, you should consider selling and then buy a place that has potential for capital appreciation. Such a sale and move might free up more cash, which could be reinvested to return more retirement income. The house will not pay you to live in it! However, if you love your home, are surrounded by friends and family, and can continue to afford the upkeep, don't sell, enjoy it. Certain decisions should be looked at with the heart and not the pocketbook.

My husband and I have just retired. Our house is fully paid for and is now worth $175,000. We could really use some more money for retirement living, but we don't want to move. This has been our home for thirty years. Is there anything we can do to get some more money without selling?
For people who need some extra cash but don't want to sell their home, there is a relatively new financial product available that may help. It's called a reverse equity mortgage. This allows you to spend the equity in your home and still keep ownership. If you were to take a mortgage out on this home to get extra money, you would have to make mortgage payments every month to pay back the loan. A reverse equity mortgage gives you

monthly payments. You pay back what you've borrowed plus the interest at the *end* of the reverse equity mortgage term, when you sell the house or when your estate receives the house and sells it after your death. You receive payments instead of making them. Check availability of these types of mortgages in your area.

My wife and I are getting ready to retire and after long discussion have decided to move to Florida. The trouble is neither of us has any idea where in Florida we'd like to live. Everybody we talk to has a different opinion. What should we do?

Don't take your friends' opinions as anything more than opinions. Since your friends aren't you, they can't know what you and your wife will enjoy. Here's what we recommend you do *before* picking a spot to live:

- When you've chosen two or three possible areas while sitting in your armchair, contact the areas' chamber of commerce and try to locate copies of local newspapers through your local librarian. Subscribe to the papers for a few months and read about the areas.
- Now that you've done some research while still at home, begin to vacation-test the most promising spots. Since you are specifically interested in Florida, go down in season as well as during the summer to see the difference.

A methodical, educated search should keep you from choosing the wrong place to retire.

I have worked hard during my lifetime and have a comfortable nest egg, but I guess we could use a few extra dollars. My next-door neighbor's son has a great idea for improving an electric lawnmower that he thinks will make a million dollars. All he needs is $10,000 start-up capital. Should I invest?

This is not the time of your life to begin investing in get-rich-quick schemes. He may have invented the greatest moneymaking idea of this century, but let him risk someone else's money! For the sake of good neighbor relations, if losing $500 won't hurt you but would help him, do it. But no more than that.

Times are pretty tight for my son and daughter-in-law. They have asked my wife and me to lend them $10,000. The good news is we can afford to take the money out of the bank, but the bad news is we hesitate to make it a legal transaction by signing papers. We are such a close-knit family. Do you have any suggestions?

Yes. Unless you just want to give them the money and forget about it, you must take the necessary steps to make it a legal, binding transaction so that there will be no surprises or hard feelings in the future. Remember, any loan should be committed to writing, especially between relatives and friends. A simple promissory note is all you need to document the loan, signed by each party and notarized. You can obtain a simple promissory note form from any bank or lending institution, which can help guide you in writing your own loan agreement. The note should state:

- the amount borrowed
- the repayment terms
- interest charged
- the penalty for default, such as a piece of property in lieu of the money, etc.
- whether the amount owed is to be paid to inheritors in the event of the lender's death.

As long as a loan to your children will not be a drain on your own retirement income, do it. However, do it in a formalized way.

What interest rate must I charge my children if I lend them money?

For a loan of $10,000 or less, the IRS has very little to say concerning how much you must charge. Loans of larger amounts are governed by more complicated rules. Check with your lawyer or accountant during the process of setting up this loan. The IRS will expect a competitive interest rate.

SUMMARY

Many people dream of a day when they can stop work and spend their time doing things they want rather than things they must. Although not everyone wants a full-time retirement, even those people who hate the thought of retiring often dream of leaving their present job to begin new ventures. Whether you consider yourself a member of the first group or the second, both options take careful planning to achieve. There are certain ingredients we need to mix up a recipe of security and comfort in our golden years.

- Make sure you know how much money you'll need before you stop work. You need a money plan.
- Retirement planning should be the most detailed financial plan you undertake.
- From the day you begin to work, put aside funds for those later years.
- Take full advantage of IRAs, Keoghs, and other available retirement plans.
- Take the time to understand your company's pension and savings benefits.
- Keep track of your Social Security record of earnings on a regular basis.
- Make provisions for inflation. Prices will not hold still because *you* are retired.
- Plan to live longer than estimates suggest. It's better to die with too much money left than to live with none.
- Start pulling together all the necessary components of a comfortable retirement (good credit, housing requirements, insurance, etc.) today.

- Look for a preretirement course offered by some community colleges and other organizations. It could be very helpful.

Dr. William Russell once said, "Leisure is the most challenging responsibility a man can be offered." Be responsible. Plan for a wonderful retirement!

FURTHER INFORMATION
ORGANIZATIONS

American Association of Retired
  Persons (AARP)
1909 K Street, N.W.
Washington, D.C. 20049
(202) 728–4300
($5 annual fee for booklets,
  seminars, and one-year
  subscription to *Modern Maturity*
  magazine)

Pension Rights Center
1346 Connecticut Ave., N.W.
Washington, D.C. 20036
(202) 296–3778
*A Guide to Understanding Your
  Pension Plan* ($3)
Your Pension Rights at Divorce ($2
  with a self-addressed stamped
  envelope

BOOKS

The Complete Retirement Handbook
Forest J. Bowman
Perigee, 1983

*Your Guide to a Financially Secure
  Retirement*
C. Colburn Hardy
Harper & Row, 1983

Prime of Your Life
Joseph Michaels
Little, Brown, 1983

*What to Do with What You've Got:
  The Practical Guide to Money
  Management in Retirement*
AARP Books
Dept. 800
400 S. Edward Street
Mount Prospect, Illinois

Places Rated Retirement Guide
Richard Boyer and David Savagean
Rand McNally

PAMPHLETS

New Choices
850 Third Avenue
New York, New York 10022
(212) 715–2785
(212) 715–2787
Planning Your Tomorrow Kit
  includes:
"Money," "Health Leisure," "The
  Law," "Planning and Working in
  Retirement"
Realizing Your Full Potential
65 Mistakes to Avoid in Retirement
Your Social Security Benefits
*Finding the Right Place for
  Retirement*
*What I Wish Someone Had Told Me
  About Retirement*
50 Plus Money Plan for Retirement

*A Consumer Guide to Life-Care
  Communities*
National Consumers' League
815 15th Street, N.W.
Washington, D.C. 20005

NEWSLETTER

The Retirement Letter
Peter Dickenson
47 Chestnut Street
Larchmont, New York 10538

10

Choosing a Financial Adviser

William R. Travers, a nineteenth-century lawyer and wit, was watching the end of a yacht race at Newport, Rhode Island, with a group of friends. As each fantastic boat passed the finish line, the owner's name was called out. Each owner was a *stockbroker*! Gazing at this dazzling array of boats, Travers asked, "And where are the customers' yachts?"

More people than you can imagine believe the implied idea hidden in the story. Unfortunately, in some cases it's true that financial advisers earn more from a person's investments than the investor does. This is why we have written this book. You may be relying on your financial adviser more than you need to or should. With the information we have provided, you can become your own financial adviser and use the broker or planner as an order taker and nothing more.

In speaking with radio, television, and seminar audiences, we constantly hear, "How can I find someone I trust to handle my money?" No one can be trusted to handle your money the way you will. Our hope is to educate you enough to be your own financial adviser. You won't worry as much when you understand what you are doing.

Achieving financial security is a goal to which we all aspire. Unfortunately, too many of us do nothing for fear of making a mistake or we jump into investments thoughtlessly on hot tips from friends or we follow the crowd.

We often select brokers or financial planners the same way. No wonder so many people feel they're not being dealt with fairly. Finding the right financial adviser *is* a tough job, but it can be accomplished if you're willing to make some effort in understanding the many types of financial professionals available and learn what the alternatives are all about. With your newfound knowledge of available investment alternatives, you should need a financial adviser more to execute *your* choices rather than accepting his or hers. This will give you a greater comfort factor. You won't have to worry if you are getting the complete story. When you finish this book, you'll know most of the story yourself.

What is a financial adviser?

Typically, a financial adviser is someone on whom you rely for direction through the minefields of financial alternatives. Your broker, banker, financial planner, insurance agent, and, to a degree, your lawyer and accountant can serve as your financial adviser.

Do I need a financial adviser?

This book should give you the tools to handle your own financial affairs. But the truth is, everybody can use expert help in certain circumstances. Even the Dolans turn to others for information on new products and to place an order for stocks or bonds. Unless you are licensed to transact business on a stock exchange, there are certain investments you can't make by yourself.

My broker calls himself a full-service broker. What does that mean?

A full-service broker offers a wide variety of financial products and services. He or she will charge you a higher commission to transact your business because, along with the transaction, you can receive day to day assistance with your finances if you need it and investment recommendations if you ask. Your commissions also pay for research reports on stocks, the cost of developing new products, and other services. The important point to keep in mind with a full-service broker is that he or she makes money only when you buy or sell something. A lot of the broker's time can be yours for no fee.

Is there a difference between a full-service broker and a discount broker?

There are some big differences! With a discount broker, you're basically on your own. You make the decisions; you do the stock research; you decide which products are best for you. However, because you are receiving bare-bone assistance, you generally pay much lower commissions than at a full-service firm. For example, buying 100 shares of stock at $5 per share could cost you $35 in commissions at a full-service firm or as little as $29 at a discount firm. The spread widens as the price of the shares goes up. One hundred shares of a $20 stock might cost you $57 in commissions at a full-service firm or $30 at a discounter's. On a $70-per-share stock, 100 shares can carry a commission of $95 at the full-service firm and as little as $33 at a discount firm. However, we offer a word of caution concerning discount-brokerage firms. Shop the discounters, too. There are wide swings in price among these firms, and with some trades of lower priced stocks, you may actually pay more at the discount firm than at a full-service one. Shop before you buy . . . or sell.

Which type of broker is best for me?

The answer depends on your circumstances. If you are comfortable making your own investment decisions, then why pay full-service commissions? On the other hand, if you are new to investing or you don't have the necessary time to devote to your investments (shame on you!), then the extra cost of a full-service broker makes sense. In our opinion, the best solution is:

- Have a full-service broker to keep you abreast of the latest financial information and ideas, for which you'll pay full commissions.
- Have a discount broker to transact the investment decisions you make on your own *without* consulting anyone else.

What is a financial planner?

A financial planner is someone who generally does not sell you individual investments on a piecemeal basis but who will program all your assets in a unified plan. To deal with current needs right through your retirement, financial planners will structure your insurance, tax strategies, college-funding needs, and retirement planning. They can assist in estate planning and may even negotiate home mortgages.

Can't my broker do the same things as a financial planner?

Some brokers will do the same job, but they're harder to find. In fact, because there are no legal restraints as yet, almost anybody can call himself a financial planner.

How can I tell the difference between a real financial planner and someone who just calls himself one?

If you really want a financial planner who has had the educational training necessary to become one, be sure the word *certified* or *chartered* is in front of the words *financial planner*. Those terms say something about the person's training but not necessarily about his or her competence.

I've run across the terms *account executive, investment broker*, and *financial consultant*. How do these titles differ from *stockbroker* and *financial planner*?

Account executives, investment brokers, and financial consultants are nothing more than stockbrokers. Many Wall Street firms have tried to take the "broke" out of broker by disguising the term with other names.

Do certain types of financial advisers have better financial products than others?

Basically, no. Most financial advisers are selling the same mutual funds, insurance products, stocks, and bonds. The products, for the most part, are no different. The advice and the follow-up are what make the difference!

If my broker or planner is not a certified financial planner, does that mean that he doesn't know what he's doing?

Not necessarily. The probable success of your financial adviser is not dictated by a designation but rather by experience, an intelligent approach to finance, and other factors.

But do you think I should do business only with a certified financial planner?

The designation CFP does not ensure infallibility. You should do business with the investment professional with whom you have good rapport, who takes the time to answer all your questions, and who has been recommended by other satisfied clients. He may turn out to be a CFP, but it isn't critical.

Where can I find a list of qualified financial planners in my area?

A list—yes; qualified—not necessarily. The International Association for Financial Planning (IAFP) will send you a list of its members. This list will enable you to begin the process of finding a qualified financial planner. The IAFP neither recommends nor endorses its members. Write to:

> IAFP
> 2 Concourse Parkway
> Suite 800
> Atlanta, GA 30328

Ask for a copy of its *Registry of Financial Planning Practitioners*.

How does a financial planner charge me for his work?

There are three typical ways to be charged for a financial plan:

- *fee only:* Usually this type of planner sets a one-time charge dependent upon the size of your portfolio. It could be a flat rate or a typical hourly rate of $100 to $150. This planner may or may not execute his recommendations. You might have to go elsewhere to purchase the products.
- *fee plus commission:* This planner may use the same fee scale as the fee-only planner or he may elect to take 1 to 2.5 percent of the portfolio's value on a yearly basis. He will also sell you the products recommended in his plan and take the sales commission.
- *commission only:* Here there are no charges for the plan. Like a full-service broker, the commission-only person makes money if and when

a financial product is sold. The commission generated by the sales is the compensation.

Is one method of payment better than another?

The method that produces the best financial plan is the best. If the investment recommendations aren't good, all three methods cost too much! If the investment ideas are sound and profitable, the fee and/or commission structure doesn't make much difference. The personal chemistry between you and the prospective adviser, as well as your confidence in his or her ability, is more important than the cost. You can *always* find someone who's cheaper, but maybe cheap is what you'll get!

Before you do business with any financial planner, understand the fees and/or commission schedules and do some homework. If the financial planner is a commission-only person, familiarize yourself with the costs of other products that have the same objectives as those recommended by the planner. You need to know before you buy if you are being sold an investment for its merits or its commission structure. Shopping the plan with other professionals will tell you what you need to know before you buy. Just as we'd warn you to avoid a broker who churns an account for more commissions, avoid planners who work on commissions and constantly present high-price products.

I'd like to start investing through a broker or financial planner, but I don't know how to begin. Since I don't know anyone in the business, do I just walk in off the street and talk to anyone?

You can walk in off the street and you might get lucky. But the smartest way to begin a relationship is to call the branch manager of a brokerage firm or the senior officer of a financial planning firm and make an appointment.

After I've mustered enough courage to contact the senior person, what questions should I ask that will give me the peace of mind to leave my money with that firm?

First of all, remember one very important fact: You're interviewing them; they're not interviewing you! You are looking to employ them and not the other way around. Your initial meeting with an officer of the firm is to determine the firm's financial integrity. If a company is smaller and not as well known as Merrill Lynch or Smith Barney, you want to know:

- *How long have you been in business?*
  It should be at least three years.
- *How much working capital does your firm have?*
  It should be at least $500,000.
- *What type of clients does the firm specialize in?*
  It should be your type of client, i.e., molded to your investment objectives whether you are conservative, aggressive, income-oriented, etc.

With both large and small firms, you should also ask if the monthly/ quarterly statement of account activity is easy to understand. Ask to take a look at one, and ask questions if you need to do so.

All right, I feel comfortable with the firm after meeting the person in charge. Now how do I find the right professional to assist me on a day to day basis?

After discussing your particular situation with the person in charge (the size of your portfolio, your needs and objectives), he or she will recommend that you meet a specific broker/financial planner. Your purpose in meeting this individual is to test the personal chemistry and ask some specific questions designed to give you the confidence to entrust your hard-earned money to someone else. But never forget that ultimately, *you* are responsible for *your* money. The professional is only an overseer. Don't ever promote him or her to something more.

What questions do I ask the financial adviser?

Here's the list:

- *How long have you been in the financial business?*
  It should be at least three years, in some capacity.
- *What is your source of financial information?*
  This should be a combination of the firm's research, company contacts, friends in the business, professional publications, and material that would *not* be easily available to you. If you both read the same information, you probably don't need the professional!
- *What type of accounts do you specialize in?*
  Your needs should match his or her answers.
- *How many clients do you service?*
  More than a hundred clients is too many. He or she probably won't have enough time for everybody.
- *How often will you meet with me to discuss my portfolio?*
  You should meet at least quarterly.
- *Are your transaction costs (commissions) and fees competitive with those of other similar firms?*
  Have it proven with real examples.
- *How well have you done for other clients?*
  Make sure you see some real figures concerning investment performance.
- *May I have the names of several of your clients so that I may discuss your performance with them?*
  Beware of any professional who will not let you speak to two or three of his or her clients.

Those are some great questions to ask, but I don't think I'd have the nerve to ask them!

We're not suggesting that you will feel comfortable asking *all* these questions, but be sure to ask *most* of them. Go through this screening process at several firms, and you'll feel more comfortable with the process each time. Don't forget *you* will be the benefactor of this most important exercise.

Is it possible to ask if the broker/planner will give me access to other specialists in the office?

It's possible to ask anything within the dictates of good taste! This question is a good one to ask, because if the answer is yes, it can be a great perk for you as an investor to be able, for example, to talk to the firm's municipal bond specialist or the senior research analyst. But don't expect to have your request granted unless you do enough business with the firm.

How can I find out more about a particular firm and its standing before doing business there?

Check the financial (business) section of your newspaper. If the firm is publicly traded (that is, if it has stock available to the public, bought and sold on a stock exchange), you will find it listed on the stock pages. You may request the Standard and Poor's report on the company from a full-service broker. The S&P report is known as a tear sheet. This report will provide you with the company's rating and pertinent financial information. Even if it's not a publicly traded company, any reputable firm will give you its annual report upon request. This will tell you the current financial condition, some historical background, and short-term future goals.

How can I find the best financial adviser for the smallest out-of-pocket cost to me?

Prior to May 1975, the brokerage industry had fixed commission schedules everybody followed. But in 1975 the industry was deregulated, allowing for the emergence of discount brokers and different commission schedules in stock and bond trades. For the best prices, you will have to shop professionals just the way you shop for a new car. All other brokerage firm products, such as mutual funds, limited partnerships, insurance products, and unit investment trusts, remain basically the same from firm to firm. So *ask* the cost before you buy.

Are friends or acquaintances a good source of referrals when looking for a financial adviser?

Friends and acquaintances are a great place to start the search. We all love to share good news, and you will get a good inside track on who's happy and who's not by asking around.

None of my friends is in a position to do business with a financial adviser. Is there anyone else I could ask for a referral?

There is. Another great place to check for referrals is with your lawyer and accountant, who have reason to work on a regular basis with financial professionals. Lawyers and accountants who do estate settlements often use brokers to update them on the portfolio of the deceased.

Should I have more than one financial adviser?

We give you an emphatic *yes* as our answer. No one adviser has all the good ideas and perspectives to totally round out your financial plan. But make sure you tell both advisers your total portfolio, so that you don't end up too heavily invested in one area.

My brother-in-law is a broker. What do you think of having a family member as my financial adviser?

We generally believe that you can get too close to home. A family member can lack an overall perspective when dealing with a close relative. You may want to do some business with your brother-in-law when he presents an interesting idea, but we'd do the majority of our business with someone else.

My broker has asked to have discretion over my account. What does that mean?

It probably means trouble! Discretion is the granting of power to your financial adviser to buy and sell securities in your account without your specific permission for each transaction. We do not recommend that you grant discretionary powers to your financial adviser. It is too great a temptation for abuse when you grant such wholesale power. Your financial adviser should have to call you *before* any changes are made in your portfolio so that you can both discuss the whys and wherefores. The final decision to buy or sell something should always be yours.

My broker has offered me lower commission charges if I will give him 25 percent of the profits generated by him in my brokerage account. Is that legal?

No. A broker may not share in the profits or losses of a client's account. Report this offer to the branch manager *immediately*.

What are the most common abuses by brokers?

Since no one can be expected to care more about your account than you, watch out for:

- *churning:* excessive activity in your account for the purpose of generating commissions
- *unauthorized trading:* transactions that take place *without your permission*

What's the biggest mistake investors make?

They allow themselves to feel intimidated by the complex process and don't object when there is a deviation from their wishes. For example, if you sell a stock position and end up with less money from the sale than you expected, ask why!

My broker has been executing trades without my permission. What should I do?

The best answer we can give you is: *Take action immediately.* Contact the branch manager. All firms must send out confirmation slips as soon as a buy or sell takes place. If you receive a confirmation for something you didn't authorize, call immediately. Don't wait. The biggest mistake investors make is to let the transaction ride. It could be construed as positive acceptance at a later date.

I found an unauthorized trade in my brokerage account yesterday. I called my broker and told him to cancel the trade. He gave me some garbled reason about how it was too late to do anything about it. What should I do?

If your broker refuses to reverse a trade that you haven't authorized, contact the branch manager and explain the situation. A good branch manager will immediately reverse the trade at no cost to you.

I have a major problem with my broker. He has been making trades in my account without my permission, yet neither he nor his branch manager has responded to my correspondence. Help!

It's time to get tough! Since you have received no satisfaction from the local branch office, your next step is to contact the firm's director of compliance. This person can be found at the firm's main headquarters. If you live in the city where the main office is located, call and make an appointment to talk with the director. If you can't go there in person, send a letter stating your problem clearly and concisely.

I've tried your suggestion about contacting the firm's director of compliance and I haven't heard a word in over a month. What do I do now?

Now you bring in the *heavy* artillery! Since you have received no satisfaction from the firm, you will have to contact the National Association of Security Dealer's Arbitration Department, which exists to protect investors. Write or call:

NASD
1735 K St., NW
Washington, D.C. 20006
(202) 728-8000

This office will ask for documentation, so start the information-gathering now! Get out all the transaction slips, monthly or quarterly statements from the firm, and any copies of documents you may have signed pertaining to the account.

My broker never answers my phone calls. What should I do?

It is possible that your broker is too busy because his or her clientele is too large. If you are generally pleased with the broker's performance to date, sit down and try to work out a suitable solution; if not, move on and find a broker who will give you the time that your account deserves.

Why do some accounts get more attention than others with some brokers?

Well, the larger the account and the more often a person does business with a broker, the more attention an account usually will receive. It may not seem fair, but the broker makes money from activity. The more often you do business with a broker, the more attention you'll get. On the other hand, you should get the service and the time you need.

Brokers and other financial advisers are always cold-calling me and, I must admit, are presenting what sound like some very interesting investment opportunities. Should I buy over the phone without having met the salesperson?

No! You wouldn't buy a house or car without a careful inspection, so why should your investments be any different? If an investment idea sounds interesting, make an appointment to sit down face to face with the caller and make your decision after you've met and carefully considered the proposal. When we were brokers, we were always amazed at the number of people who became clients whom we never met in person!

A financial adviser called me the other day. I asked him how he got my name, but his answer was very vague. Should I be put off by this?

No, not really. Many brokers and other types of salespeople feel uncomfortable about admitting that they had to buy names from mailing lists or used the phone book as a source. This does not mean they are untrustworthy or incompetent. However, we would prefer that our names are given on a referral basis by a friend who is happy with this adviser and wants to share the good news. Admittedly, most financial advisers using phone books and lists can be newcomers to the business, who lack both experience and a large family of satisfied clients. By asking callers how long they've been in the business and for referrals of other clients you can check with, you can weed out the new kid on the block.

When I pay a fee and/or commission to brokers or financial planners, don't they become responsible for my investments?

You are responsible. No one takes care of your money more carefully than you. Your financial adviser may take the initiative in suggesting an investment and he or she can help and advise you along the way, but you pay or profit from the ultimate consequences. Never turn control over to a financial adviser. Keep on top of the situation.

How much money do I need to open an account with a broker or financial planner?

It's very hard to attract an experienced professional to assist you if you don't have a lot of money. That's an unfortunate fact of life. An account of $25,000 will help you find an experienced person. However, even small accounts are attractive to financial advisers who are relatively new in the business. Because a person is new doesn't mean he or she is incompetent. Many new people join because of their own investment success in dealing with their own account. Never assume your account will be too small to attract someone talented. To a real professional, even a small account today may be a large account of the future. Get some education, and then start your search for talent.

Now even my insurance agent is calling himself a financial planner! What's going on?

Insurance companies and banks are becoming much more involved in selling financial services. It's no longer the exclusive domain of Wall Street firms. Treat your insurance agent the same way you would a broker or financial planner. Ask the same questions we recommend in dealing with brokers and planners.

I buy and sell a lot of stock on a regular basis. I prefer to trade rather than to sit and hold stock for the long term. How often should I hear from my broker?

A very active trader should hear from his or her broker daily. If you trade often but not constantly, a weekly call from your broker should not be too much to expect.

I consider myself a conservative investor. How often should I hear from my broker?

You should expect to hear from your broker once a month if you buy stock and mutual funds. If you are more involved in very long-term investments such as bonds and limited partnerships, you should still expect to speak with your broker quarterly.

How closely should I monitor my own investments after I invest?

In the case of stocks and mutual funds, the price quotes appear in the newspapers every day and some cable-TV systems run stock quotes, usually with a fifteen minute delay. Stocks and very aggressive mutual funds should be looked at every day. More conservative funds should be looked at once a week.

Some of the investments I have aren't listed in my newspaper's financial section. What can I do?

Tell your financial adviser that you would like to be updated every month or twice a month. If your account isn't large enough to merit this kind of service, call the financial adviser yourself once or twice a month for the figures.

Am I better off doing specific kinds of business (stocks, bonds, options, tax shelters) with different brokers who only specialize in one area?

You wouldn't go to a podiatrist for heart surgery, so why should you go to a broker who specializes in mutual funds to do a sophisticated options transaction? You should always try to deal with someone who specializes, though that's not easy to accomplish. Most brokers are generalists, i.e., they try to diversify their business in order to handle all kinds of clients. In some areas, though, you should deal *only* with a specialist: options, commodities, junk bonds, and short-term trading strategies, to name a few.

I'm interested in a career in financial planning. Would this be a good career move?

The financial services field is clearly one of the hottest of the 1980s and 1990s. The more people become aware that they must have greater control of their finances, the greater the demand will be for qualified advisers.

Where can I get more information about becoming a financial planner or broker?

The College for Financial Planning offers a six-part course leading to the certified financial planner (CFP) designation. The self-study courses are offered through nearly one hundred colleges around the country. Further information is available by writing to:

> The College for Financial Planning
> 4695 South Monaco St.
> Denver, Colorado 80237-3403
> (303) 220-1200

Brokerage firms continually search for new people. Additional information about hiring and training is always available from a branch manager in a local office, and some colleges and universities offer undergraduate as well as graduate degrees.

SUMMARY

The search for a qualified financial adviser is *not* easy, but it *is* possible if you:

- don't believe everything you hear.
- don't take an adviser's track record as gospel without written proof.
- interview prospective advisers before signing up with anyone.
- don't lose control of the interview process. Remember, you're hiring them; they aren't hiring you!

- don't make the final selection without interviewing at least three candidates.
- don't even *start* the search for a financial adviser until you have set your own personal financial objectives.
- don't depend on the financial adviser to tell you every little detail. Keep your own eyes on the portfolio. It's your money, so stay on top of the situation.
- don't ever lose control!

The search for a competent financial adviser becomes even easier with this book as your reference guide. Once you've mastered the concepts we talk about, you will in essence become your own financial adviser.

FURTHER INFORMATION
ORGANIZATIONS

International Association of Financial
  Planning
2 Concourse Parkway
Suite 800
Atlanta, Georgia 30328
"Consumer Guide to Financial
  Planning" (free)

National Association of Personal
  Financial Advisors
1130 Lakecook Road
Suite 105
Buffalo Grove, Illinois 60089
(They will send you a list of *fee only*
  planners in your area.)

National Association of Securities
  Dealers
2 World Trade Center
New York, New York 10048
(212) 839-6200

Securities and Exchange Commission
450 Fifth Street, N.W.
Washington, D.C. 20549
(202) 272-7440

BOOKS

*Tools & Techniques of Financial
  Planning*
Stephan Leinberg, et al.
National Underwriting Co.
Cincinatti, Ohio

Investors' Rights Manual
N.Y. Institute of Finance

11
Your Home

While visiting London, Benjamin Franklin was invited to tour a house an English peer had built for himself. The house had a fantastic facade, but because of the narrow and odd-shaped property, the inside of the house was very badly laid out. Franklin, after inspecting the inside, turned to the peer and said, "All you need to do to enjoy your house, my lord, is to rent a spacious apartment directly across the street."

One man's castle is not always another man's home! But historically, Americans have treasured owning their own home. Our home symbolizes our success and security and is one of the few items that we can buy, use for as long as we want, and, generally, sell for *more* than we paid.

For most of us, our home is the biggest purchase we will make in our lifetime. This has never been more true than now. Cheap housing is a thing of the past. The average price of a home today is between $100,000 and $200,000 in most areas of the country. How different from the days right after World War II, when William J. Levitt sold Cape Cod tract houses to returning veterans for $6,990.

This appreciation in price has made it more important than ever for home buyers to shop wisely and search out the best financing rates available. Price appreciation has also encouraged people who already own homes to sell, take their profit, and begin looking for newer and larger homes. But whether it's your first home or your fourth, inflation is no longer escalating housing prices at the rapid rate of the seventies. Today's home buyer must do some in-depth studying and unemotional planning to survive and thrive.

In this chapter we will show you how to choose the right housing, finance or refinance it properly, and maintain it for resale and profit. Owning your own home doesn't have to be an unattainable goal. Home ownership is one of the few true tax shelters left to many of us. Let's find a way to profit from that. Home ownership is the best investment you can make if you do it wisely.

When is a good time in a person's life to buy a first home? My wife and I would like to take the plunge, but we can't quite get ourselves to do it.

Do it! There really isn't a bad time to buy that first house. Home ownership, favored under tax law, should be the cornerstone of almost everyone's financial plan.

How do you start looking for a home?

Don't put the cart before the horse. Find out how much house you can afford first. In other words, see a mortgage lender and find out how much money you can get before you start touring available homes.

How do we know how much house we can afford?

There's a general rule of thumb followed by most lenders that we think makes a lot of sense. After you determine how much of a down payment you can afford, no more than 28 percent of your single or joint gross income (before taxes) should be used for mortgage payments (principal and interest). Included in this 28 percent must be other home-related expenses, such as real estate taxes, home association dues, mortgage insurance, and homeowners' insurance. For example, you and your husband earn $64,000 per year.

$$28 \text{ percent} \times \$64,000 = \$17,920 \text{ a year}$$
$$\$17,920 \text{ divided by twelve months} = \$1493 \text{ a month}$$

Let's assume approximately $250 per month is allocated toward real estate taxes and insurances, etc.

$$\$1493 - \$250 = \$1243$$
available for the monthly mortgage payment

By using a loan-amortization schedule available at your local bank, you will find that you can afford: a 10 percent, thirty-year mortgage for $140,000 that costs $1230 a month, or a 10 percent, fifteen-year mortgage for $115,000 that costs $1236 a month. These calculations assume a steady $64,000 income. If one of you should stop working for any reason, those monthly payments could be jeopardized.

Please help us take some of the emotion out of looking for our first home. Everything we see looks good to us!

That doesn't happen just to first-time home buyers! Too many of us buy homes because of emotional reactions instead of educated reactions. Here's a list of questions to ask yourself *every* time you look at a house:

- Will I be able to afford the upkeep?
- Will I be able to keep up the payments?
- If the house needs repairs, can I afford to make them?
- Are rooms where I want them to be?
- Are the rooms accessible easily from all parts of the house?
- Are kitchen appliances modern and in working order?
- Is the house structurally sound?

What do you consider the most important consideration in buying a house?

We hate to bring up an old real estate chestnut, but the most important consideration was, is, and will continue to be location, location, location!

How can I determine that I've picked the right location?

To decide whether you've picked the right location, you should judge the area by the following list:

- How good are the schools?
- What type of municipal services are offered, i.e., trash pickup, clean streets, good security, sewers?
- Are transportation systems convenient and in good repair?
- Is there shopping close at hand?
- Are cultural and recreational facilities near?
- Is the area well cared for and zoned carefully?
- If you have small children, are there other small children living there? If you have no children, are there too many children?

Do you think that most people should use a real estate agent when searching for a home?

We *strongly* suggest that you use a real estate agent. A good agent will be familiar with the local real estate market, understand your personal needs in a home, and be knowledgeable about the various mortgage options and how you can qualify.

How can I find a real estate agent that I'm comfortable with and can trust?

There's the million-dollar question! It's not an easy job. But there are some guidelines to make the job easier.

- If you have friends who have recently moved, ask them for a referral.
- Telephone the local board of realtors and ask for the names of a few "salespeople of the year." This is a designation awarded to the very best real estate people in the area.
- Attend open houses. You'll find pages of these in the real estate section

of your local paper every weekend. You might meet an agent you like, and you'll also get a look at a house that's for sale.
* Question people in the area in which you're interested in buying about who their broker was and whether they were pleased with the service they received.

When we find an agent, what kinds of questions should we ask to be sure that this person has the ability to help us in our search?
Here are the questions:

* *How long have you worked in this area?*
  It should be at least eighteen months.
* *Do you know the housing market in the area we're interested in? How many houses have you sold here? (Do you live here yourself?)*
* *Do you have access to a multiple listing service so that I can see as many houses as possible?*
  This will provide you a greater selection.
* *How much time do you have available to spend with me?*
  This should be on an as-needed basis, within reason.
* *Do you have houses in our price range?*
  Save time for both you and the agent by establishing what you can pay.

Most agents represent the seller. Is there such a thing as a buyer's agent, who would be more concerned about my wife and me as we begin looking for a new home?
Yes, there is. What you are looking for is called a buyer's broker. A buyer's broker will represent you and protect you from conflicts that might arise between the buyer and the selling agent and seller.

Is there any point in getting a buyer's broker?
Buyer's brokers can be extremely helpful by ensuring that a house is thoroughly inspected by a professional before you buy. They can obtain a deed, containing the original price, which might give you an edge in negotiating price. They can help you keep a healthy perspective, because they're not trying to sell you the house.

How are buyer's brokers compensated?
Buyer's brokers can take a percentage of the purchase price, work for a flat fee, or charge by the hour. The best arrangement is to deal with one who charges by the hour. The broker will have less temptation to lead you toward more expensive houses when he or she doesn't receive a percentage of the price.

Where can I find a buyer's broker?
It's not an easy job. There are only a little more than six thousand buyer's brokers in the country. The best way to find one is to ask your local board

of realtors, local insurance company, or real estate attorney. If that fails to produce one, send $25 plus $2.40 postage to:

> Who's Who in Creative Real Estate
> P.O. Box 23275
> Ventura, California 93002
> (805) 643–2337

They'll send a national directory of over a thousand buyer's brokers' names and addresses.

Is it worth $150 to $200 to have a home inspector go through a home we're considering buying before we buy it?
Yes. A home-inspection specialist is *trained* to look for possible trouble spots and will surely take more time than you, and probably have more expertise to dig in and find potential problems. Let's say you're going to buy a $100,000 home, maybe the biggest purchase of your life. It's well worth $200 to protect that investment.

Are there any good books available about home inspection?
A book that will prove very helpful in evaluating a house before you buy is *The Home Inspection Handbook*, by Hugh Howard and Home Renovation Associates, Doubleday ($5.95; softcover).

Where can I find a list of accredited home inspectors in my area?
If you'd like a list of accredited home inspectors in your area, just write to:

> American Society of Home Inspectors
> 3299 K St, N.W.
> Suite 700
> Washington, D.C. 20007

When you receive the list, look for inspectors with a minimum of three years in the business, and ask for referrals.

The owner of a home we want to buy claims that he has purchased a one year home warranty to protect the new owners from surprise repairs. But he won't show us the warranty or tell us what it covers! What should we do?
If he won't show you a copy of the warranty, then we have to say we doubt strongly that one really exists! If you really love this house, pay to have it inspected and proceed from there.

What does a home buyer's warranty usually cover?
A home buyer's warranty usually covers wiring, plumbing, and built-in

appliances. Generally, the new homeowner will still have to pay $25 to $50 for the service call if something breaks down.

We've found a beautiful old home in our area. We are both handy and can do *almost* any repairs. What are the key areas to check for in an older home before buying? We want to avoid major problems.

The best places to check are the areas that are extremely expensive to repair or replace, such as:

- *water pipes:* It could cost over $1000 to replace clogged or leaky pipes.
- *water heater:* A new forty-gallon tank costs more than $500.
- *roof:* 100 square feet of asphalt shingles cost $125; wood roofing shingles, $400.
- *storm windows:* New windows can cost almost $100 per window to buy and have installed.
- *insulation:* Insulation can cost upward of $1 per square foot to install.
- *furnace:* New ones can cost over $2000.
- *electrical wiring:* Rewiring a two-story, four-bedroom house will cost over $5000.

The house I'm looking at needs a new roof. The home inspector I hired says that will cost about $3000. Should I pass the house up even though it's exactly what I want?

Not at all. Use the figure for a new roof as part of the bargaining process with the current owner. You may be able to lower the asking price enough to fix the roof and have the home of your dreams.

There has been a lot of publicity lately in our local papers about home repair, building, and renovation scams in which homeowners were really taken to the cleaners. Are there any guidelines to protect us from a similar fate?

To protect yourself:

- Ask for references and double-check the quality of work by evaluating a job already completed.
- Make sure the person you're considering hiring has been in business for at least three years *in the same area.*
- If your state requires licensing, make sure the contractor has one.
- Get all assessments in writing. They should include the grade of materials to be used, brand names, and model numbers.
- Check the contractor's credit with suppliers and ask the local Better Business Bureau if any complaints have been lodged against him.
- Make sure a lawyer reviews all contracts before you sign.

My wife and I are recently graduated from college. We'd like to buy a small condo, but we have no credit history, good or bad. How can we prove credit-worthiness to get a mortgage?

Sometimes it's harder to prove credit-worthiness on a first loan application than it is to explain a history of bad credit! Take a look at our chapter on credit (page 254) to help you get started. Your best bet in this situation, if you need the loan sooner than later, is to find someone to co-sign the mortgage for you.

My husband and I are very interested in buying our first home, but we've encountered our first major stumbling block—we have very little money for a down payment! My father recommended we look into a VA mortgage. How can that help?

A VA mortgage can be a great strategy for someone with little or no money to put down. For qualified veterans, VA mortgages up to an amount of $144,000 are available for no money down. Over $144,000 requires a small down payment. Don't forget to save some money for closing costs, though, because they will apply. Closing costs include your lawyer's fee, documentary stamps, accrued property taxes, etc. VA mortgages are available in both fixed rate and adjustable rate terms and can be assumed by a future owner of your house.

I've been told the best deal in mortgages is available from the VA. Unfortunately, I'm not a veteran. What about an FHA mortgage?

FHA mortgages are also a good bargain—again, if you can see your way through all the paper work. FHA mortgages require only low down payments, usually of 5 percent.

I've heard that foreclosures are a good way to get a house for little money down. How do I find one?

Foreclosure occurs because the homeowner fails to make timely payments of interest and principal on a mortgage. The holder of the mortgage goes to court, gains the right to seize the property, and the homeowner loses title. These homes are then sold to satisfy the claims on the mortgage, sometimes for less than market value. There are many foreclosures and distressed properties available for little or no money down. The best sources of these bargains are local banks, savings and loans, the VA and FHA, and through the Federal National Mortgage Association (FNMA). Often, you will find several local real estate agents with foreclosure expertise. Usually, a lender will want a down payment of 10 percent, sometimes less, with thirty-year financing available.

It is possible to trade off something I own in lieu of a down payment?

It is possible and often works with a very motivated seller. If you have something the owner wants or needs, such as a boat, mobile home, car, stocks, or bonds, the owner may be willing to take that instead of cash for the down payment. Give it a try.

Can I borrow a down payment for a new home against something I already own?

You sure can. This is called the equity-release method of financing:

1. Brokerage firms will lend you money using stocks, bonds, or mutual funds as collateral. Some will even lend you the money without securities on deposit.
2. If you have a cash value life insurance policy, you can borrow against its cash value.
3. Another piece of real estate, classic car, or other big item can be borrowed against.
4. A last resort would be to tap into a credit line with your credit card company. Don't even consider using this method unless you can pay back that *high* interest very quickly.

My wife and I want to buy our first home and we have *no* money for a down payment and no assets to borrow against or trade. I'm not a veteran, so I don't qualify for a no-down-payment VA mortgage. Is there anything I can do?

Believe it or not, you can check your local real estate pages and your local real estate agents for houses that can be leased with an option to buy.

How does a lease with an option to buy work?

This is a very effective way to get into that new house in a painless way. It's most often used in areas where there are many houses available and motivated sellers who are tired of waiting for their houses to sell. You are guaranteed the right to buy the home that you are renting at a pre-agreed purchase price for a pre-agreed period of time.

Suppose I lease with an option to buy and then after a few months decide the house isn't for me? Am I still obligated to buy it?

There is no obligation for you to exercise that option. You rent the house to have a place to live and have an on-scene opportunity to evaluate the house and neighborhood without tying yourself down.

While I lease with an option to buy, could the owner get a better offer and sell the house out from under me?

The owner cannot sell the house to anyone else during the period of your option to buy.

How does leasing with an option to buy help me get a down payment together?

In the agreement you make with the homeowner, part of the rent you pay is applied to the down payment needed to buy the house. In some cases, the rent may be *all* that's needed in the way of a down payment.

If I lease with the option to buy and agree to a purchase price, what happens if the house's value *declines* while I'm renting? Don't I get stuck paying too much for the house?

Not at all. If the house falls in value or you find serious structural defects while you're renting, simply don't exercise your option to buy! On the other hand, if while you're renting, the price of the home goes up, you end up coming out with a real bargain.

Should I use a lawyer with a lease-to-buy option?

Yes, you should. Make sure that all facets of the option arrangement are reviewed by a lawyer before you sign.

My husband and I have finally found a house that we like and can afford. The seller is willing to hold the mortgage for us. Is this a good idea?

Seller financing is usually very good for the buyer. You'll encounter few closing costs and no points (see page 208). It's especially attractive for people who might find it hard to meet the income requirements of various lending institutions. Sometimes a motivated seller will even allow deferred payments, interest only or graduated payments.

If we choose to use seller financing instead of a bank or mortgage company, what should we watch out for?

Make sure that you receive from the seller all the documentation regarding property taxes as well as a record of the interest and principal payments that you make during the year, just the way you would receive from a bank. Make sure that your lawyer reviews the mortgage agreement thoroughly.

My parents have offered to help my husband and me get into our first home. We feel funny about taking their money. Is there some way we can get around this?

Parent-child equity sharing will get you and your husband the home you want and also benefit your parents. Your parents can make the down payment for you and then take an ownership share of one third to one half of the house. They will then rent their share to you and your husband. You'll pay the mortgage and taxes and keep up repairs. Your parents get to depreciate their share of the house for a tax benefit, and you own your own home with your parents as partners.

I'd like to buy a house, but I'm a little short of the down payment. What is the broker equity our real estate agent mentioned?

Your real estate agent is offering to loan you a small down payment to close the deal on a house. Take a good look at the offer. It could be a good deal for you if you really want the house.

We are a newly married couple looking to buy our first home. We can't borrow money from a conventional lender because we really can't afford a big mortgage payment. Do you have any suggestions?

If you have exhausted family, friends, and other personal sources of help, there are two alternatives, but remember to *consider* and *research* before you make a commitment to either of these options:

1. *graduated payment mortgage (GPM):* Down payment is low, monthly payments are kept low at the beginning and rise at a set rate over a period of time.
2. *growing equity mortgage (GEM):* Again, you have low payments at the start, with payments increasing over a period of time. The higher payments go toward principal pay-down.

Are there any bad features to be aware of with a graduated payment mortgage?

You should commit to a GPM *only* if you can obtain it with a *fixed* rate of interest. If it has an adjustable rate and interest rates rise you may find yourself in a real payment bind. Beware!

What's the bad news with a growing equity mortgage?

The problem with a GEM is its lack of flexibility. You are obligated to meet the rising monthly payments whether or not your income goes up at the same rate over time.

May I take money out of my individual retirement account (IRA) to pay for a down payment on a home?

Yes, you may, but you'll pay ordinary income tax on the money you withdraw, as well as a 10 percent penalty, at this writing. However, the costs may (we repeat, *may*) be outweighed by the tax deductions that the home will generate. Check with your accountant before withdrawing any money from your IRA.

How about this for a no-down-payment strategy? We don't have a lot of cash, although my wife and I have good jobs. We'd like to offer to make much-needed repairs on a run-down house that we have our eyes on rather than make a cash down payment.

That's a great idea! It may be attractive to the owner because if, in the future, he had to foreclose on the property, it would be in better condition and therefore more salable than when he sold it to you.

Do you have an answer to a question that's been troubling us? Do we put a small or large down payment on our new home?

You're lucky to have a choice. Many buyers are scrambling around for every penny they can find! Generally speaking, we recommend a smaller down payment for several reasons:

1. One hundred percent interest deduction on a primary residence is still one of the best personal tax shelters left to Americans. The bigger the mortgage, the bigger the deduction.
2. If the value of the house increases, your percentage return on the initial investment is greater, since you've been using someone else's money.
3. By making a smaller down payment, you can invest the remainder of your savings in other types of investments.

What kinds of information will I need to provide my lending institution when I walk in off the street to apply for a home-mortgage loan?

A real estate agent will provide you a lot of helpful guidance in this area, but here's some help from us:

- your W-2. The lender wants to know what you (and any cosigner) earn before taxes.
- signed copies of your last two federal tax returns and a financial statement if you're self-employed. You may also be asked for an audited profit and loss statement.
- a complete list of your assets—stocks, bonds, homes, boat, cars, cash value of life insurance, pending gifts, bonuses, savings and checking accounts, etc.
- a current list of liabilities
- your Social Security number (and the cosigner's)
- your previous address if you've lived at your current address for less than two years

What does a mortgage loan officer look at when you apply for a loan?

The loan officer wants to see the three *C*'s:

1. *Credit or credit-worthiness:* This is a record of payment of other loans. Don't fudge the facts. They're going to check!
2. *Capacity:* Are you going to be able to make the monthly payments, and is your current level of income likely to rise?
3. *Character:* This is pretty subjective. It becomes most important if your income just meets the minimum needed to borrow the amount you want.

We're shopping around for the best rate on a mortgage loan. We check the newspaper every week for the rundowns on local banks and mortgage brokers. Where else should we look?

If you're working with a real estate agent, ask the agent for help. A good one will have a list of lenders in your area and be familiar with the best rates. However, do some checking on your own. Some agents work exclusively with one or two lenders, who may or may not have the *best* rates. If you're buying a home from a builder, he may very well have a local bank willing to provide financing for his clients. Again, shop around before you sign. Searching for the right loan is a long, arduous process but can produce big rewards. For example, the difference between a 9 percent and a 9¼ percent mortgage on a $125,000 thirty-year loan is $8100 over the life of the loan. Keep hunting, and save money!

I don't have as much time as I would like to check out all the different mortgage lenders and rates. Is there a service that will do this for me?

There is a mortgage service worth checking into to help you out. It's a company called HSH Associates. Each week, this company compiles mortgage data from different parts of the country. For $18 it will provide information relating to mortgage rates, terms, and costs in your area.

> HSH Associates
> 1200 Route 23
> Butler, N.J. 07405
> (800) UPDATES

What does the term *amortization* actually mean?

We all use the term, but we're not all sure of its exact meaning. *Amortization* describes the process whereby your mortgage payment stays the same every month but the breakdown changes. In other words, early in the life of your mortgage, most of the money you pay goes toward the interest and little pays off the principal. In later years, more of your monthly payment goes to pay off principal and little of the interest.

What are points?

A point is a charge of 1 percent of the total amount borrowed, levied by the mortgage lender. For example, a 2-point fee on a $100,000 mortgage is $2000.

How do I calculate the effect of points on the interest rate of my mortgage?

Each point charged is equal in cost to about one eighth of 1 percent interest on a thirty-year mortgage. On a shorter mortgage, calculate a point as one quarter of 1 percent. For example, a 10 percent mortgage with a 3-point origination fee is the equivalent of a 10⅜ percent mortgage over a thirty year period.

Are points on a mortgage for our first home tax deductible?

Up-front interest, better known as points, that you pay in advance for a mortgage is still fully deductible in the year of purchase of a principal residence. Points representing closing fees must be amortized over the life of the loan.

I'm having a lot of trouble deciding between a fixed rate mortgage and an adjustable rate mortgage. What do you think?

A *fixed rate* mortgage is best for you if:

- you want predictable housing costs.
- your income is stable.
- you can afford to pay the higher interest rate of a fixed rate mortgage.
- you don't plan to move for at least five years.

An *adjustable rate* mortgage makes sense for you if:

- you don't qualify for a fixed rate.
- your income is consistently going up to outrun payment increases.
- the mortgage has caps on how often and how much the rate can be adjusted.
- you are not planning to stay in the house for more than a couple of years.

For a number of reasons, I feel that an adjustable rate mortgage is best for me. What confuses me are the different indices used for calculating changes in the rate. What index should my mortgage be pegged to, or does it matter?

It does matter. The interest rate on your adjustable rate mortgage should be pegged to a *stable* index, like the bank board's contract mortgage rate or the Federal Home Loan Bank Board's rate. The Treasury bill index used by some banks changes every day and is not nearly as stable.

A lender quoted me an adjustable rate mortgage 3 points higher than the index being used. Is that good?

It could be better. The lender's profit should really be no more than 2 to 2½ percentage points above the index used. Keep looking. You'll find a better deal.

I can't get an answer from my lender on the type of index being used for its adjustable rate mortgages. What should I do?

Take your business somewhere else! *Some* savings and loans and *some* state chartered banks use an index based on their own cost of funds. The information about this is not available to the public and therefore could be subject to manipulation. Stay away from these kinds of loans and the people who offer them. It could cost you a bundle.

Do I really *need* a lawyer for the closing on my house? I hate the idea of spending the money.

Considering the fact that your home will, in all likelihood, be the biggest purchase you ever make, our answer is an emphatic yes! More than that, get a lawyer who specializes in real estate transactions. Don't shortchange yourself!

We've been told to bring our checkbook with lots of money in it (!) to pay all the closing costs for our new home. Since we're running short

after the down payment, could you give us a rough idea of how much we'll need?

It's not as bad as you may fear, but we do subscribe to the old saying "Forewarned is forearmed." Be ready for:

- a loan application fee—$100–$300.
- loan origination fees
- points
- mortgage insurance (if your down payment is substantial, you may be able to forgo this)
- title search and insurance
- lawyer's fees—$500–$1500
- homeowners' insurance
- mortgage tax
- survey—$125–$300
- recording fee—$40–$60
- accrued property taxes

We can't give you a dollar amount. Depending on the size of the mortgage, the amount of property taxes your area levies, and other variables, it is impossible to calculate. The mortgage lender, however, will provide a full breakdown for you prior to closing.

Is there any way to cut back on the fees and charges at the closing?

Yes, there is. The more money you have tied up in the home (the bigger the down payment), the more comfortable the loan officer will feel about your ability to keep up the payments. You may be able to forgo mortgage insurance, which could cost from $450 to $1000 right off the bat.

What is a loan application fee?

This is a charge that many lenders insist you pay just to apply for a mortgage. It pays the costs for processing your application, obtaining your credit report, and, in some cases, for property appraisal. If your lender doesn't charge a loan application fee, expect to pay separately for an appraisal and a credit report.

What is a loan origination fee?

A loan origination fee is generally a flat charge of 1 percent of the loan amount to cover the overhead the lender incurs in processing your loan.

Do I really have to bother with the expense of title insurance and a title search?

If you want to be smart and avoid potential trouble at a later date, yes. Most mortgage lenders want proof that the seller has a clear title to the property you're buying. That's why you need a title search. The title insurance is another protection for both you and the lender that if something was missed in the search, you will be covered by insurance at a later date.

We were just about to close on a new home when we were told that the seller is unable to deliver a marketable title to the property. This sounds serious. Is it?

A property with a marketable title is a property free of liens, easements, encumbrances, or other title defects. If your seller has a title problem but it's not serious, a good sit-down between the seller and a title attorney should clear things up.

How do I know if the title we receive at our house closing is a marketable one?

The best evidence of a marketable title is an owner's or lender's title insurance policy. If during the title search a mistake is made, the title insurance company must pay damages to the mortgage lender or the insured owner. The title insurance policy that you pay for at the closing is well worth the money!

Is is true that most lenders require mortgage insurance?

It's true in many cases, particularly when a down payment of less than 20 percent is made. The lender wants assurance that it will be repaid.

Where can I get mortgage insurance?

You may qualify for Veterans Administration or Federal Housing Administration mortgage insurance. Your local banker also can provide information on mortgage insurance provided by private companies.

Could I do without homeowners' insurance until after I get back on my feet from the expense of buying the house and closing on it?

Sorry, but you can't. True, it's up to you to provide home insurance, but at the closing, the lender will ask for proof of the policy before you get the money to pay for the house.

I'm having trouble finding an insurance agent who really understands the ins and outs of homeowners' insurance. Can you give me a short course?

So many people try to save money on their homeowners' policy that they sacrifice coverage for a few dollars. Just let something calamitous happen to your castle and you'll learn too late how foolish that is. Here are some guidelines to get you the proper coverage and not cost you an arm and a leg:

- Insure your home for *at least* 80 percent of its replacement value.
- Choose the highest deductible you can possibly afford.
- Make sure your policy's home-replacement value keeps rising with the value of your house.
- Insure the contents of your home for replacement value, *not* cash value.
- Make sure your liability coverage is for at least $100,000, not the $25,000 that most policies offer.

I thought I heard a friend mention that you can get a discount on your homeowners' policy premiums for certain items. Did I hear right?

You sure did. Discounts on premiums are available for new houses (up to 20 percent), 5 percent for installing dead bolts and smoke alarms, and 20 percent discounts are available for sophisticated fire- and burglar-alarm systems.

I use my home for business purposes. Do I need additional insurance besides my standard homeowners' policy?

If you run a part-time business out of your home or a full-time business, we really recommend that you add a business option to your policy. Many homeowners' policies don't cover commercial activities—although some of the newer policies do offer minimal business coverage.

We rent out our house during the summer months. Do we need any special insurance?

In addition to standard insurance on your home for such things as fire, theft, etc., we strongly recommend you consider buying an umbrella policy, which will cover you or anyone else staying in your house from personal damage liability. These policies can usually be obtained for much less than $200.

We have purchased a home on an as-is basis; that is, the seller is not responsible for any problems that may arise *after* the sale. How can we protect ourselves from the possibility of future surprises?

An as-is sale, when so stipulated, does not hold the seller liable for possible defects. Technically, when purchasing an as-is house, the buyer is taking his or her chances. The seller has far less liability in this type of a sale. When most of us buy a home, it's not on a stipulated as-is basis. In your case we recommend you buy, for around $350 (or, if you're a good negotiator, the seller might purchase for you), a one-year home warranty through your real estate agent. This policy pays for repairs to heating, built-in appliances, plumbing, wiring, and other items.

What isn't covered in a home warranty policy?

Windows, foundations, and the roof are not covered. Before closing on the house, be sure to have these items inspected by a professional home inspector. With the warranty policy and an inspection, you should be able to avoid any surprises.

The interest rate on my current home mortgage is 13 percent. I can get a 10 percent mortgage at a bank near where I live. Should I refinance?

If you plan on staying in your home for the foreseeable future, refinancing is definitely an alternative to consider, but mortgage rates have to be 2 to 3 percent lower than your current mortgage for it to make the most sense. That is because it takes three to five years to offset the expenses involved in refinancing. If you don't expect to stay in your home that long, you really shouldn't bother.

If I have a prepayment penalty in my current mortgage should I forget about refinancing?

Maybe and maybe not. For a specific answer, you need to run the numbers. But generally speaking, a prepayment penalty of 1 to 2 percent can substantially lower the benefits of refinancing.

I'm seriously considering refinancing my 12.5 percent mortgage. What's keeping me from doing it is a fear that I won't be able to afford a new set of closing costs. Can you give me a ball-park figure to throw into my calculations?

Unfortunately, when you refinance you'll have to pay many charges, such as points, title search fees, appraisal, and credit report, again. It's a pretty safe bet to "guesstimate" closing costs of 2½ to 3 percent of the loan amount.

My wife and I went to the bank to refinance our mortgage and got the shock of our lives. After all the paperwork was finished, the bank told us we'd have to come up with another down payment! What gives?

This happens to many people when they try to refinance an existing mortgage. Most refinancings are done for 80 percent of a home's value. If you originally put down very little cash and your home hasn't appreciated substantially in the interim, you will get a request from the bank for more down payment before it will refinance.

I have a thirty year $80,000 mortgage at 13 percent with a $885 monthly payment, which I can easily afford. Is refinancing really worth the trouble?

If you could refinance at 10 percent, your monthly payment on this particular mortgage would drop to $702—a savings of $183 a month, or $2196 every year. Enough said?

Using this example, how long would I have to stay in my home to make refinancing worthwhile?

Figuring refinancing charges of 2½ to 3 percent of principal, it would cost you approximately $2400 to refinance. You wouldn't have to stay much longer than a full year to have it make sense.

I have a rather high interest rate mortgage, but refinancing is going to mean paying costs that I can't afford. I guess there's nothing I can do. Right?

Wrong! Call your bankers. Although you don't hear much about it, lenders are often willing to renegotiate the terms of a high interest loan. This process probably won't reach a rate as low as you'd receive from refinancing, but it will be lower than your present rate, if you succeed, and you won't be faced with closing costs. Try it!

My husband and I have an adjustable rate mortgage, which we took when fixed rate mortgages were at much higher levels. Now that fixed rate mortgages are so much lower, should we refinance?

Switching to a constant mortgage payment offered by a fixed rate makes a lot of sense if you'll be staying in your home long enough to recoup new closing costs and if the cost of switching makes financial sense. In other words, if you plan on staying in this house for at least three to five years more, we recommend locking in a fixed rate now, while rates are lower. Being conservative by nature, we like the idea of predictable expenses for long-term residents.

I have a thirty-year mortgage with no prepayment penalty. Should I pay it off before thirty years?

Your principal residence is still your best personal tax shelter. One hundred percent of the mortgage interest you pay is deductible. So we recommend you consult your tax advisor before considering early prepayment of your mortgage. It can make much better sense to go on "owing" this money.

There has been a lot of talk lately on radio and television shows concerning the monthly prepayment of principal to greatly reduce the life of a fifteen- or thirty-year mortgage. Is it advisable and realistic to do this?

Some people would rather own their residence free and clear instead of having a tax deduction. If your mortgage carries no prepayment penalty, you can pay off your mortgage in almost half the time by employing this simple strategy: Add the principal portion of your next month's mortgage payment to your current payment of principal and interest.

By making an "extra" principal payment, you bypass the interest payment. Prepayment accelerates the pay-down of your principal amount. Each month, the bank recalculates how much of a monthly payment goes for interest and how much toward the principal. By lowering the principal amount outstanding, you are being credited with more toward principal and less toward interest, thus saving yourself money. Earmark the "extra" payment as "pay-down of principal."

What happens if I start prepaying my mortgage and have to stop because of an unexpected bill?

You can prepay only as you can and want to do so. If you get into a financial bind, you don't have to prepay at all.

I'd like to prepay my mortgage, but I can't afford the full principal amount. Can I do anything else?

Of course you can. If your principal payment is too large for your budget, send what you can afford. Even a $25-a-month principal payment will save you interest and time. However, keep in mind that the faster you pay off your mortgage, the faster you lose the interest deduction on your income tax.

My sister told me about a biweekly strategy for prepaying a mortgage. Can you explain that to me?

A biweekly payment of your mortgage is another way to cut down the time it takes to pay off your mortgage. You divide your monthly mortgage payments in half and pay the mortgage every two weeks instead of monthly. By paying every two weeks, you end up making a full extra month's payment every year. This extra payment can reduce the life of your thirty-year mortgage by nearly ten years!

We're tired of paying apartment rent, but I don't think we want the responsibility of a house. My father recommended we look at some co-ops and condominiums. What's the difference between the two?

Entire books have been written to answer your question! But we'll give it a try.

CONDO	CO-OP
• You own your individual unit, much the way you own a home.	• The co-op corporation holds title to individual units. You are a shareholder of the corporation.
• You can sell at any time.	• You can sell with board approval.
• You may sell to whomever you wish.	• Co-op board must approve the potential buyer.
• You carry a mortgage on your condo.	• The corporation is the mortgagor. If a co-op owner misses payments, all shareholders are liable.
• You pay monthly dues for upkeep of common areas.	• You pay a monthly fee for upkeep of common areas.

Do you recommend buying a condo or a co-op?

That's a question only you can really answer. Condos are easier to buy, because no board qualification is required, and generally easier to rent or sell, again because there is no need to pass a board opinion. Before you make the choice, you need to decide on your preferences and needs. To help you decide, pick up a copy of *A Home of Your Own*, by Alan Hughes, et al., published by Acropolis Books Ltd. It costs $9.95 and is well worth the money.

My husband and I have found a co-op we want to buy. Is there any way we can get prequalified by the co-op board?

There are no guarantees that you will be accepted by the co-op board, but there is a way to in effect prequalify yourselves and avoid disappointment. Tell your agent not only to make your offer, but to include your economic and social standing. The agent should also say that you can receive financing at a moment's notice, but you won't proceed without an indication of board acceptance. Have the broker ask if the seller will call a board member and ask for an evaluation of your qualifications. If your desire for a prequalification statement is ignored, you can then move on to other co-ops with less wasted time and emotional turmoil.

Our offer for a co-op has been accepted. Now what do we do?

Go see your lawyer. Make sure your lawyer receives the building's original prospectus and amendments. (In the case of an older co-op, the prospectus may not be available. Then you should get a copy of the building's proprietary lease, bylaws, and rules.) Your lawyer should also see the financial information, building surveys or studies that have been distributed to shareholders, and the sales contract. *You* should try to review minutes of the board meetings to see what matters have been discussed and ruled on that may color your opinion of the co-op. There's a lot of paper work to be reviewed by both you and your lawyer. Make sure you are informed.

I plan on buying a condominium in New York City. I've been told my lawyer and I should review the "black book." What is that?

The black book is a large document that discloses details about the co-op or condominium offering. You should pay special attention to:

- *the sponsors:* These are the owners of the building. Check the reputation of these people by looking into other projects they have been involved in.
- *proprietary lease:* This states payment schedules and penalties for late payments of maintenance charges, as well as building restrictions.
- *projected budget:* This may reflect only the first year's projected budget, but you want to see how realistic it was. Don't buy until you review three years of financial statements, if they are available.
- *engineer's report:* The engineer is hired by the sponsors, so you may or may not get an unbiased report. However, sometimes a tenants' committee hires its own engineers. This report would also be in the black book.

I've just been informed that my building is going co-op. The owners are sending out a "red herring." What is that?

This is the first document issued by the sponsors for a building conversion. This offers many, but not all, details concerning the upcoming offer. Parts of this document may be changed before the final black book is issued.

I've lived in the same apartment building for ten years. Yesterday I was told that the building is being turned into condominiums. What should I do?

You should seriously consider buying if:

- you can afford the price and find it to be competitive with others in the area.
- you have enjoyed living there and like the neighbors.
- you know of no serious building defects.
- you can afford the common fees and real estate taxes.
- you consult with a team of professionals, including a lawyer and accountant.

I'm interested in buying a prefabricated home. Do you think it's a good buy?

It can be if you do your homework. But keep in mind the "ifs":

- you have the necessary time and skills to supervise construction.
- your bank will finance this type of house.
- the company will give you names of other people who bought their homes, for references.
- there is specialized expertise of construction for this type of job in your area.

If you've answered no to any of these questions, then reconsider prefabricated homes.

Where can I get some more information about prefab homes to help us make a wise decision?

Send $6.25 to:

Home Manufacturers' Council of the National Association of Builders
15th and M Streets, N.W.
Washington, D.C. 20005

and ask for the *Guide to Manufactured Homes*, which lists the market areas for each member company on a state-by-state basis. This booklet will also prove to be very helpful for anyone considering the purchase of a log cabin.

After a long, exhaustive search for our dream house, we've decided to build it! Are we crazy?

You're not crazy at all. However, the National Association of Home Builders estimates that custom-built houses cost up to 30 percent *more* than comparable development houses, even if you don't use an architect. Architects' fees can add 10 to 15 percent more. Another way to go about this is to buy preexisting plans, which will be less costly. There are literally hundreds of plans available. One place to check is:

Bloodgood Architects, P.C.
3001 Grand Avenue
Des Moines, Iowa 50312
(515) 283-0404

They have hundreds of different blueprints for new homes and multifamily dwellings available in all shapes and sizes. The cost of the plans depends on the type of house, its size, etc., but here's a quick overview:

House size:	1800–2799 square feet	
Set of:	1 plan	$155
	4 plans	$255
	8 plans	$285

Are there accredited professional organizations from which I can receive lists of architects/building designers, contractors, and interior designers in my area? I really need help as I put my building team together, but I don't know whom to trust.

There's a wealth of information available from the following groups, including lists of professionals in your area:

- *Architects:*
  American Institute of Architects
  1735 New York Avenue, N.W.
  Washington, D.C. 20006

- *Building designers:*
  American Institute of Building Designers
  1412 19th Street
  Sacramento, California 95514

- *Contractors:*
  National Association of Homebuilders
  National Remodelers Council
  15th & M Streets, N.W.
  Washington, D.C. 20005

- *Interior designers:*
  American Society of Interior Designers
  1430 Broadway
  New York, New York 10018

We're going to design and build our own home. Typically, what are the charges for architects, interior designers, and contractors?

Although fees vary from place to place, here are some guidelines:

- *Architects/building designers:* will charge either a flat, negotiated fee, an hourly charge of $50 to $125 per hour, or 10 to 15 percent of the total construction price.

- *Interior designers:* may charge $40 to $125 an hour or a fixed fee of up to 25 percent of the total cost of decorating.
- *Contractors:* typically charge 15 to 25 percent of the construction cost.

Is there any way we can save some of the cost of having a home custom-built?

There are ways to cut costs, but do so only if you have time and some expertise to manage it. You can save:

- 20 percent if you act as your own general contractor.
- 40 percent if you do most of the work yourself and subcontract for the basic shell construction and foundation.
- 58 percent if you do *everything*.

Is getting financing for a home that we plan to build ourselves more difficult than conventional financing?

Generally, yes. Before you can get a *mortgage* on a home, it has to be built. But before you build it, unless you have lots of cash on hand, you'll probably need money to pay for the construction. This will make a short-term construction loan necessary. The construction loan is usually good for less than one year, but get some sound construction experience before you apply for such a loan. The loan officer won't be very impressed to hear about the set of bookends or tool rack you made when he asks about your building experience.

I own a condo with a friend who has become permanently disabled and is deteriorating mentally. What can I do to protect our investment? He's joint owner with me.

You can get a power of attorney from him with respect to any matter relating to your jointly owned property so that you can make decisions without having to consult your partner.

My family is outgrowing our present home rapidly. We are torn between moving and renovating. What do you suggest?

If more space is all you really need, then we would suggest you price the cost of renovation first, before you move out. The costs of moving, a sales commission if you use a broker, new mortgage closing costs, and other related expenses may make staying put and adding on a smarter idea.

Are there any rules for deciding whether it's wiser to remodel than to move? We have enough property to make additions, but don't know if it's worth all the trouble.

There are no rules, but these are suggestions to consider. If you still love your home and you have enough property to accommodate an addition, you should consider remodeling when:

- your need for more space can be met by adding on or redesigning.
- you're happy with the location of your home.
- moving to a larger house or better neighborhood would seriously strain your monthly budget.

My husband wants to remodel our home, and I want to move! Can you give me some good ammunition to use in our next "discussion" about this situation?

Far be it for us to come between a husband and wife (!), but here are some valid thoughts to consider. Moving makes more sense when:

- the cost of remodeling will put your home's market value 20 percent or more over that of other houses in your neighborhood.
- property values in your area have declined or not kept up with the appreciation of other areas.
- your home is too large.
- it's costing you more than you want or can pay for maintenance and upkeep.
- you would find it almost impossible to live with the confusion and dust and dirt that construction would cause.

My husband and I have decided to remodel some of our home now in hopes of getting a better price for it a couple of years from now, when we sell. What changes would help us get a better price?

Remodeling to increase your investment is a wonderful idea. Just be sensible about it, and use moderation. The best three investments you can make in your home are the addition of a fireplace, converting the attic into extra bedrooms, and interior face-lift. Modernized kitchens always help, too. A modernized bathroom won't increase your home's resale value, but adding a new bathroom will.

I've heard that some remodeling doesn't add much at all to the resale value of a home. If this is true, what should I forget about doing?

It is true. If you're looking to increase the resale value of your home, you'll get little back from new storm windows and doors, a swimming pool, or interior decorating. A new heating system won't return extra money either, because a home buyer *expects* a good heating system.

We've been trying to sell our home for an awfully long time and so far no luck. It's crossed my mind that maybe our house doesn't look so good to prospective buyers. Is there something we can do without spending much money to improve our chances of selling?

Yes, there is. Because first impressions are so important, spruce up the front-yard landscaping. Pull the weeds, keep the lawn trimmed, and sweep the sidewalks. If the rooms in your house are small, make the most of them by storing any unnecessary furniture. Clean out the closets to make them look larger. Offering a home warranty policy for a year and a decorating allowance can also prompt more interest. If the kitchen and bathrooms are in really bad shape, you may have to spend a few dollars to get them in better condition. These are two areas that most home buyers go over thoroughly.

My real estate agent has approached me to have an open house to help her sell my home. Is it worth the effort?

It's worth a try, especially if you have had trouble selling your home. Although walk-in traffic is encouraged, make sure your agent does her best to prequalify potential buyers before you throw open your doors. An open house will give you the opportunity to showcase the house. Use this opportunity wisely. Do a little extra yard work, invest a few dollars in some fresh flowers or plants, and give the place a good cleaning, including closets. A few minutes and a few dollars can go a long way.

When selling a home, do you prefer a real estate agent who is a member of Multiple Listing Service (MLS)?

Yes, we like the idea of many agents having access to your home information in the MLS program. Why not have many brokers trying to sell your home instead of one or two?

How important is a commitment from an agent concerning advertising support?

It's very important to obtain an advertising commitment from an agent interested in selling your home. Without some creative advertising, a home sale is difficult. While we're on the subject of commitments, you should insist on a weekly progress report from your agent. If that's a problem, then the commitment is just not there.

I've decided to sell my home myself. One major problem, however, is that I know nothing about the art of negotiating. Can you help?

Negotiation is a part of every real estate transaction, simply because real estate prices very often consist of *perceived* worth. Although we generally recommend using an agent to handle negotiations, here are a few guidelines:

1. Don't let your emotions take control.
2. Know comparable prices of similar homes in the area, and stick with the norm.
3. Never reveal your personal bottom price as a seller, not to a prospective buyer or to your real estate agent.
4. Never denigrate a reasonable offer. This may stop the communication process.
5. Don't be afraid, as a buyer or seller, to offer creative financing alternatives.
6. Before you start negotiations, establish your negotiating parameters, such as price, down payment, timing of closing, what's included in the sale, etc.

Negotiating is the process of identifying the buyer's and seller's needs. Don't make the process harder than it has to be.

What are some other factors to consider when negotiating, as either the buyer or seller?

While factors specific to your particular situation may slightly change your negotiating technique, remember:

- A negotiation should be little more than two parties sitting down and getting the transaction done!
- You should be respectful at all times. Never denigrate the property.
- Always evaluate the buyer's/seller's needs. For example: How quickly does the sale have to happen? How much cash does the seller really need?

I've heard that skillful negotiation can add 20 percent or more to the selling price of my home over comparable sales prices in my area. Is this true?

It is possible, but only if you have really made the effort to understand the market value of your home as compared with others that have sold and that are for sale in your area. Include in your calculation what their asking prices were.

I've heard that there are over 1 million real estate agents in this country. I know that there are some very good ones around, but how do I find him or her?

The way to find a competent agent, responsive to your needs, is to ask some questions before you hire the agent.

- *Are you licensed?*
- *How long have you been licensed?*
- *Do you work full-time as an agent?*
- *Do you live in the area I'm interested in or have you sold many houses in that area?*
- *Can you refer me to some recent clients of yours?*

I hate to bring up this subject, but I need to talk about taxes! I really disagree with the last assessment the county appraiser did on my home. Is it possible to appeal?

You can appeal an assessment that in your eyes seems unfair. You really have to stay on your toes these days because many cities and towns are reevaluating assessed value more often in order to keep up with escalating real estate values.

- Check the breakdown of your assessment. Busy appraisers can sometimes make mistakes. Are there too many bathrooms listed?
- In order to get your assessment changed, you must prove that other

houses similar to yours are appraised lower. Check the property tax records for the appraisals of other houses in your neighborhood, and check with local real estate agents for their estimate of your home's value.

- If you unearth some strong evidence, request a meeting with the property appraiser.
- If the assessment is lowered, great! If you feel you haven't gotten proper satisfaction, you can appeal to the county board and then to the state board if it becomes necessary.

Give it a try! Many homeowners are paying more property tax than is necessary.

What tax benefits do you get from owning your own home?
Among the many tax benefits are:

- a 100 percent deduction on mortgage interest
- a deduction for property taxes
- a deduction for mortgage points if they are separately charged on a loan origination fee
- a deferral of capital gains on the sale of your principal residence if you buy another within two years that costs at least as much as the one you sold
- an exclusion from capital gains taxes up to $125,000 from the sale of your principal residence if you're fifty-five years of age or older and have lived in the home for three of the last five years

I'm fifty-three and my husband will be fifty-five later this year. We are scheduled to close the sale of our home two months before the date he turns fifty-five. Can we take the once-in-a-lifetime exclusion?
You can take it *only* if you postpone the closing. One of the joint owners must be fifty-five or older on or before the closing date. Talk to the people who plan to buy your house. They may be willing to wait two months to help you out. If they're not, you may have to consider selling to someone else. There's a lot of money involved here.

Is the mortgage interest on my second home fully deductible?
That depends. Owning and maintaining a second home has great tax advantages, but a second home also used as an investment has fewer.

We own a second home and keep it only for our own use. We don't rent it out. What is the tax situation?
Since your second house is used exclusively by you and your family, the tax law allows you two deductions: property taxes and mortgage interest.

My wife and I bought a second home as an investment property. We rent it out most of the year. Do we get any tax break?

If you are an "active" investor, in other words, if you manage the property and don't rely on someone else to do it, you may deduct up to $25,000 of losses a year from that property. However, this $25,000 is not particularly generous for higher-income individuals. If the adjusted gross income of an individual or couple filing jointly is more than $100,000 per year, the $25,000 figure is reduced by 50 percent of the excess. That means with a yearly income of $150,000 or more, *no* tax deductions are allowed.

What constitutes active management of a property?

You must own at least 10 percent of a property and be able to document that you make final decisions relating to approving tenants and authorizing repairs.

Will I still be considered an active manager by the IRS if I use a real estate broker to help me rent the house?

Yes, as long as you meet the other requirements.

I rented out my home for less than fourteen days last year. What's the tax status of the rental income?

Rent received for no more than fourteen days per year is tax free; you don't even have to report it! If you rent it for longer, any income left over after you have deducted your expenses is taxed at the same rate as your regular income.

I intend to rent my second home for investment income. I know that to have it qualify as an investment, I can't use the house more than fourteen days or 10 percent of the time it is rented, whichever is greater. What other restrictions should I be aware of before I make my final decision?

There are many restrictions. Let's check some of the most important ones:

- If your property is newly purchased, you must use the 27½-year straight-line depreciation method unless you bought the property and put it in service before January 1, 1987, in which case you can take advantage of the old nineteen-year depreciation schedule. That would give you bigger write-offs in the early years.
- Rental expenses may be used to offset your regular income, assuming that you actively participate in the management of the property. People whose adjusted gross income is $100,000 or less a year may deduct $25,000 in rental losses from wages and other income. Over $100,000, the deduction benefits begin to phase out, and they disappear at $150,000.
- The tax law allows you to deduct the rental expenses against income from other properties you do not actively manage or from real estate limited partnerships within certain limits, but not against wages, salary, or portfolio income, such as dividends and interest.

Are mortgage prepayment penalties deductible?
Yes, they are.

How about tax deductions for an office in my home?
Consult your accountant. The IRS has recently relaxed some rules on home office deductions. It's well worth a call to the accountant to find out if you qualify.

Under tax reform, is the mortgage interest on our two homes still tax-deductible?
Yes, as long as they are both primarily for personal use.

Is the interest paid on a home-equity loan deductible?
Although this remains a fairly murky area, here goes:

You may fully deduct interest in a home equity loan if the amount borrowed is the *lesser* of:

(1) the fair market value of the residence reduced by the amount of indebtedness (in most cases, the original purchase money mortgage).

OR

(2) $100,000 of such debt

See if I understand this: I can borrow money using my home as collateral and fully deduct the mortgage expense even though the interest deductions on consumer loans is being phased out in 1991?
Right. If you borrow against your home within the specified limits, the interest expense is deductible.

I want to buy another home and use the residence rollover provision again. I used the deferral when I bought my present home eighteen months ago. May I use it again so soon?
You may use the residence rollover again *only* if you are buying the new home for a job related reason. Generally, you can't take advantage of the rollover rule more than *once every two years*.

We're having trouble calculating the actual profit we will realize when we sell our home. We know that it's important to take maximum advantage of the residence rollover rule. Can you help?
We sure can. Here are three steps to consider:

1. Take your *original* purchase price and add to it any fees paid at the closing for insurance, legal fees, etc. Also add to that the cost of any capital improvements, such as a new addition, air conditioning, etc.— any improvement that will preserve the structural value of the house.
2. Next, determine the *adjusted sales price* of your home by taking the sales price and subtracting legal fees, brokers' commissions, and any

allowable fix-up costs, like painting and landscaping work done within
ninety days of entering into a sales contract.
3. The difference between the basis (step 1) and the adjusted sales price
   (step 2) is your taxable profit.

**My husband and I just sold our principal residence. We're not old
enough to take advantage of the once in a lifetime exclusion. Do you
have any suggestions to help us minimize Uncle Sam's tax bite?**

The simplest way to defer any profits is to buy a house of equal or greater
value within two years (before or after) of your sale date.

**We bought a home of lesser value than the one we sold last year. What
is our tax liability?**

You are liable for taxes only on the amount of capital gain that exceeds
the purchase price of the new house. For example, if you purchased the first
house for $50,000, sold it for $75,000 and bought a new house for $60,000,
you must pay taxes on the $15,000 capital gain.

**My wife and I just sold our home. Now we'd like to live on a boat as
our principal residence. Does a boat qualify for the residence replacement rollover rule or will we be taxed on the capital gains from the sale
of our home?**

As long as the boat will be your *principal* residence, it does qualify for
the residence replacement rollover rule. Condos, co-ops, houseboats, and
mobile homes also qualify.

**I'm selling my home and moving into an apartment closer to work. May
I buy a vacation home and take advantage of the twenty-four-month
residence replacement rollover rule?**

Sorry, but the answer is no. The rollover replacement rule applies only
to a *principal* residence. A vacation home does not fall into this category.

**We're about to sell our home. Unfortunately, we're fifty and fifty-three
years of age, not old enough to take the once-in-a-lifetime capital gain
exclusion. To complicate matters further, we don't plan to buy another
home within the two year time limit. Is there anything we can do to
avoid a heavy tax burden?**

Aren't you lucky! There is a strategy that you can use. If you were close
to the age of fifty-five, we'd recommend you put off the closing as long as
possible to run into your fifty-fifth birthday. But at age fifty-three there is
another option available to you, too. Consider taking back a note or mortgage on the house. A portion of your gain becomes deferred because you
are not yet receiving the full amount of the sale. You'll pay tax only on the
gain as you collect principal payments from the mortgage. So, for example,
a fifteen-year mortgage will spread the tax liability on your gain over a
fifteen-year period.

My wife and I are getting divorced. We'll be splitting all our assets fifty-fifty, including the sale proceeds from our house. The house is being sold for $250,000, with an original purchase price of $100,000. Is there any way I can defer tax on the profit I'm receiving?

Even in this unfortunate situation, each spouse can defer tax on the sale of a jointly owned home by using the residence replacement rollover rule. This rule states that a person may defer tax on the profit when another principal residence of equal or greater value is bought within two years before or after the sale of the old house. In your case, your share of the home is $125,000. Buy a new principal residence within a twenty-four-month period costing at least that amount and the tax on your approximate profit of $75,000 will be deferred, not eliminated.

I have a chronic respiratory ailment. Consequently, the doctor has prescribed that I install central air conditioning in my home to minimize my discomfort and keep my ailment under control. Is the cost of the air conditioning tax-deductible?

In your case, it is most likely that the IRS would allow the deduction as a medical expense, but to be deductible, your total medical expenses for the year must exceed 7½ percent of your adjusted gross income. You can use the air conditioner as part of those expenses.

What other kinds of medical expenses are deductible to homeowners?

Depending upon your particular circumstances:

- special bathroom and bathing facilities for a handicapped person
- an elevator for a person with a heart condition
- a swimming pool when swimming is prescribed as therapy and a public facility is not easily accessible

I'm thinking about taking some equity out of my home to catch up on bills and do some home improvements. What's the difference between a home-equity loan and a second mortgage?

That's a great question because the terms are often used interchangeably, although they have distinct differences.

A *home-equity* loan allows you to establish a line of credit and pay only for the money that you find necessary to borrow. The payback time is generally seven to twenty years, and some lenders allow interest-only payments for up to ten years.

A *second mortgage* is a lump-sum loan. The interest payments on the *entire* amount begin immediately. The payback time can be as long as thirty years.

Since interest on loans secured by my home is still 100 percent deductible, should I restructure my personal debt to take advantage of that fact?

Yes! The Tax Reform Act of 1986 completely phases out interest deductions on credit cards, personal loans, car loans, etc., by 1991. Loans secured by your home and a second home will still be deductible in many cases. So it makes sense at least to consider paying off some of your nondeductible (or partially deductible) loans by borrowing against your home and paying *fully* deductible interest. But do check with your accountant before you borrow.

I thought that there were certain limitations placed on the deductibility of home loans.

On a first mortgage, there are no limitations. You may have it confused with the limitations on a home-equity loan. (See page 225.)

What happens if I borrow more on a home-equity loan than the stated limits?

The excess you borrow over the allowable amount becomes subject to the same phase-out treatment of consumer-loan interest.

SUMMARY

Owning your home is your best personal tax shelter and probably your best investment. Finding that special home, negotiating its price, and making the necessary improvements can be a very arduous process, but it can also be the major cornerstone of financial security for a lifetime. As with any investment, there are certain rules of the road to keep in mind:

- Your first home doesn't have to be your dream home. Getting into the game on even a small scale is the important step.
- Take your time when looking, and ask questions.
- Put together a team made up of an agent, a real estate lawyer, a lender, and an accountant. Don't try to do everything yourself.
- A small house in a good neighborhood is much better than a big house in a poor neighborhood.
- If you're buying an existing home, have it inspected before you buy.
- Insure the house properly. Don't try to cut corners on insurance.
- Deal with agents, contractors, and remodelers who have a track record and can give you referrals.
- When trying to sell your house, do some housekeeping and make it look attractive.
- When negotiating to buy a house, find out what the seller needs, not what he wants. Usually, these are two different figures.
- Your home is a source of credit, but use it *wisely.*

Your home can and should be the building block to a firm future.

FURTHER INFORMATION

Federal Housing Administration (FHA)
U.S. Department of Housing and Urban Development
451 Seventh Avenue, S.W.
Washington, D.C. 20250

Veterans Administration (VA)
810 Vermont Avenue
Washington, D.C. 20420

BOOKS

Selling Your Home Sweet Home
Sloan Bashinsky
Monarch Press

The Mortgage Manual:
Questions and Answers (4th edition)
Albert Santi
Probus Publishing

How To Buy A House With No (or Little) Money Down
Martin Shenkman & Warren Boronson
Wiley & Sons

The Common Sense Mortgage
Peter G. Miller
Harper & Row

How to Buy a Home While You Can Still Afford To
Michael C. Murphy
Sterling Publishers, Inc.

Home Sense: A Year-Round Practical Guide for the Homeowner
Mike McClintock
Charles Scribner's Sons

Buy Your First Home Now
Peter G. Miller
Harper & Row

Buying and Selling a Home
Editors of Kiplinger's
Changing Times magazine
1729 H Street, NW
Washington, D.C. 20006

Consumer Information Center
P.O. Box 100
Pueblo, Colorado 81002
"Consumer Handbook on Adjustable Rate Mortgages"
    Publication 428V (50¢)
"A Consumer's Guide To Mortgage Lock-ins"
    Publication 426V (50¢)
"A Consumer's Guide to Mortgage Refinancing"
    Publication 427V (50¢)
"The Mortgage Money Guide"
    Publication 137V ($1.00)
"Wise Home Buying"
    Publication 163V ($1.00)

Buy Smart! A New Homeowner's Inspection Checklist
R. Edward Brown
McGraw-Hill

12

Investing
in Real Estate

John Jacob Astor, once called the richest man in America, sold a lot near Wall Street for $8000. The buyer, thinking he had bested Mr. Astor, bragged after the close that the lot would be worth $12,000 in just a few years. Mr. Astor retorted, "True, but with your eight thousand I will buy eighty lots above Canal Street, and by the time your lot is worth twelve thousand, my eighty lots will be worth eighty thousand!"

Growth is one of the prime benefits of a sound real estate investment. John Jacob Astor knew this, and many investors in real estate today recognize this fact as well. If you browse through *Forbes* magazine's list of the four hundred richest people in America, you will find that 47 percent of the fortunes listed there came from investing in real estate. As Will Rogers so aptly put it, "They ain't making any more!" What better investment can you make than to buy something that has a finite supply?

As with all investments, real estate presents good and bad opportunities. The smart investor will learn as much as possible to avoid potential pitfalls *before* investing. Stories abound of the man who bought land in Florida only to find, upon personal inspection, that it was six feet under water. The Brooklyn Bridge has been sold hundreds of times since its completion!

Real estate investing can be one of the most lucrative avenues for your investable cash, and sometimes little or no cash is needed to get you started. But it can also be no better than throwing cash into a ditch and shoveling dirt over it. Too many would-be investors think that *any* investment in real estate is a sure-fire winner and that anyone can make a million dollars. The bankruptcy courts are full of such dreamers.

In this chapter we will show you the myths and the realities of real estate and help you learn some hard facts so that you can enter this world armed and ready to invest wisely.

I'm a novice in real estate investing. How do I know what to buy?

Here are some guidelines to use when evaluating a property:

- *Look for market value appreciation potential.* The days of depending on runaway inflation to guarantee resale profits on *any* real estate are gone. These days you have to buy property at below market value and/ or add to its intrinsic value by remodeling, good management, etc., if you are going to make a profit.
- *Calculate the return on investment.* If a real estate investment can't beat the return of other investment vehicles that may have more liquidity and safety, then why buy property? Nobody needs a real estate investment with the potential of equaling the return on a *guaranteed* certificate of deposit!
- *Check the construction quality.* Before even considering a home or building for investment purposes, have it thoroughly checked by a home inspection professional. Three hundred dollars spent now is better than a $10,000 surprise down the road!
- *Know market conditions.* Do your homework when investing to find the good areas. Consult real estate agents, the chamber of commerce, local business people, homeowners, etc. Have properties in the area been for sale for more than six months? Are more people moving into the area? Is industry moving in?
- *Location, location, location!* Seek out properties with ready access to highways, shopping centers, schools, etc. In the case of urban properties, important considerations are proximity to transportation, cleanliness of neighborhood, safety, child/pet restrictions. These areas tend to cost more but usually rent faster, hold their value, and sell faster.

I don't even know how to calculate return on a real estate investment! Can you help?

Rate of return, in the most general sense, applies to both current yield (rent payments, etc.) and longer-term yield, which is best defined as probable rate of future price appreciation of the particular property.

Current rate of return: You pay $50,000 cash for a single-family house that you rent for $600 per month, or $7200 per year. Your return on investment is 14.4 percent annually, minus insurance, upkeep, etc. ($50,000 divided by $7200 equals 14.4 percent).

Long-term return: This represents possible future appreciation. Five years later, that rental property is worth $75,000. You sell it for a $25,000 profit, or a 50 percent return on your initial cash investment of $50,000. The $25,000 capital gain plus current annual income, in this case 14.4 percent, is called *total return*. Both are important when assessing the viability of a real estate investment.

I've been bombarded with all sorts of real estate deals lately, but I'm so confused that I don't know what's a reasonable rate of return for each! Can you give me some idea of what to expect?

Here are some benchmarks of annual returns for several high-quality real estate investments.

- single-family homes—10 to 12 percent
- apartments/commercial buildings—8 to 10 percent
- regional shopping malls—7 to 8 percent
- hotels—10 to 12 percent
- strip shopping centers—9 to 10 percent
- mini-warehouses—12 to 13 percent

I'm interested in investing in real estate, but returns seem too low for me. Am I being too aggressive?

No, although the average returns sound pretty attractive to us! If you have earmarked a small portion of available cash for risk-taking, then you may find returns in excess of 12 to 13 percent. But we stress that you use only a small part of your available cash for this. There's no free lunch. Proceed with *caution*, and know what you're doing before you invest.

I've been told that buying a single family home and renting it out is a great way to start in real estate. What are your thoughts?

We agree that for many first-time investors it's a great way to start. Single family houses:

- are easy to manage, have low turnover.
- have good resale opportunities, especially lower priced homes.
- can return 10 to 12 percent annually as a good yardstick.
- are much easier to finance than commercial properties or apartment buildings.

One key point to keep in mind as you begin is *start small*. Leave the big deals to someone else or for when you're more experienced.

We're considering purchasing our first rental property. Can you give us some guidelines to follow?

Sure. Here are a few factors to consider before buying your first rental property:

- Consider property within a reasonable distance of your home, either by car or mass transportation.
- Don't jump at the first opportunity. Take three to six months to investigate various general areas and specific neighborhoods.

- Look for residential areas with no more than a 10 percent vacancy rate.
- Don't shy away from houses that are run down. You'll be surprised how far a lot of work and some paint will go!
- Choose a neighborhood convenient to transportation, schools, employment, and shopping.
- Buy a home with the largest number of rooms you can afford, and ask about seller financing—very often the best kind.
- Don't forget government sources of mortgage money like the VA and FHA.
- The rental income should under most circumstances cover the cost of your mortgage, insurance, taxes, repairs, and other related expenses.
- Keep costs down by doing repairs yourself, if you can, wherever possible.

A friend of mine buys houses, which she fixes up and then rents. She claims that she buys only homes that she would live in herself. How important a consideration is that?

We find that to be a very significant consideration. If you go about choosing and refurbishing an investment property with the same care and concern that you would have for your own primary residence, that touch will be evident when a potential renter is looking for a comfortable, well-cared for place to call home.

You don't recommend buying a property with negative cash flow. Are there any exceptions to your rule?

Yes, but beware. Negative cash flow means your expenses are greater than the income from the property. If you are considering buying a property for a quick fix-up and resale in a fast-moving real estate market, negative cash flow for three to six months is acceptable. However, be prepared. Real estate cycles sometimes change rather quickly. The last thing you need is negative cash flow in a declining real estate market.

I don't trust the home appraisers I've talked to. How do I find another one?

The best source of names for trustworthy and professional appraisers is the mortgage department of local banks. An appraiser who gives inaccurate information doesn't last long at a bank. A member of the American Institute of Real Estate Appraisers or the American Society of Appraisers is preferable.

I don't feel comfortable with the appraiser recommendation given to me by the bank. Is there another source?

Yes. There is a national organization that we have selected because it demands both high levels of excellence and periodic recertification:

The National Society of Real Estate Appraisers
1265 East 105th Street
Cleveland, Ohio 44108
(216) 795-3445

If you were looking for good buys for rental homes, where would you look?

In order of preference, we would check out:

1. *Our own neighborhood:* Yards and houses in disrepair may signal a willing seller.
2. *Local bankers:* They often have a list of foreclosed homes; called REOs (real estate owned). The banks don't want to be in the real estate business, so typically, they will offer excellent terms to potential buyers.
3. *Government foreclosures:* Call your local Veterans' Administration, Federal Housing Administration, and the Federal National Mortgage Association offices for more information.
4. *Estate sales:* The liquidation of a home in an estate usually follows after long periods of neglect of the home. Some good prices are available here.
5. *Local real estate agents:* Good agents often know who's facing a foreclosure, a job transfer, or a divorce. Oftentimes you can negotiate better prices in these situations.

There is a great deal of industry moving into our area, and rental homes are in demand. We're in our sixties, have no mortgage on our home, and are thinking of moving into an apartment. What do you think of the idea of renting out our home?

It's good thinking. By taking out a mortgage on your home, you will make it a bona fide rental investment. The rent income will be offset by mortgage interest and depreciation deductions. If you and your wife's adjusted gross income is under $100,000 a year, you can write off losses up to $25,000 per year.

Are there any other benefits to renting out our home?

There certainly are. By renting the house instead of selling it, you will still be the beneficiary of future appreciation on the property. You won't have to pay any taxes on a capital gain because you haven't sold the house. Because you are in your sixties, you can still qualify for the once-in-a-lifetime exemption if you decide to sell the house within two years. (Refer back to the once-in-a-lifetime exemption in the previous chapter.)

I'm about to rent a house I own, and I'm trying to figure out what is a reasonable rent. I know there are always individual considerations, but is there some rule of thumb that can help?

Currently, three fourths of 1 percent of a home's market value is a likely figure for a monthly rental. As you say, many factors might make it wise to raise or lower that amount. Will heating be included if you're in a cold climate? Does the area have a very good school system? Check your local newspaper ads, which will give you an idea of rental rates for similar homes.

There is no campus housing available to our daughter, who begins college in the fall, and the rents off campus are atrocious. Do you have any suggestions?

You might consider buying an apartment or home for your daughter, perhaps large enough to rent extra space to other students. Charge your child and the other tenant(s) a fair rent. You, as the owner of a rental property, get all the tax shelter benefits that it produces, and you'll have a sound piece of real estate property. You can even pay your daughter to oversee the home, and when she graduates, you can either sell the home in the open market or maybe sell or rent it to the college, which appears to need additional housing facilities.

I needed $6500 for my son's college tuition, and because I'm unemployed, I was unable to borrow the money. What I did was give a five year option to buy my house to my next-door neighbor for $6500. If he doesn't exercise his option, I can keep the money. What are the income tax ramifications on the $6500 payment?

Option money is not taxable until:

- the option expires unexercised. At that point, it's taxed as ordinary income.
- the option is exercised and he buys your home. The option money becomes part of the down payment and is taxed as capital gain.

Is there any tax advantage to me if I buy my parents' home and rent it back to them? We help support them, although they're not dependents in the tax sense.

Absolutely. Buy the house from your parents on the installment method. Make monthly payments to them and then rent the house back to them at a fair market rent. If you've been contributing to your parents' support as well, your installment payments should be equal to the rent plus the amount that you had been giving them every month. The rent you receive from your parents is sheltered from taxes by property taxes, depreciation deductions, upkeep, etc. Your parents' capital gain on the sale may be tax free because of the $125,000 once-in-a-lifetime exclusion. Another alternative would be to obtain a bank mortgage and purchase an annuity that will give your folks a healthy monthly income for the rest of their lives.

Can I take any write-offs if they exceed the amount of rent I receive?

If the write-offs exceed the amount of rent, you can deduct up to $25,000 of losses against your salary and other taxable income if your adjusted gross income (AGI) is under $100,000. If your AGI is between $100,000 and $150,000, you can deduct *some* of your losses against taxable income.

My broker told me to be wary of the redemption period when considering a foreclosure purchase. What is that?

That's a *good* broker! Generally speaking, the original owner of a foreclosed property has six months to a year to pay the amount owed and reclaim the property. This is known as the redemption period. Be sure that it has passed before you consider buying a foreclosed property.

What is a distressed property?

A distressed home is one, most usually, that is in need of a lot of work. But some houses look in worse shape than they actually are—even though it will be hard work for you or a contractor to restore.

How can I find distressed properties?

Some sources of leads for these properties are IRS seizures and sheriffs' sales.

I'm about to buy a three-family home as my first rental property. There is only one family currently living there, so I have to find two more tenants to make my investment pay off. Any suggestions?

Yes. Buy an excellent book entitled, *Landlording*, by Leigh Robinson, Express Publishing, El Cerrito, California, 94530, $17.95.

What other suggestions can you make for finding good tenants?

Finding *good* tenants can be difficult, but having your act together before you begin interviewing people will make the job a whole lot easier.

- *Establish rent and security deposits.* Survey the area for comparable rents, and make the security deposit more than one month's rent. By making the security deposit *more* than a month's rent, tenants won't use up the security deposit as the last month's rent and leave you uncovered for any damage.
- *Compose a thorough rental application.* Make sure the application includes Social Security number, driver's license number, bank accounts, previous landlords' names (and check them), employer's name and address, etc.
- *In some areas of the country it's common to charge a $100 rental application fee.* It can later be applied to the first month's rent if you accept the person as a tenant. A prospective tenant who can't afford $100 is not the type of tenant you want.
- *Ask personal questions.* Find out why they are moving and if they got along with the previous landlord. Ask if they have pets, what kind of business they're in, and a lot of friendly questions that will give you some idea of whether they're going to take good care of your house, be noisy, etc.
- *Check the rental application and credit report(s).* Don't be lazy. You can avoid a lot of trouble later by doing the groundwork now.

I am most interested in buying a three-unit apartment building. The cash flow is positive and the financing attractive. Should I invest?

Rental property is not like buying a stock or CD. It generally takes your *active* participation for both profit and peace of mind. If you don't have the time or inclination to respond to a 2 A.M. call that a toilet is overflowing, can you find dependable on-site management or local workmen? Are you handy enough to know when repairs need to be done and by whom? We are not trying to discourage you. We're merely pointing out specifics that you need to address before you invest.

My brother and I are just beginning to negotiate for a small, nine-unit apartment building not far from our home. But let me say, we feel like babes in the woods when dealing with these pretty slick real estate people in our area. How can we protect ourselves?

As a buyer or seller, it's important that you take into consideration both your needs and the needs of the person across the table. You want to buy low and they want to sell high! Those are wants, not needs. By delving deeper, you'll uncover what the seller needs to get from the property. The more you know about the seller, the better off you'll be. Find out if:

- the seller needs cash to fund another project.
- the property has been for sale for a long time.
- the economic trends in the area are good.
- it's an estate settlement or divorce or separation settlement.

Use time as a tool, the way the best negotiators do. Don't tip your timing to the seller. If you have no time constraints, take the time and flush out the other person's position.

I have an opportunity to buy a four-unit apartment building with three units already rented. If I move into the fourth and pay the same rent that I am currently paying, the building will have a positive cash flow. What do you think?

You may have found real estate heaven! As we previously mentioned, if you are financially and psychologically prepared to buy this real estate, then you have found a good deal. To live on scene is the best way to watch and manage an investment. Couple that with a good neighborhood, positive cash flow, and a good shot at capital appreciation, and you have found a perfect investment.

I'm negotiating to buy an apartment building, but I'm having a great deal of trouble getting accurate income and expense reports from the real estate agent. How can I find out the real numbers?

Ask the real estate agent for a copy of the seller's Schedule E income tax return, because rental income is rarely overstated and expenses are rarely understated to Uncle Sam!

Prospective tenants look good except for one thing—they have no references from previous landlords. What should I do?

We recommend you take a cautious stance. Ask if the parents of the prospective tenants or another relative will cosign the lease or rental agreement. This is a tough call to make, but being overly cautious rarely hurts.

My wife and I own two small apartment buildings and we're really confused by the passive activity rules in the tax law. Can you help clear up the confusion?

We'll try. By 1991 no actual or paper loss from rented property will be deductible except for a $25,000 annual allowance, if you materially participate in property operations. Material participation consists of approving of repairs, checking out tenants, etc. To receive the full $25,000 allowance, your adjusted gross income must be no more than $100,000 a year. Over the $100,000 limit, you will have a phase-out of the allowance, which disappears completely at the $150,000 level.

I want to buy a condominium in Boca Raton, Florida, stay in it for two weeks a year, and have a management company oversee the property and rent it out for the balance of the year. The rent will nearly offset my mortgage payments, and I'll get tax breaks as an investment property. What's the catch?

There may not be a catch if you want to vacation there every year and the management company can prove to you through past performance that it can rent it for you. The bank wants its monthly mortgage payment whether the condo is rented or not. Check the sales prices of similar units for the past three years to make sure the trend has been *up*. This type of investment can be very attractive, but *all* the pieces have to fit!

How much will the management company charge me to manage my condo when I'm not staying there?

Typically, a management company will charge 7 to 15 percent of yearly rental income as a management fee.

I have an opportunity to buy a piece of undeveloped land that is situated fairly close to an emerging downtown area. Would this be a good investment?

The purchase of undeveloped land is tricky. It's hard to predict how long it will take for the property to appreciate, or if it will. The major consideration is, is it worth your tying up money that throws off no income or using that money for a more predictable return? It's your choice, but remember, time is money!

Is farmland a good real estate investment?

Land values in some farming areas have dropped 35 to 50 percent since 1981 and many real estate experts think that acreage prices appear to have bottomed out around 1987. In our opinion, farmland represented a great contrarian strategy in the early '80s. Investors could buy low, earn a respectable yield on the land by leasing it to local farmers, and sell high when the market rebounded.

Where can I find some professional help in evaluating an investment in farmland?

Real estate companies, agricultural experts, and local bankers in the geographical area of interest are excellent sources. Oppenheimer Industries' Management and Consulting Division in Kansas City is the country's largest farm sales/management specialist. Among other things, it will match investors with available properties.

How much money might it take to invest in farmland?

The initial cash outlay is large, typically $50,000 or more.

I hate to kick a guy when he's down, but how about acquiring farm property for little or no money down by taking over the payments on a long-delinquent mortgage?

Don't lose any sleep over this thought! These kinds of deals are few and far between but worth looking for, *if* you can find them.

How does my rehabilitation of an old building qualify for a tax credit?

The law requires that at least:

- 75 percent of the building's external walls remain in place as either internal or exterior walls.
- 50 percent of the building's external walls remain in place as external walls.
- 75 percent of the internal structure framework remain in place.

Don't take this process lightly. There's lots of red tape, inspection, and certification that's necessary as you go along.

Are there tax benefits to rehabilitating an older and historically important building?

There sure are. The Internal Revenue Service in effect will help pay the cost of refurbishing an old building, typically in a part of a city experiencing new growth. The largest tax benefit is the saving of 20 percent of your certified rehabilitation expenses. This savings applies only to the renovation of certified historic structures. The certification of the historic value comes from the Department of the Interior and the Historic Preservation Office in your state capital. To be deemed historic, the building must have architectural and historical significance.

The rehab building I want to buy and fix up is not old or historic enough to be certified by the Department of the Interior. Can I still get some tax benefits from the rehabilitation process?

Yes! Tax credits for nonhistoric, nonresidential buildings constructed before 1936 can save you 10 percent of the certified rehabilitation expenses.

What is a property exchange or swap?

The Internal Revenue Code 1031 defines exchange or swapping as property "held for a productive use in trade or business or for investment . . . exchanged solely for property of like kind to be held either for productive use in a trade or business or for investment." The code authorizes tax deferral when this occurs.

Can you give me an example?

Sure. Here goes. You sell a small apartment building that originally cost you $600,000. You depreciated it down to $400,000 and have held the property long enough but don't need the cash from a sale. You would like to invest in another property and avoid the tax ramifications that a sale of the building would create. You may be a good candidate for an exchange or swap.

Suppose I can't find someone who wants to swap with me?

There's still a way to derive the same benefits of an out-and-out swap. You may arrange for an intermediary (see your real estate lawyer) to take the property and sell it to a third party for, let's say, $750,000 cash. The intermediary uses the $750,000 to buy the new property for you and then transfers title to you. You won't have to pay the IRS on the $350,000 of taxable profits until you sell the property. Check with your accountant first.

Real estate swapping seems pretty good to me under the new tax reform. Am I right or wrong?

In some cases. Swapping properties can be better than buying them outright because a properly executed trade of one property for another is *not* considered a taxable event. A sale is. Do we have your interest?! Essentially, the liability is deferred if the owner swaps his income-producing real estate, such as a rental home, for a "like" property of equal or greater value. So instead of selling your rental home, trade it. You defer taxes and keep your money in good income-producing real estate. But check with your accountant. The IRS has gotten much stricter with the definition of "like" property.

How is a real estate swap arranged?

One way is to advertise in your local paper and/or inform local real estate agents that you are listing your property for sale or trade. Specify the type of property that you desire in exchange. For example, you're selling a four family dwelling and would like to trade it for a small apartment building.

If the owner of such a building likes your four family, you can close the deal by swapping deeds and the appropriate cash.

Swapping sounds easy. What's the catch?

No catch, but because this strategy is a tax-deferred technique, the IRS has set rules and standards that must be strictly adhered to. For this reason, we strongly recommend that you find a real estate agent or lawyer who specializes in property trades. The standards for what designates a true swap are getting tougher.

In order for an exchange to be tax-free, what requirements have to be met?

These specific requirements must be met or the transaction will be taxable.

- The properties must be of like kind.
- An apartment building for another apartment building plus a $10,000 stereo system doesn't quite work. The stereo is taxable because it's personal property, not real property, and is considered an unlike exchange.
- It must be real property held for investment, trade, or business. Almost any kind of real estate except a principal residence or property owned by a contractor/developer (dealer) can qualify for a tax-deferred exchange.
- A tax-deferred exchange requires that you *trade up* to a more expensive property without receiving any taxable "unlike kind" of personal property or cash.

Is there any way that a principal residence could qualify for a tax-deferred exchange?

Yes, there is. If you want to exchange your personal residence for, let's say, an income property, you must first convert your home into qualifying property, i.e., something being used in trade or business. Rentals are a business. Rent it out to tenants, and then exchange it.

What is a signature loan?

A signature loan is exactly what it sounds like—a loan your bank makes to you when you simply sign a note to repay the bank. There's no collateral involved, but such factors as your income, good credit rating, home ownership, and history of repaying loans are taken into consideration. This type of loan is especially helpful for small real estate down payments or to complete a down payment.

I just received a call from my lawyer. He says that one of his clients is being divorced and is selling a prime piece of land for $100,000. My bank will lend me only $70,000. How can I raise the rest?

Consider this: Borrow $5000 on a signature loan from a bank. Then ask the seller to take back a $25,000 purchase money mortgage. What this means is that the seller will take a promissory note from you for $25,000, using the property as collateral. Effectively, you are buying a $100,000 piece of land for no money down. But remember, there's no free lunch. Make sure you can afford the heavy monthly payments that this strategy will demand in both mortgage payments to the bank and payments to the seller.

Can I use this strategy for any other real estate transactions?
Yes. This strategy could be appropriate for:

- a motivated seller looking for a quick sale for whatever reason
- an estate settlement

Should I use my credit cards to help me get some cash for a down payment on an income-producing property?
As long as you are very sure that the positive cash flow from the building will allow you to pay off these 15 to 22 percent loans as soon as possible, you can borrow on the cash limits of your credit cards. Have your lawyer and accountant review the numbers before you make this move, though, and use it only as a last resort.

What is a discounted mortgage?
A discounted mortgage is an existing debt sold by the lender for less than the balance owed.

Is there money to be made in discounted mortgages?
Yes, there is. Here's an example that we think will illustrate the point: Mr. and Mrs. Smith sold their home several years ago and took back a second mortgage for $10,000. Now they need the cash to buy a second home. A discounted mortgage buyer would offer the Smiths less money for the mortgage than they would have expected to receive over the life of the loan, but it could cost the Smiths much more money to borrow the needed amount from the bank now.

I'd like to buy my first discounted mortgage. How do I find one?
Notify the real estate brokers in your area that you're interested in buying mortgage debt. Also advertise in the real estate classified section of your local newspaper that you're willing to buy mortgages.

What type of return can I expect from buying discounted mortgages?
Typically, returns range from 15 to 25 percent.

Doesn't that rate of return to the investor violate the usury laws in some states?

No it doesn't, because the transaction did not change the borrower's terms or payment.

What precautions should I take before buying a discounted mortgage?
Here are some things to check before you invest:

* Study your state's foreclosure laws to avoid any surprises, like a five- or six-month grace period for the owner to make payments and avoid foreclosure on the home you *thought* you had purchased! Check with a local real estate lawyer to learn the local/state law.
* Check the borrower's credit record.
* The borrower should have at least 20 percent equity in the home—too much to walk away from.
* Insist on a title insurance policy paid by the mortgage seller.
* Make sure the property is worth the appraised value.
* The home must be occupied.

Remember that buying a discounted mortgage is like buying the home!

I've heard about zero coupon bonds, but I'd never heard of a zero coupon mortgage before. What is that?
A zero coupon mortgage is an investment in which the lender gives up periodic interest payments now in return for a lump-sum payment of principal and interest in the future.

How can I invest in zero coupon mortgages?
You can invest in partnerships formed to make zero coupon loans. These are available from some brokerage firms, which have packaged these instruments, working in conjunction with large real estate development companies. You can also invest in equity zero coupon mortgage partnerships, which buy properties already financed by zero coupon mortgages.

Can I also go directly to the real estate developer to participate in zero coupon mortgages?
If you can find a developer who deals directly with the public. However, we don't recommend this, because a large brokerage firm has the expertise to evaluate this investment far more effectively than the average investor.

What types of yields do these investments produce?
The interest rates on these mortgages tend to be higher than conventional mortgages, to compensate the lender for loss of immediate return. In the case of zero coupon mortgage partnerships, there's higher leverage because of borrowed money to purchase the properties and, therefore, even higher yields.

How do I evaluate zero coupon mortgages in order to make a wise investment?

Here are a couple of guidelines that will help you evaluate a zero coupon mortgage:

1. It's important to find a property with good growth potential so that the value of the property will keep pace with, or exceed, the debt load.
2. Make sure that the amount of the mortgage plus all accumulated interest doesn't exceed 80 percent of the property's original value.

You can get more information about zero coupon mortgages by contacting a financial adviser or real estate broker who deals in them.

There must be some potential problems with zero coupon mortgages. What should I be aware of when looking at one?

The most important caution is that when a property financed by a zero coupon mortgage is sold, the accrued interest and deferred taxes have to be paid *before* you receive your money. That puts you in line behind the bank and the IRS. You must also be able to wait, usually a number of years, for this investment to pay off. A third point to remember is that the partnership may have to sell or refinance a property to make payments when the accumulated interest comes due.

I've decided that I don't have the cash needed or the ability to deal directly with real estate investments other than my home. Is there any other way I can include real estate in my investment portfolio?

Of course there is. Take a look at real estate investment trusts as an alternative.

What is a real estate investment trust?

A real estate investment trust, or REIT as it is commonly called, consists of shares in real estate companies that buy, sell, and manage properties, mostly of income-producing varieties.

Do REITs make sense as an investment in real estate?

REITs are an excellent alternative for many investors. Because the shares in these companies are publicly traded on major stock exchanges, they offer a liquidity not often available in real estate transactions. You may sell your shares any business day to raise cash if it's needed. A second attractive feature of REITs is that they offer ownership in a company that is experienced in the buying, selling, and managing of properties for a person who may not have that expertise.

Do REITs have any other attractions?

They certainly do. REITs distribute at least 95 percent of their earnings to their shareholders. A REIT investor, therefore, has both income and growth opportunities with this type of investment.

Are there different kinds of REITs?

Yes, there is an array of different types of real estate investment trusts. Three of the most important kinds are equity REITs, mortgage REITs, and hybrid REITs.

What is an equity REIT?

An equity REIT is a real estate investment trust that has the highest potential earnings and dividend growth because it shares in the appreciation of properties in which it invests.

What is a mortgage REIT?

A mortgage REIT offers relatively low growth potential but good current yield, as long as the borrower doesn't default. This type of REIT really acts as a mortgage lender on the various properties in the portfolio.

What about a hybrid REIT? It sounds like it might be a combination of both.

You've hit the nail right on the head! Hybrid REITs invest in *both* property and mortgages. This type of REIT might own an office building in Boston and lend money to a office park developer in Florida.

How can I check the value of my shares if I buy a REIT?

Many REITs trade on the major stock exchanges. Simply look in the financial pages of your local newspaper in the alphabetical list of the exchange on which the REIT trades. There you will find the closing price of a share for the previous trading day.

I own a number of stock mutual funds and I'm quite satisfied with them. Now I understand that I can dabble in real estate by purchasing a real estate mutual fund. Is this a good idea?

It's well worth considering. A real estate mutual fund allows you to invest in real estate by buying *shares* of real estate companies that buy, sell, and manage properties. A fund offers you diversification because of the many investments in the portfolio, as well as experienced professional management.

Would it be a good idea for me to invest in a real estate mutual fund?

The major benefit of this type of real estate investment is that, like REITs, mutual funds offer you the liquidity that traditional real estate investing does not. You can sell your shares on any business day if the need for cash arises. Secondly, while most traditional real estate investments require a substantial amount of money, real estate mutual funds can be purchased for as little as $500, although some funds require $2000 to $5000 as an initial investment.

Who should consider investing in a real estate mutual fund?

Anyone looking for a real estate investment that doesn't require hands-on expertise but who wishes income and long-term growth should consider a real estate mutual fund.

How about a real estate limited partnership? My broker is trying to sell me one, but I don't understand what it is.

A real estate limited partnership (RELP) is an organization made up of a general partner, who manages the project, and limited partners, who invest their money but whose financial liability is limited to the amount of their capital contribution.

What kind of return can I expect from a real estate limited partnership?

Limited partners are generally promised an annual yield of 4 to 12 percent, partly shielded from taxes by depreciation deductions.

I understand that there are leveraged and nonleveraged RELPs. What's the difference?

A leveraged partnership is one in which the limited partner will borrow funds (typically up to 50 percent of the participation) in order to receive yield income that is, to a certain degree, tax free. A nonleveraged partnership is generally more conservative because all the properties in a particular pool of funds are bought for cash, with no mortgage debt. The return of the nonleveraged limited partner is mostly taxable.

How can I determine if I'm investing in a sound limited partnership or one that's a waste of money? I've heard some real horror stories from friends!

The first item to check is the general partner's track record. He or she should have five to seven years' experience in the stages of development and management, including the acquisition and sales of properties.

It's also important that a limited partnership fit into your investment objectives. This is not a short-term place for money. It is not a liquid investment. You must also carefully determine your ability to withstand risk.

Where can I get more information about real estate limited partnerships?

For a complete analysis of how to choose the right RELP for yourself, see: *How to Evaluate Real Estate Limited Partnerships*, by Robert A. Stanger and Keith D. Allaire, Robert A. Stanger and Company Shrewsbury, New Jersey.

It will cost you $48, but in our opinion, it's the finest book written on this subject.

I bought a RELP in 1985. May I still use deductions generated by the partnership to offset salary and other earnings?

You may now use only 10% of the deductions to offset salary and other earnings, *if* the RELP was purchased before October 22, 1986. For 1991 and beyond, there is no deduction allowable against salary and earnings. But remember, tax losses are less important than the ability of the project to make profits.

How about partnerships purchased after October 22, 1986?

For RELPs and other types of limited partnerships purchased after October 22, 1986, write-offs may be deducted only against income from other passive investments, primarily other limited partnerships.

What is the IRS's definition of passive real estate investments?

The IRS defines a passive real estate investment as one in which you make no decisions concerning tenants and do not participate in management decisions.

Do you prefer a leveraged real estate limited partnership where we would have to borrow money and pay in over a longer period of time or a cash/nonleveraged partnership?

In general, we prefer nonleveraged partnerships because the primary aim *now* of a RELP should be to generate income and profit, not tax losses as in past years. By purchasing a nonleveraged partnership, you should be able to ensure that properties are purchased in a timely manner, so that all your money goes to work immediately rather than sitting in an escrow account until enough capital is accrued. Another important plus is that because there is no mortgage debt, profit from the rental or leasing of properties should flow more quickly to you in the form of distributions.

When I invested in a real estate limited partnership, I knew that liquidity (the ability to sell and get my money out) was not one of its benefits, but I really thought I wouldn't need the money. Now I'm in a bind. I lost my job six months ago and I'm having trouble finding another. I need the money in the partnership to pay my mortgage. Can you help?

There may be some light at the end of the tunnel for you. Raymond James and Associates, a regional brokerage firm in St. Petersburg, Florida, makes a market in about 160 partnerships. This means that the company buys and sells partnership units on a daily basis. It is worth a try for someone in your position. Call the company at (813) 381-3800 and ask for the limited-partnership trading desk. The data that Raymond James and Associates provides can also give insights to other partnership units for someone looking to buy.

Another source to try is:

The National Partnership Exchange
(800) 356–2739

I'm reading more and more about master limited partnerships (MLPs). Are they better than RELPS?

Better is not really the right word to use; *different* might do it. MLP units trade on major stock exchanges and over the counter, much like stocks. This gives them a liquidity that isn't available in RELPs.

What's the aim of a master limited partnership?

Its aim is the same as a RELP: to invest in real estate (or oil and gas ventures, another type of MLPs) to pass along income to investors.

Are the yields on MLPs competitive with those of other investments?

Yes. Currently yields of 10 percent per year can be found.

How come MLP yields are so high?

MLP income is taxed *only* to investors, unlike corporations, which pay taxes before distributing dividends to shareholders, who then must also pay taxes. At the present time, MLPs eliminate double taxation.

What determines whether the value of my MLP shares will appreciate or depreciate?

The market value of shares often depends upon the income return to investors rather than the worth of the underlying assets. The potential weakness in MLP investing is that share prices could drop if the MLP sponsor decides to reduce distributions temporarily, even if the cash is used for long-term investments that would eventually benefit investors.

MLP units interest me. Please give me some guidelines to follow when choosing this type of investment.

That's a smart way to approach any investment. Here are some guidelines:

- Make sure that the MLP sponsors have a successful track record in managing the types of properties included in that particular MLP.
- Find out if the properties have been generating steadily increasing income.
- Look for MLPs that own buildings in areas where vacancy levels are below 10 percent.

We believe that it is important to locate a real estate professional at a major brokerage firm who has the experience and expertise to evaluate MLP investments, as well as other real estate investment options. Ask the branch manager for a referral.

Are MLP shares a better investment than shares of a real estate investment trust?

It's a question many people ask. Although both REITs and MLPs share one common benefit—i.e., the dividends are taxed only once to the shareholder—REITs are less risky than MLPs because there's little chance that the IRS will abolish the REIT structure or change it. The IRS jury is still out on MLPs. REITs are presently more strictly regulated than MLPs; consequently, we believe the IRS will generally leave REITs alone.

Are there any other tax advantages to MLPs?

Yes. Thanks to some rather complex accounting rules, the tax you owe on your MLP distributions may not be due immediately, because some or all of the distributions may be considered a return of capital, which is tax-free. You would receive these tax-free returns of capital payments until your cost basis per unit is $0. After that point, future distributions are taxed as regular income, but you might consider selling your unit at that point.

Tax laws assume properties depreciate in value as they age. There's more good news, too. In reality, the market value of income-producing real estate generally increases over time. Even though part of your MLP distribution may be counted as a return of capital, the value of your shares my still increase.

Where can I learn more about MLPs, REITs, and RELPs?

Some brokers are well versed in all three and able to make appropriate recommendations in keeping with your stated investment objectives. However, if you'd like to know more yourself, see "Further Information" at the end of this chapter as well as Standard & Poor's and Value Line (two respected advisory services), which have a broad range of information available.

Can you explain timesharing?

The concept that spawned the idea for timesharing is a simple one. Instead of paying many thousands of dollars to buy a vacation home that you might use for only a couple of weeks each year, timesharing allows you to pay a fraction of the purchase price to use the property each year, usually from one to four weeks, for a twenty- to thirty-year period.

We are considering getting involved in timesharing. What should we know before we do?

Here are some guidelines to follow before you put your money on the table:

- Check out the developer's reputation by asking for and checking references from *other* projects in which the developer has been involved. If there have been no other projects, be especially wary.
- Never buy on the spot. Strong-arm tactics can be the norm in this type of transaction rather than the exception.
- Check with the developer's lender and the state attorney general's office to see if any complaints have been filed.

- Take home copies of the proposed contract, offering memorandum, and disclosure statement and have them reviewed by your lawyer. Don't try to do it yourself.
- Look at the sales contract for a statement of your rights if the resort/ developer runs into financial trouble.
- Make sure that the developer sets aside a portion of your maintenance fee in a reserve fund for major repairs and replacements. Also make sure that the developer is paying his proportionate share of maintenance fees for the units not yet sold.
- If you make the purchase, call the court clerk in the timeshare's jurisdiction to make sure that the title is recorded.

Rumor has it that you two aren't big fans of timesharing. Is that true?

It is true. We're not big fans of timesharing for a number of reasons:

1. If, for whatever reason, you decide that you're unable or unwilling to take a vacation at the same time every year and want to sell your timeshare arrangement and recover part of your investment, you may or may not find a willing buyer. Timeshares have a liquidity problem.
2. Maintenance costs are not fixed at the time of sale. They probably will go up.
3. If you need the money back for some emergency, it's unlikely (although possible) that you'll find someone willing to buy it from you. Not everyone can plan his or her annual vacation that far in advance.

Is it necessary to have a lawyer review the legal papers before we buy the timeshare that we have our eye on?

It is an absolute necessity to have not just a lawyer, but one who specializes in timeshares, review the document.

We're considering buying a timeshare, but we don't understand two terms that have been thrown around: *right to use* and *taking title*. Can you define them?

Sure we can. *Right to use* means you have no ownership in the building, no right to any capital appreciation that may occur, and you have the right to use the unit in which you have invested only for a particular time each year. *Taking title* gives you ownership of the particular unit in the building for which you receive a deed.

Do you recommend the taking-title alternative or right to use?

Given a choice (although we don't particularly like either), we prefer taking title (outright ownership) with some rights if the developer defaults. If you can't get title, then try for a nondisturb clause, which gives you the legal right to use your unit even if the developer fails and the management reverts to another company.

Is there any tax advantage to taking title to a timeshare unit?

Check with your accountant, but our guess is that you'll save pennies rather than dollars in taxes, because of your fractional ownership of the unit.

The developer has promised exchange privileges if we buy his timeshare unit. What does that mean?

You have the right to swap your timeshare arrangement in a given year for a comparable period of time at another timeshare resort. This is sometimes used as a come-on; but it is not guaranteed. To have any chance of this exchange privilege working, you'd better be buying in a very popular resort area that is attractive and desirable to many people.

We live in Baltimore and have been promised an all-expense-paid weekend in Florida if we merely sit through a ninety-minute sales promotion for a timeshare resort when we arrive. Is this legit?

Legit, perhaps, but it could be a very uncomfortable ninety minutes or more, where high pressure tactics are used. Very often these presentations are uncomfortable and distressing to sit through. We recommend that you make sure that you won't have to pay the travel expenses if you don't buy! We have three words for you: beware, beware, beware!

Well, it happened! I really need cash for an operation, and my only source is my timeshare unit. What are my chances of selling it? I have a right-to-use arrangement.

It's going to be a tough job, but let's give it a try. The following company specializes in timeshare resales. We're not recommending this company, but rather listing it as a place to start.

> Holiday Condominiums Condo Link
> 7701 Pacific Street
> Suite 300
> Omaha, Nebraska 68114
> (402) 392-0468

I don't see much in the newspapers or magazines about timesharing pros and cons. Please recommend a source of information for more study.

Contact:

> Resort Properties Owners of America
> 175 W. Jackson
> Suite 1901
> Chicago, Illinois 60604
> Tel: (800) 446-7762
> Tel: (312) 939-0141

After hearing so many negatives about timesharing, why would anyone become involved?

We can only surmise that timesharing is attractive to some people because they need the discipline of forcing themselves to take a vacation every year; they like the idea of going to the same place every year; or timesharing allows some people to afford a resort area that they might not be able to afford otherwise.

We say, save your vacation money and shop for vacation bargains to where you want to go, when you want to go.

SUMMARY

Real estate investments have been the cornerstone to wealth and security for many smart investors. Single family homes, apartment complexes, commercial property, and mortgages can bring great rewards when used wisely and with understanding. Real estate investing, however, is not a get-rich-quick, sure-fire way to make money. Thoughtful appraisal and knowledge of the marketplace are just as important and, often, more important with real estate investments than with other investment opportunities. We recommend that you always keep in mind:

- Smart negotiation, not money, is the most important ingredient to successful real estate investing.
- Location is the most important asset in real estate.
- Choose properties for rental that you would like living in yourself.
- Being a landlord can be a time-consuming job.
- Negative cash flow should be avoided in most cases.
- A team made up of a real estate agent, a real estate lawyer, and a good accountant is a must.
- Never sign a contract without having your lawyer review the terms.
- There are many sources of creative financing. Look around for them.
- Your most important tool is a good education in real estate.
- If you don't want to get your hands dirty, there are packaged products for real estate investment.
- Take time before you jump into a real estate deal. Look at it from every angle.
- Make your first real estate investment close to home.
- Don't be afraid of your first investment.

A well thought out real estate investment can be made at any time. There is no right or wrong time to begin, so get educated and get started!

FURTHER INFORMATION
BOOKS

*The Dow Jones-Irwin Guide to
 Property Ownership*
Margaret Shulman
Dow Jones-Irwin

*The Smart Investor's Guide to Real
 Estate*
Robert Bruss
Crown Publishing

*The Common Sense Guide to
 Successful Real Estate Negotiation*
Peter Miller and Douglas Bregman
Harper & Row

The Total Real Estate Tax Planner
Martin M. Shenkman
Wiley & Sons

Investing in Real Estate
Andrew McLean
Wiley & Sons

Real Estate Investment Trusts
N.Y. Institute of Finance

Inside Real Estate
H.I. Sonny Bloch
and Grace Lichenstein
Weidenfeld and Nicolson

*Investing in Real Estate: How to Do
 It Right*
Dennis Brouner
Longman Publishing

*Financial Security Through Real
 Estate*
Marc Garrison
Simon and Schuster

Landlording
Leigh Robinson
Express Publishing
El Cerrito, California 94530

Dictionary of Real Estate Terms
Friedman/Harris/Lindeman
Barron's Publications

*How to Evaluate Real Estate Limited
 Partnerships*
Stanger/Allare
Robert A. Stanger, Co.
Shrewsbury, New Jersey

TIMESHARING

Resort Property Owners of America
175 West Jackson Boulevard
Chicago, Illinois 60604

AUDIO CASSETTES

Foreclosure Research of America
P.O. Box 10236
Rockville, Maryland 20849
(301) 294–2274 (MD)
(800) 627-3393 (outside MD)
"The 8 Steps to Making Money
  With Foreclosures" (free)

13

Consumer Credit: A Powerful Tool

When a well-known Roman nobleman died, leaving behind an enormous amount of debt, Augustus, the first Roman emperor, told his personal agent to attend the estate auction and buy the nobleman's pillow. When asked why he wanted it, Augustus replied, "That pillow must be particularly conducive to sleep if its late owner, in spite of all his debts, could sleep on it!"

So begins the chapter on credit! You may have charged the price of this book on your credit card. You're not alone. Over sixty million Americans use their credit cards to charge purchases every year, and there's nothing wrong with that. An important part of everyone's financial planning revolves around knowing when to pay cash and when to use the least amount of money with the proper use of credit.

Credit can help increase your wealth and your standard of living when wisely used, but if indiscriminately used, it can grease the slide to personal bankruptcy. In this chapter we will show you the many types of credit available, how and where to get credit, how to use it wisely and *profitably*, how to regain a good credit rating, what to do if your credit situation is out of control, and how to clear up credit discrepancies.

Are there any advantages to using credit instead of paying cash for everything?

Nowadays, with so many people in debt over their head, it's hard to believe that there are advantages to using credit! But here's the good news:

- Credit allows you to make major purchases for little or no money down, with small, affordable (we hope) payments over an extended period of time.
- The use of credit allows you to preserve money you've been able to save—and we all know how hard that can be!
- Credit gives you the immediate use of a product without having to pay for it all at once.
- In cases of financial emergency, credit gives you access to ready cash.
- Credit is convenient. You don't have to carry a lot of cash or write a lot of checks.

What are the disadvantages to using credit?
Here's the bad news:

- Credit used today becomes a drain on any future income throughout the life of the repayment agreement. Continue to factor in that cost until the debt is paid.
- Easy access to credit can sometimes lead to overspending. A $399 VCR may be too expensive for you if you have to pay cash, but with the use of credit, it may cost you only $25 a month for the life of the loan. Suddenly, the VCR seems very affordable. But with this kind of thinking, you might stock up on too many "bargains" for your monthly budget and wind up in financial trouble.
- It costs money to borrow—sometimes lots of money.
- If you don't keep up the payments, the creditor may repossess the goods.

Could you explain what you mean when you say it costs money to borrow?
Sure, although you may not like the facts! Let's look at the most often used form of credit, a home mortgage. Assume you are buying a $100,000 house and you have $20,000 to use as a down payment. You will have to mortgage $80,000.

After shopping around for mortgage rates (and we recommend that you *do* shop around), Bank ABC quotes you the best rate for a thirty-year fixed-rate mortgage at 10 percent. The monthly payment is $702.06 for principal and interest. Over the life of the loan, you will pay Bank ABC a total of $252,741.60.

But I borrowed only $80,000!
Exactly. But don't forget it is costing you 10 percent to borrow the money. So over the life of the loan you will pay Bank ABC $172,741.60 for the use of its money. You will repay that $80,000 more than three times over! If you borrow less for a shorter period of time or pay off the mortgage sooner, it will cost you less. But never forget that credit costs money.

What type of credit is the easiest to get?
The easiest credit to get is a retail charge account, which allows you to

purchase a particular store's merchandise on credit. If you pay off your account in full within thirty days of the billing date, no interest is charged. Any balance over thirty days old is usually charged monthly interest of 1 or 2 percent.

Is there any difference between an American Express card and a Visa card?

There aren't as many differences today as there were when these cards first came out. The major difference is that American Express cards, like Diners Club and Carte Blanche, are considered travel and entertainment (T&E) cards, while Visa and MasterCards are called bank cards because they're issued by banking institutions. The Visa card will generally accept a lower annual income to qualify. Travel and entertainment cards expect higher annual income from members. However, bank credit cards are very quick to initiate interest charges, while American Express and other T&E cards do not. Many business people are able to hold off paying the monthly bill until expense checks have been issued without incurring interest charges.

Why is the interest rate on credit card purchases so high?

Because the lender is really making you an unsecured loan with no hard assets as collateral. The loan is backed by your honesty and promise to repay—two great qualities, but hardly salable if you miss payments! This puts the lender at greater risk and so you pay more; generally, a couple of percentage points higher than a secured loan.

What are secured loans?

Secured loans are backed by a real asset, such as a car or boat. If you fail to make payments, the creditor may sell the asset to recoup his money. Less risk for the lender means lower interest rates (cost) for you.

I've just graduated from college and started my first job. I'd like to get a credit card, but I've been turned down because I have no credit history. Help! How can I get started?

Welcome to the real world! You have just bumped up against the Catch-22 of the credit world. Lenders seem willing to lend you money only after you've proven that you don't need it! There is a four step procedure to follow that will show creditors that you are willing and able to handle credit:

1. *Open a checking and a savings account.* When you apply for credit, you'll be asked about these accounts. This action alone will not make you credit-worthy, but it does indicate that you do handle money in a responsible way.
2. *Next, apply for a retail charge account.* This is the easiest to get. Begin making small purchases you would ordinarily pay cash for, and pay the bill promptly when you receive it.
3. *Now you're ready to apply for a bank credit card.* Again, charge only

what you can reasonably pay each month, and pay the bill promptly when it arrives.

4. *Finally, take out a small loan.* If you've followed the first three steps, you should be eligible. Take the money that you borrow and put it in an interest-bearing account. This way you can offset some of the finance charges of the loan. After six months, pay off the loan in full. By paying the loan ahead of time, you accomplish two important goals: 1) you've decreased the total amount of dollars charged for the loan; and 2) you've earned yourself an A-1 rating as a good credit risk.

Is there an easier way to get a credit card than the four-step process?

There is an easier way if you have some cash on hand that you're willing to tie up. Some major credit card companies do offer a secured credit card. You give a preset amount of money to the company (in some cases as little as $500), and it will issue you a card. Five hundred dollars may not seem like a high credit limit, but it gets you started. The money in escrow earns interest and the amount you may then charge is pegged to the amount you have on deposit with the company. If you miss a payment, the credit card company will take the amount out of your account, which then lowers your line of credit (the amount you may charge). The key here is the same, however, as with the retail charge card. Always pay the bill promptly so that your credit history will reflect responsible handling of money.

I want to get a credit card, but I'm so confused by all the different types available. Interest rates and fees vary. What is the *best* credit card?

The best credit card is the one that matches you and your objectives. For almost everybody, the best deal is a card that has a low interest rate, no annual fee, and a thirty-day grace period (the time in which you can pay your bill in full and not be charged interest).

Can you offer some guidelines for smart credit card selection?

Here are four guidelines to follow:

1. Interest rates can range from 9.5 to 22 percent. Don't accept a card that has a high rate even if you pay your bill in full every month.
2. Annual fees can range from nothing to $250. Small and medium-sized institutions generally keep fees low and often charge no annual fee, just to get your business.
3. The grace period should always be noted before you accept a card. Some institutions charge a low annual fee or no fee but compensate by eliminating grace periods. Twenty-five to thirty days' grace is best.
4. Be aware of any other fees and charges. These might include a small transaction fee every time the card is used or late-payment fees and charges for exceeding your limit.

When I opened my credit card bill today, I found a $54.25 charge I never made. How do I go about getting this fixed?

The Fair Credit Billing Act passed in 1975 helps people like you in just such a situation. There are five easy steps to follow:

1. Don't phone.
2. Send the creditor *written* notice within sixty days of receipt of the bill. The address for billing error notices is right on the bill.
3. Send the letter registered mail, return receipt requested, so you'll have proof of the dates of mailing and receipt.
4. Send photocopies of sales slips or other documents that might pertain.
5. Keep the originals for your own records.

I don't agree with the balance on my latest credit card bill. I wrote to the company, but I was wondering if I should have paid the bill anyway. Do you know?

Until you clear up the problem with the credit card company, you may withhold payment only for the amount that is in dispute. You must pay any amount that you find correct.

I wrote to my credit card company when I was charged for something that I had returned unused. I still haven't heard back from them. What are my rights?

You may not have given the credit card company enough time to respond. By law, the creditor must acknowledge your letter within thirty days after receiving it. The creditor then has up to ninety days to investigate and correct the error or explain why the bill is correct. If you haven't heard from the creditor within the allotted time, contact the Federal Trade Commission's Division of Credit Practices in Washington, D.C.

How can I protect myself and my credit cards from theft?

To avoid both misuse of your credit cards by a thief and credit card fraud:

- Sign new cards as soon as they arrive and destroy those that are replaced.
- Record your card numbers, expiration dates, and the telephone numbers and addresses of the companies that issued the cards.
- Keep the card in view after giving it to a store clerk. Retrieve the card promptly after using it.
- Don't sign a blank receipt. Draw a line through blank spaces above the total before signing the receipt.
- Void or destroy all carbons and incorrect receipts.
- Save card receipts to compare them with the billing statements.
- Open billing statements promptly and reconcile accounts each month, just as with a checking account.
- Report any questionable charges to the card issuer in writing.
- Notify card companies in advance of a change of address.

Our son has the same name as my husband. Since living on his own, he has gotten into trouble with his credit cards. Last week my husband

was denied a new car loan because of mistaken identity. How can we make the creditors aware of the difference?

Contact all your creditors, banks, and even the credit bureau to explain the situation. Then have them make a notation on all the records of your husband's address and Social Security number and anything else that might distinguish him from your son.

My daughter used my department store credit card after I told her not to. Today I received a bill for $210. Do I have to pay it?

If your daughter uses your card on a regular basis and you didn't notify the store not to honor her charges, pay the bill and take steps so that this won't happen in the future. You are responsible. If, however, you notified the store ahead of time, you owe nothing.

A local department store is offering teenage charge accounts for limited chargeable amounts. Would this be a good way to teach our teenage children to manage credit?

A teenage charge account might be a wonderful way to teach your children about credit as long as you make them pay the bills when they arrive. If the parents pay, the kids won't benefit at all from this opportunity!

I've received a solicitation in the mail from a company that will keep track of my credit cards and notify the companies if they are lost or stolen. I will be charged only $12 a year for this service. Is this a good deal?

For its fee, the only real service this company is providing is the telephoning of creditors should your cards become lost or stolen. You still have to make a list of cards and card numbers. If $12 a year is worth your not having to call each company separately, then subscribe. However, we don't think it's worth it.

What about insurance on credit cards?

Don't bother! It's an unnecessary expense. Remember that federal law protects you in cases of loss or theft of credit cards. Your maximum liability is $50 per card if charges are made *before* you report the loss or theft. If you notify the company immediately, then you don't have to pay anything. Save your money.

What happens when I reach the spending limit set by the credit card company?

An embarrassing situation could arise if you don't keep track of your credit limit and it happens in front of a friend or business associate! Your charge is rejected until you pay off some of the outstanding balance.

A charge I was about to make wouldn't go through because someone had placed a credit hold on my card. What is that and who could have done it?

Some creditors, usually hotels and car rental companies, may impose a credit hold on your card without your knowledge. A credit hold adds $200 or more above the billed amount for deposit against potential damage. This amount is then removed after you check out of the hotel or return the car. Sometimes they forget to mention this hold and, worse, sometimes they forget to remove it.

I need a new washer and dryer, but I don't have enough money to pay cash. The appliance dealer offered me an installment sales contract. Is that a good idea?

Yes and no. Since you can't afford the appliances if you have to pay cash, buying on time (installment sales) will get you what you need for little money down. But installment sales contracts are usually more expensive than other loans, so make sure you can afford the monthly payments *before* you sign on the dotted line.

Besides the extra expense, is there anything else I should know about installment sales contracts?

A point to keep in mind is that the dealer will often sell your contract to a finance company so that he can collect the money from the sale as soon as possible. If something goes wrong with the appliances before you finish paying for them and the dealer is hard to work with, you'll have to negotiate repairs through the finance company, not the dealer.

What's the cheapest way to borrow money?

The cheapest way to borrow money can be found right in your life insurance policy. Life insurance companies have several types of policies (discussed fully in Chapter 7) that build up cash value along with providing death protection. Borrowing on the cash value of your policy gives you inexpensive rates and flexible repayment terms.

How can I find out how much it will cost me to borrow on my life insurance?

The interest rate the insurance company charges is stated right in the policy.

What should I know before I borrow on my life insurance?

You can't borrow more than the amount of cash value that has built up in your policy. Then, if you should die before you repay the loan, the amount that you borrowed will be deducted from the face value before your beneficiary is paid.

Instead of borrowing on my life insurance, should I just cash in the policy and use the money?

If you have reached the stage in life where you no longer need the protection, you can turn in the policy and receive the amount that has accrued.

If you still have family obligations that might not be met if you were to die uninsured, then by all means *don't* cash in the policy. Borrow against it instead.

I belong to a credit union. I plan to borrow some money in the near future. Should I check the rates at the credit union?

By all means, yes! A credit union is an excellent place to look for inexpensive loans. They have very good rates and their repayment terms are usually better than those of other sources.

What types of loans are available from credit unions?

Credit unions offer secured and unsecured loans and overdraft accounts. Overdraft accounts, mentioned in Chapter 2, loan you money to cover checks written for more than the funds in your checking account. Many credit unions are now making first and second mortgages available for members as well.

Should I go to a commercial bank or a savings and loan when I want to borrow money?

The answer to your question depends largely upon the type of loan you want. Savings and loans concentrate the bulk of their loans in the housing area, although since deregulation they are becoming more competitive in personal loans too. The rates between the two banking groups are competitive.

What is a debt consolidation loan?

A debt consolidation loan allows you to gather all your outstanding debts together, pay them off with money borrowed from a lender, and only have *one* payment to face each month.

Who should consider a debt consolidation loan?

Anyone carrying high balances on credit cards at 18 percent plus should look into a debt consolidation loan. It can certainly be a less expensive way to get your bills under control and put you on the right track to sensible credit management.

What is a passbook savings loan?

A passbook savings loan allows you to use your savings as collateral for a loan. With this loan you are really borrowing from yourself. The bank charges a much lower rate of interest because the money is already on deposit with the lender should you default. However, the interest paid on these loans is no longer tax deductible and therefore not as good a deal as it once was.

What types of loans are available from finance companies?

Finance companies make both secured and unsecured loans. Their specialty is small installment loans to individuals. But they also lend money for second mortgages and can also provide credit counseling.

Should I borrow money from a finance company instead of a bank?

If you can find somewhere else, we would advise you to avoid a finance company. Of the top five sources of credit (also life insurance, credit unions, commercial banks, and savings and loans), finance companies are far and away the most expensive. One suggestion, which we discussed in some detail in Chapter 8, even outlines alternatives for borrowing from your company's retirement plan, in certain cases. Review this material with your benefits officer before rushing off to a finance company.

Why are finance companies so expensive?

They are willing to take greater risks in lending practices. Someone with a bad credit history may be able to borrow money from a finance company when no one else will lend to him or her. For this, you pay a high price— considerably higher rates.

I've been turned down for a loan by several banks. Should I go to a finance company?

If you've been turned down for a loan by the banks, maybe you shouldn't be borrowing money at all!

I've been thinking about selling some stock to buy a boat. But I don't really want to sell the stock and I don't want to go to the bank for a loan. Do you have any suggestions?

Why not sit down with your broker and discuss using your stock as collateral for a loan right in your brokerage account? There are two good reasons for this: 1) since you don't really want to sell the stock, borrowing, using your securities as collateral, allows you to raise the money you need without going through the banks; 2) because brokerage firms are considered good risks by commercial banks and other lending institutions, they are able to borrow money relatively inexpensively. In turn, the firm passes the savings on to you.

I've been thinking of pawning a few items I own to raise some quick cash. Is this a good idea?

Pawnshops should be used only as the last resort after other lenders have been tried. Interest costs are very high and repayment periods are generally very short (sixty to ninety days) because most items are never reclaimed. The pawnbroker, after appraising the item, will lend you only a fraction of its value and if you can't repay within the short time allotted you, the item will be sold to recoup the pawnbroker's money. If the sale price is higher than what was loaned to you, the pawnbroker is supposed to give you a refund. Enough said. Please look in other areas for money first.

I read an ad in a magazine for mail-order loans. It sounds like a good thing. They promise you the money very quickly and with complete confidentiality. What do you think about this?

We don't think much of the idea! These loans are usually very expensive, and the mail-order firm you deal with may not be required to follow the laws in your particular state. Because these companies are so loosely controlled, if you have a problem with them, you may have no one to turn to for help.

We have a remedial loan society in our town. What is that?

A rose by any other name is still a pawnshop, although this type of pawnshop has a different twist to it. Because the society is operated by a nonprofit organization, interest rates charged are generally quite reasonable and, as with a pawnshop, if an item is sold to cover the loan and it sells for more than the loan amount, the difference will be refunded to you.

I know how important a good credit rating is. Do you have any tips to getting a good credit history?

We sure do. There are just three short rules:

1. *Don't borrow* unless it's absolutely necessary.
2. *Set a limit* to how much you can charge and don't go over it.
3. *Discipline yourself* so that you are always aware of how much you owe.

How can I maintain a good credit rating?

Good credit histories take work and discipline. If you follow these five rules, you should never have a problem:

1. Use only as much credit as you can afford.
2. Pay bills promptly.
3. Tell the truth when you apply for credit.
4. Fulfill all the terms of the credit agreement.
5. If you can't meet your payments as agreed, immediately get help from credit counselors.

Isn't it always best to pay cash and not borrow?

No, there are times when borrowing is too good a deal to pass up. A perfect example of that is when auto makers and car dealers offer financing on new cars at 2.5 percent. Even with your savings sitting in a passbook-savings account earning only 5.5%, it is foolish to use your own money to buy a car. Leaving your savings alone, you were still earning 3 percent after borrowing. Sometimes it's just *too good* a deal *not* to borrow.

What's the biggest mistake people make in dealing with credit?

In our opinion, the biggest mistake is borrowing on your credit card. Most major credit cards are still charging 18 percent or more per year.

That's extremely expensive! The second mistake is not shopping around and comparing rates before you borrow.

I know what a credit union is, but I'm confused by the term *credit bureau.* **Is it the same thing?**

You've probably never been denied credit or you'd know exactly what a credit bureau is! Credit bureaus are companies that sell businesses information about how you handle your financial obligations. There are about two thousand credit bureaus around the country. They do not make decisions about who gets credit and who doesn't. All they do is open the chapter on you when a potential creditor asks, and then let your actions speak for themselves.

What is included in my file that the credit bureau keeps?

Your credit file includes reports from previous creditors, information from public records about bankruptcies, lawsuits, tax liens, judgments against you, and anything else that might influence your credit-worthiness.

I have a spotless credit record, but I was turned down for a loan last week. I checked my record, and there was no reason why I shouldn't have been granted the loan. What happened?

Even a glowing report does not guarantee that a new request for credit will be granted. The potential creditor, after reviewing your file, may have decided that another loan would be too much for you to handle. Sit down and talk with the creditor. There may be a small loan or two that you could pay off to get the new request for credit.

My credit history wasn't too good, but I have really cleaned up my act in the past couple of years. Do you think I should apply for a loan now?

Go for it! Past mistakes could very well be overlooked if you now look like a better risk.

My application for credit was turned down. What are my rights?

There is a federal law that requires you be told why you were denied. You must also be told if your credit report was the reason for denial. The potential creditor must also tell you the name of the credit bureau he used. Call the credit bureau and make an appointment to review your file; ask for a copy to be sent to you so that you can review it or authorize someone at the bureau to discuss it with you over the phone.

After being denied credit, I asked for and received a copy of my credit file. There was incorrect information in it. What can I do about that?

Tell the credit bureau to investigate the incorrect information. Once the credit bureau begins the investigation, it is obligated to delete from your file any information that cannot be verified. If the bureau is able to verify the information and it remains in your file, you have the legal right to attach a statement that tells your side of the story. This may help minimize some of the damage.

What about creditors who may have been given the file before a deletion or an attached letter from me?

If your report was changed after review either because the bureau dropped the information or you attached a letter, you may request that the credit bureau resubmit the amended file to any creditors who received the un-amended file within the past six months.

How long can bad news on my credit record follow me?

Your credit history should not extend back any further than seven years for negative information. The only time this doesn't hold true is if you've been declared bankrupt by a court. This information may remain on your credit file for ten years. Credit bureaus must delete these negative reports at seven and ten years, or financial problems would follow you for the rest of your life. Bear in mind, however, that most creditors are interested only in the last two years of your file.

How much does it cost to review my credit file?

There is no charge for any credit bureau service if you have been denied credit, but you must request your file within thirty days of the denial. If you put it off longer, the credit bureau will usually charge you a $10 to $20 fee, as it will do if you just want to see what your credit file says about you.

I've heard that you should check your credit file every year to make sure there are no mistakes in it. Is that true?

Some professionals recommend you check your file every year; others say it isn't necessary because mistakes rarely occur. We recommend a peek into your file every two years, because accidents can happen!

How can I find the credit bureau that has my file?

You can find your local credit bureau by looking in your Yellow Pages under "Credit Reporting Agencies." If you live in a major city, there will be more than one listing, so you'll have to place a few calls to see who has your file. If you've been turned down for credit, you don't have to go through all that. Just ask your potential creditor which agency made the report, and he or she will supply the name.

What if the credit bureau refuses to show me my file?

If the credit bureau refuses your request—and by the way, it is not re-quired to provide it by law *unless* you have been denied credit—write to the Federal Trade Commission's Division of Credit Practices, FTC, Washing-ton, D.C. 20580. The FTC will inform you of your rights concerning credit matters, and you may even find an FTC representative who will write a letter for you requesting the information that you want.

How much credit can I afford?

What a great question! With consumer debt at an all-time high, we're afraid too many people forget to ask this. The rule of thumb is: no more than 35 percent of your gross pay. Included in this 35 percent rule are mortgage payments, car payments, unpaid educational loans, etc.

Are there any danger signals to warn me when I've gotten in over my head?

There are a lot of danger signals many people unfortunately ignore until it's too late. Here are a few:

- You are near or at the limit on your credit lines.
- You are paying bills in sixty or ninety days that you once paid in thirty.
- You make only the minimum payments on your revolving charge accounts.
- More of your paycheck is being used to pay bills every month.
- You are working overtime to pay bills.
- You are charging for items you used to pay cash for.
- You are always late paying your bills.
- You are using your savings to pay current bills.
- You don't know how much you owe.
- You worry all the time about money.

When I borrowed money from the bank, I was quoted an interest rate of 8 percent. That was fine, but then the banker told me the annual percentage rate on the loan was 14.5 percent. Where did that figure come from?

By advising you of the annual percentage rate (APR) of the loan, the banker was only doing what, by the federal truth-in-lending law, he must do. APR is probably the most misunderstood rate around. The definition doesn't help much either, but let's give it a try:

Let's assume that you borrow $1000 from the bank and pay $100 in interest in one lump sum at the end of the year. The loan is also repaid at the end of the year. Under these circumstances, your APR was 10 percent.

But now let's assume that you paid the $1000 back in twelve equal monthly installments over the course of the year. You had use of only approximately one half of the $1000 because principal was being repaid every single month. In this case, your APR is almost 20 percent because you lost use of some of the money every single month.

The 14.5 percent APR quoted by your banker reflects the situation that you didn't have use of the full amount you borrowed for the entire year. The interest charged and the APR will usually not be the same amount.

I'm buying a new car and financing its cost. The lender suggested that I buy credit insurance, which will pay off the loan if I die unexpectedly. My wife thinks this is a good idea. Do you?

Credit insurance surely benefits the lender. It may or may not benefit you. Credit life insurance, on an estimate, will add to the cost of borrowing about 1 percent to your loan amount. Many consumer groups are dead set against this type of insurance because they believe it is too expensive. However, there are certain circumstances that make credit insurance a wise buy.

What are those circumstances?

The time to consider credit insurance is if:

- your family would be unable to continue payments if you unexpectedly died.
- you don't have enough other life insurance and can't afford to buy it.
- you're in ill health and ineligible for other insurance.
- you're at an age where straight term insurance would cost you more.

If you fit any of these profiles, then do look into credit insurance; but be sure to compare prices among insurers before you settle on the first policy offered.

Being a full-time housewife, I have no salary. Is there any way I could still get a credit card in my own name?

If you own any stocks or bonds in your own name, have a bank account or an inheritance or own your own car, you may be able to get your own credit card. Make a list of your personal assets on the form when you apply, and if you're still turned down, try another creditor. There's no need to give up with the first no.

What steps can a woman not employed outside the home take to assure herself credit?

The passage of the Equal Credit Opportunity Act in 1975 prohibits discrimination based on sex or marital status of a credit applicant. Yet a number of women are still turned down for credit when they shouldn't be. Here are ways to avoid that disappointment:

- *Use your own name when applying.* If you're single, this is no problem. However, if you're married, use your own first name with your legal last name. Never apply for credit as Mrs. Thomas Jones, for example. This is merely a title and any credit information under this name would be put in your husband's credit file, not yours.
- *Make sure that accounts currently being used include your name.* Any account opened after June 1, 1977, automatically reports under both the husband's and wife's names, but accounts opened prior to that date may not. To be absolutely sure that all accounts are reporting two separate credit histories, write to your creditors requesting that reports also be done in your name.

I've been asked to cosign a loan for a friend. Should I say yes?

Before you decide, make sure the contract is complete—there should be no blank spaces—before you sign. Make sure that the contract agrees to notify you as soon as any payments are missed. Don't pledge your home or your car as security for the loan. Be aware that cosigning a loan for a friend could adversely affect your own ability to borrow money for the life of the loan.

It's important for you to evaluate how likely it is that your friend will be able to pay back the loan without putting you in jeopardy. The friend is asking a great favor from you and should review carefully with you how he or she expects to pay the loan back and what assurances he or she will make to keep you intact.

I've heard people talk about the rule of 78 in regard to loans. What is that?

The rule of 78 is a type of prepayment penalty that some lenders use. If you decide to pay off a loan early, your rebate (the amount of interest you won't have to pay) may not be as much as you expected if the lender calculates it with the rule of 78. This basically charges you a lot more interest in the early months of the loan, when you have use of more money, and less interest in the last months. Prepaying a loan calculated by the rule of 78 guarantees you will have paid more interest back than the time you had use of the money may warrant. If you are entitled to a rebate for pre-payment of a loan, be sure to ask how it will be calculated before you sign.

I've decided to pay off my car loan sooner by making two payments every month instead of one. Can I cut back the cost of the loan this way?

No, you can't. By doubling up your payments, you will pay the same finance charges each month. But don't give up the thought. There's more than one way to skin a cat! Since you're able to pay more on a regular basis, first be sure there are no prepayments penalties in the loan agreement. Second, ask your loan officer for a breakdown of monthly payments in principal and interest amounts. Once you know how much principal is paid each month, then you can begin to pay *principal* amounts along with the regular monthly payment, shortening the life of the loan and avoiding some finance charges. Another alternative would be to renegotiate the loan for a shorter term, which would also lessen your finance charges.

I've gotten in over my head, and my creditor informed me he turned my bill over to a collection agency. This agency is beginning to make my life miserable both at work and at home. Is there anything I can do?

There certainly is something you can do. You have protection under the Fair Debt Collection Practices Act. A debt collector may contact you by mail, phone, or telegram and he or she may contact other people, such as family or your employer, in an effort to locate you. A debt collector cannot:

- tell anyone that you owe money.
- call constantly at night or at work if you tell him or her not to do so.

- threaten or abuse you.
- use obscene language.
- use an envelope or postcard that advertises he is a debt collector.

If, after telling the debt collector to stop, any of these violations continue, report him or her to the Federal Trade Commission, Debt Collection Practices, Washington, D.C. 20580.

Charges on my credit card have really gotten out of hand. I can't possibly make payments on all my bills, and I don't know where to turn. Can you help me?

The best help we can give you is to recommend you contact a credit counselor immediately. Start at the National Foundation for Consumer Credit, 8701 Georgia Avenue, Suite 507, Silver Spring, Maryland 20910, (301) 589-5600. This is a nonprofit, impartial credit-counseling service that won't try to sell you a fancy plan. The NFCC has over 250 affiliates worldwide who counsel individuals and families with serious debt problems.

What do credit counseling services do?

Credit counseling services offer training in how to budget expenses and pay off your debt. The service will design a repayment schedule to fit your particular needs. Once you, the service, and your creditors agree on a repayment schedule, you pay the service the monthly sum agreed upon for handling your bills, and it pays your creditors.

How much does credit counseling cost?

The fee for a one-time meeting with a counselor may be as high as $50, but counselors will generally work with people who can't pay, too. If you agree to the counselor's repayment expense, the average monthly charge will be $10 or $11, although it could be more.

I don't just need help now. I seem *always* to be in debt. Any suggestions for where to get help?

> Debtors Anonymous
> 314 W. 53rd St.
> New York, NY 10019
> (212) 969-0710

I'm going to have my car repossessed if I don't pay something on the loan. Unfortunately, I can't find the money to make a payment. Is there some way I can avoid repossession?

We're sorry that it has come to this, but you may be able to avoid repossession if you can sell the car first. Once you've sold the car, pay off the loan. In this way, you'll be able to keep the stigma of a repossession off your credit history.

What does garnishment of wages mean?

Garnishment is a legal procedure that forces an employer to withhold a portion of your paycheck to send to your creditor. It is used for unsecured loans when no means of payment can be found.

Can I be fired if my wages are garnished?

You can't be fired for garnishment for just *one* debt, but we'd be less than honest if we didn't mention that garnishment would certainly start your employer looking at you in a less favorable light. Garnishment will also hurt your credit history because it will be noted on your credit history for the next seven years.

I'm up to my eyes in debt and I don't think I'll ever get out from under all my bills. Should I declare bankruptcy?

Bankruptcy should be considered only as the last resort when all else fails. Try counseling first. If the counselor finds that you're too far behind ever to catch up or if your creditors refuse to accept a repayment schedule, only then should you consider bankruptcy.

I have to declare bankruptcy. After being hospitalized for six months, I have huge bills and no income. My problem is, I don't know which type of bankruptcy to declare. What's the difference between Chapter 7, Chapter 11, and Chapter 13 bankruptcies?

Unless you're a corporation, you can forget about Chapter 11. So let's compare Chapter 7 and Chapter 13. Chapter 7 is straight bankruptcy. Your assets are sold and the money raised is distributed among your creditors. When Chapter 7 is finished, all your debts are erased even if your creditors only receive a fraction of the amount they're due.

Chapter 13 bankruptcy includes a repayment plan for your creditors, which may mean paying the entire debt over a longer period of time, or at least as much of the debt as you can. A repayment schedule, acceptable to your creditors, should avoid a forced sale of assets.

In your case, because you are currently unemployed, Chapter 13 is not available to you. To file for Chapter 13 you must have regular employment from a job or other sources, and secured indebtedness (loans with collateral) can't be more than $350,000. Unsecured indebtedness (loans without collateral) can't be more than $100,000.

If I file for Chapter 7 bankruptcy will all my debts be taken care of, or am I still liable for some?

You'll still be liable for:

- credit card charges made within twenty days of filing
- personal loans and installment purchases made within forty days of filing
- alimony and child support payments

- certain back taxes
- certain restrictions on student loans
- money owed someone for intentional harm
- debts resulting from fraud

What debts am I responsible for if I file a Chapter 13?

You're still responsible for:

- long-term debts not fully repaid during the repayment schedule.
- alimony and child support payments.

How long does a Chapter 13 repayment schedule last?

Most Chapter 13 schedules last for three years, but if you have mitigating circumstances, you may be able to convince the judge to stretch it out to five years.

If I file a Chapter 7 bankruptcy, must I wait to file again?

Under a Chapter 7 bankruptcy, you cannot file again for six years. There is no time restriction placed on you in a Chapter 13 filing.

I understand that the court appoints a trustee when you file for Chapter 13. What does the trustee do?

The court-appointed trustee reviews your repayment schedule to make sure it's realistic. The trustee will also check your employment record, your honesty, existing hardships, and any other details that may affect your ability to repay. Once your repayment plan is accepted, you will send the trustee a monthly check and he or she will pay your creditors.

When I filed for Chapter 13 bankruptcy I thought I'd have no trouble meeting the repayment schedule, but now I'm having difficulties. What can I do?

Go back to the court and tell the trustee your problem. The court may be willing to grant you a modified plan. If a modified plan won't solve the problem, you may have to consider filing a Chapter 7.

I'm so deep in debt it seems the only way out is to declare bankruptcy, but I'm afraid to do it. I don't want to lose everything I own. What else can I do?

If bankruptcy is the only way out of your predicament, then do it. Don't be afraid. You don't lose everything in bankruptcy. The cartoon character of the naked man in a barrel is only a cartoon! Most of your assets are partially or completely exempt from judgment.

Could you give me a list of assets that are partially or completely exempt from bankruptcy?

Sure. Your house, furnishings, clothes, appliances, and household goods are exempt from the proceedings up to a certain amount. You will also be allowed to keep one car and any property you use to conduct business, up to a certain amount. Sit down with a good lawyer and work out your problems. Don't fear them.

Three years ago I had to declare bankruptcy for a number of reasons. One friend told me I could reapply for credit after four years, but another said I had to wait seven years. Who's right?

Technically, both friends are incorrect. Bankruptcy remains on credit records for ten years. However, if there was a good reason for declaring bankruptcy, such as prolonged hospitalization, you may be able to talk with potential creditors and reestablish credit without waiting for the full ten years. Have a one-on-one meeting and explain things fully. You may be pleasantly surprised.

SUMMARY

With proper use, credit can be a very important building block to financial security. With improper use, credit can undermine all your hopes and dreams.

- Use credit only to further your financial plans.
- Don't use credit for impulse buying or for things you really don't need.
- If you find yourself unable to make all your payments, talk to your creditors *immediately* and contact a nonprofit counseling group.
- Be aware of your legal rights as they pertain to credit.
- Use bankruptcy only as a last resort.

Credit is a powerful tool; use it wisely!

FURTHER INFORMATION
PAMPHLETS

How to Establish and Use Credit
Your Credit Rating
Federal Reserve Bank of Philadelphia
Public Services Department
P.O. Box 66
Philadelphia, Pennsylvania 19105

Managing Your Credit
Household International
2700 Sanders Road
Prospect Heights, Illinois 60070

The Fair Credit Reporting Brochure
Federal Trade Commission
Division of Credit Practices
Washington, D.C. 20580

Consumer Credit Handbook
(591N)—free (How to apply for
credit, what to do if you are
denied, and how consumer credit
laws can help you.)
Fair Credit Billing (419)—50¢ (How
to resolve a billing dispute on
credit-card purchases.)
Fair Debt Collection (421N)—50¢
(Methods of debt collection that
are prohibited by law, and where
to complain.)
Consumer Information Center
Pueblo, Colorado 81009

ORGANIZATIONS

The National Foundation for
  Consumer Credit
8701 Georgia Avenue
Suite 307
Silver Spring, Maryland 20910
(800) 388-2227

Bankcard Holders of America
560 Herndon Parkway
Suite 120
Herndon, Virginia 22070
(800) 638-6407 (outside D.C.)
(703) 481-1110
A private, nonprofit organization that
educates the public about the
prudent use of credit. Its annual
$18 membership fee covers BHA's
quarterly newsletter, a credit-card-
protection service, and a toll-free
consumer-dispute hot line as well
as more than twenty consumer
education pamphlets and several
different consumer information
lists. You can request:
How to Shop for a Bank Card
Solving Your Credit-Card Billing
    Questions
Women's Credit Rights

14

Taxes

I'm proud to be paying taxes in the United States. The only thing is—I could be just as proud for half the money.

ARTHUR GODFREY

The Tax Reform Act of 1986 was supposed to simplify our future tax bills. If this tax structure is simplicity, we can only pray that we be saved from complexity! In fact, if taxes have been simplified, why do we need to write this chapter at all?

As *The Old Farmer's Almanac* once put it, "If Patrick Henry thought taxation *without* representation was bad, he should see how bad it is *with* representation." We receive more questions than ever before concerning taxes since the 1986 tax reform bill became law. The blessings provided by our representatives in Washington have been at best mixed.

In each chapter of this book we have addressed the most frequently asked questions about taxes as they apply to that particular investment. Consequently, we suggest that if you have a specific tax question relating to one of the subjects in *Smart Money* you refer to that specific chapter first.

We will touch on many remaining tax questions in this chapter, but certainly not all of them. For further reference, we include at the end of the chapter a substantial list of good tax materials for follow-up work.

Unless you have a very simple, straightforward tax situation, we recommend more strongly than ever before that you find professional tax help. The "simplicity" of current tax laws makes an accountant even more necessary.

Are you ready for "simple"?

I had just mastered the difference between long- and short-term capital gains and losses. Now I understand that tax reform changed all of this. How has it changed?

Capital gains and other income, like interest, dividends, and salary, are taxed at the same rate, peaking at a marginal rate of 33 percent for married couples with taxable income over *$71,900*.

Does the Tax Reform Act of 1986 still allow for a favorable treatment of long-term capital gains?

No, it doesn't. Favorable tax treatments on investments held six months or longer disappeared at the end of 1986. All capital gains are now treated as short-term gains and therefore taxed as ordinary income, as of this writing.

What about taxes and my investment losses?

There is good news (as good as any news can be with losses!). Losses are no longer looked at as long-term or short-term. All losses, however long you held the investment, are deductible dollar for dollar up to $3000 per year.

Does this loss treatment affect the way I should treat losing stock positions?

It certainly does. Investors with long term losses were allowed to write off only fifty cents on every dollar they lost, so they sat tight in hope of upward movement in stock prices. Now it makes sense to cut losses sooner than before. One hundred percent of any loss, long term or short term, is fully deductible subject to the $3000 annual limitation.

Every December my broker starts bugging me about stocks that should be sold for tax reasons. I'm never sure of what to do. Is there a rule of thumb I should follow when considering to sell investments for tax purposes?

The basic rule to follow is to decide what you would do with the stock if you had no taxes to consider. After you've made a non-tax-related decision, you can then go back and weigh tax benefits against your investment objectives. If a sale of stock makes good *investment* sense, sell it. If a smart investor would hold on to the shares, don't sell. Investment sense first; tax sense second.

What is a wash sale? It sounds like laundry.

Wrong! A wash sale is the purchase of the same security or basically identical security within thirty days before or after selling it for a capital loss. If a wash sale occurs, a loss will be disallowed for tax purposes.

Does the wash rule apply to the sale of securities that produce a capital gain?

No, not at all. When you sell stock at a capital gain, your gain is taxable whether you buy the stock back or not.

Are there any strategies for deciding when I should take income and when I should postpone it?

Up until recently, it was a wise idea to consider putting off any extra income or bonuses to take advantage of the lower tax rate of the following year. Once the final levels of the Tax Reform Act were reached in the beginning of 1988, the strategy changed. Now it makes sense to even out your taxable income from year to year, avoiding one high income year followed by a lower income year. With income averaging no longer allowed, the steadier the stream of income can be, the smaller your tax liability will remain.

What am I allowed to deduct for medical expenses?

Your unreimbursed medical bills are deductible only when they exceed 7.5 percent of your adjusted gross income (AGI). For example, if your AGI for this year is $25,000, you will have to bear the expense of the first $1875 yourself. Anything over $1875 will remain deductible.

Is there any smart way to time the payment of certain taxes to help my annual tax bill?

Yes, there is. Choose to pay deductible taxes when it works best for you. For example, the real estate taxes on your home should be paid in December of the current tax year you've had a particularly good year for income. If, however, you expect more income next year, it would be more sensible to postpone the payment until January, even if you face a small penalty. However, the reverse strategy may apply if you are subject to the AMT in 1988 (see page 287, where AMT is defined).

I have to pay an estimated state tax. When should I make the fourth quarter payment?

If you've had a higher than normal income this year, don't wait until January to pay the fourth quarter estimated tax. Pay it in December to charge it against this year's income.

Should I overpay my estimated state income tax to give myself a bigger deduction?

Although a slight overpayment will not be looked at as suspect, any overpayment will be refunded and counted as income the following year. And keep in mind that a truly overinflated estimated tax payment could raise a red flag to the IRS and cause Uncle Sam to disallow the deduction.

What are the current tax rates on adjusted gross income?

TAX RATE SCHEDULES FOR 1989 (1)

Married Individuals Filing Jointly

If taxable income is:	The tax is
Not over $30,950	15%
Over $30,950	$4,642.50 + 28% of the excess over 30,950 (2)

Single Individuals

If taxable income is:	The tax is
Not over $18,550	15%
Over $18,550	$2,782.50 + 28% of the excess over $18,550 (2)

Married Individuals Filing Separately

If taxable income is:	The tax is:
Not over $15,475	15%
Over $15,475	$2,321.25 + 28% of the excess over $15,475 (2)

Head of Household

If taxable income is:	The tax is:
Not over $24,850	15%
Over $24,850	$3,727.50 + 28% of the excess over $24,850 (2)

(1) Starting with taxable years beginning in 1989, the tax rate schedules are adjusted for inflation.

(2) A 5 percent surtax will apply to taxable income within certain ranges as follows:

Married, filing jointly	$74,850 - $155,320*
Single	$44,900-$93,130*
Married, filing separately	$37,425-$117,895*
Head of household	$64,200-$128,810*

*Plus $11,200 for each personal exemption. For married filing separately, $11,200 must be added for your spouse.

The 1990 tax table will be indexed for inflation.

I have heard you say that certain miscellaneous deductions are deductible only in excess of 2 percent of my adjusted gross income. What expenses are classified as miscellaneous?

Among them:

- safe deposit box fees
- union dues and assessments
- small tools, safety equipment, and supplies for your job
- costs of producing or collecting income
- fees paid to a tax adviser to prepare your tax return or represent you at an audit
- dues to professional societies
- investment counselor fees and investment service costs
- certain traveling and lodging costs connected with seeking employment.

Does it ever make sense for a married couple to file separately rather than jointly?

It's hard to answer such a general question because so much depends upon a specific circumstance. But let's give it a try by setting up a situation when it might make sense for married people to file separately.

If one spouse earns a good deal more than the other, filing separately can be worthwhile if your miscellaneous deductions are sizable. For the sake of example, let's assume your income is $50,000 and your spouse's is $25,000. You have miscellaneous expenses of $3000. By filing jointly, you may deduct only any amount over 2 percent of your adjusted gross income. In this case, 2 percent of the joint income, $75,000, is $1500. Since you spent $3000, your deduction is $1500.

Filing separately, with the lower-salaried spouse taking the deduction, is a good tax savings. Two percent of $25,000 is $500, leaving a $2500 deduction, $1000 more than if you filed jointly. However, if this strategy appeals to you, plan ahead. The spouse taking the deduction must actually pay the expenses.

My husband died in January. When it comes time to file my income taxes for that year, should I file an individual return or a joint one with full personal exemptions?

You should file a joint return and claim a personal exemption for your husband.

What is meant by a marginal tax rate?

It's not as complicated as it sounds! This is the amount of tax imposed on an additional dollar of income. Contrary to popular belief, because you may be in a 33 percent tax bracket, Uncle Sam does not tax every dollar, including the first dollar you earn, at 33 percent. The actual 33 percent tax rate begins on any income you earn over $44,900 for single filers and over $74,850 for joint filers, as of this writing.

What is a standard deduction?

If you don't itemize your deductions, you can reduce your adjusted gross income by an amount the government allows everyone to deduct—the standard deduction.

1989 standard deductions:

- joint returns and surviving spouses—$5200
- head of household—$4550
- single taxpayers—$3100
- married, filing separately—$2600

1990 standard deductions will be increased for inflation.

May elderly or blind people claim a higher standard deduction?

In addition to the normal standard deduction, a single person who is elderly or blind may claim an additional standard deduction of $750. If the single person is both elderly and blind, he or she may claim $1500.

As a married person who is either elderly or blind, the additional standard deduction is $600 and it grows to $1200 if the married person is both elderly and blind.

There's no way that I'm going to be able to file my tax return by April 15. What do I do?

Get a copy of IRS form 4868 at your local IRS office. The form's official name is Application for Automatic Extension of Time to File U.S. Individual Income Tax Return. (Whew!) It allows you to put off *filing* your tax return until August 15, but you still must estimate your tax bill and pay any tax due when you file the form on or before April 15.

How long should I keep my income tax returns?

In most cases the IRS cannot audit your return after three years. However, the IRS has six years to audit if you fail to report more than 25 percent of your income. There is no limit if the IRS thinks that you committed fraud. We believe that you should *never* throw away old tax returns. You never know when you might need one or more of them.

I filed my federal tax return on time, but I have yet to receive my tax refund check, which would come in handy right now. How can I speed up the process?

The IRS has made great strides in getting out refund checks, but it looks as if yours slipped through the cracks. Contact by phone or in writing the IRS Service Center where you filed the return. First try "TELE-TAX" Automated Refund Information to check the status of your refund. If that doesn't help, contact the IRS federal tax questions number. Both these phone numbers are listed in your 1040 instructions package and include directions on how to use the system. Have handy your Social Security number, filing status, and the exact amount of your refund.

If neither of these sources is helpful, call the IRS main number (800) 424-1040, or contact the problem resolution office. You can obtain that phone number by calling your IRS district office.

I am self-employed. May I deduct the cost of health insurance for myself and my family?

You can deduct 25 percent of your premiums for you and your family. Check with your accountant about several requirements to be met for deduction eligibility.

My daughter broke her leg and, because of complications, our medical coverage ran out. We owe an additional $8350. May I write off this amount?

You are allowed to deduct only the portion of unreimbursed costs that you have paid (any cost not reimbursed by a personal or group insurance policy) and exceeds 7.5 percent of your adjusted gross income. In your particular case, if your adjusted gross income is $20,000, you will be able to deduct an amount over $1500 (7.5 percent × $20,000). In your case, you can deduct $6850.

Our home suffered major damage in a recent flood. Unfortunately, we were underinsured and we had to pay $23,000 from our savings to complete repairs to our home. May I deduct that amount of casualty loss?

You may deduct those itemized casualty losses above $100 that exceed 10 percent of your adjusted gross income. If your adjusted gross income was $20,000, you could deduct losses exceeding $2000 or, in your case, approximately $21,000. Check with your accountant for the deductible loss limitation formula.

May I deduct a casualty loss even though I was insured?

Any loss must be reduced by the insurance proceeds you collect before you calculate deductions.

My mother-in-law has a serious heart condition. Our doctor has recommended that we install a small swimming pool so that her therapy (swimming) can be done at home. I have his recommendation well documented. May I write off the full cost of the swimming pool?

Unfortunately, not the full cost. The deductible amount is the *difference* between the cost of the item and the amount by which that item raises the value of your home. That amount is deductible only if there is no public or private pool close to your home that your mother-in-law can use.

I made a loan of $1500 to my cousin for a twelve-month period. Unfortunately, his wife was taken ill and he can't pay me back. May I deduct that amount as a bad debt expense?

Yes. If you can prove no chance of collection, you may write off up to $3000 as a nonbusiness bad debt in any one year, but the IRS will want you to prove that it was not an outright gift. Proper documentation is important. You must be able to show that you made a strong effort to get the money back. Even with proof, it is often difficult to make the IRS believe you, especially if the loan is to a relative.

What is a 1035 exchange?

If you cashed in your current insurance policy and bought a new one, you would ordinarily pay taxes on the earnings from the old policy. A 1035 exchange is a swap: The insurer of the old cash value policy will send the proceeds directly to the insurer providing the new policy. The transfer is not taxable because you yourself never take possession of the funds. To qualify, it must be an exchange of the same type of policy—life insurance for life insurance, annuity for annuity.

My wife and I spent several hundred dollars for the paper work involved in refinancing our home mortgage. Unfortunately, the mortgage fell through because interest rates skipped up just before closing. May I write off the loan processing costs?

No, these costs are considered personal expenses—and aren't deductible whether the refinancing goes through or not.

What write-offs can I take for a new personal computer I'm thinking about buying?

You can write off the entire business portion of the cost of your PC up to $10,000 in *one* year, but you must be able to prove that the computer was used more than 50 percent of the time for business. Employees cannot write off computers unless their employers require them to have one.

I'm just starting to get a part-time consulting job off the ground. Are the expenses of establishing a home office deductible under tax reform?

The office at home must be the principal place of this business, though you may work somewhere else full-time. You may depreciate your home office over a thirty one-and-a-half-year period and deduct a pro-rata portion of the expenses such as repair and utility bills that would otherwise be considered personal and therefore nondeductible. Previously, you could deduct home office expenses only up to the gross income of the business. Under the Tax Reform Act of 1986, you may carry forward into future years any of the unused tax losses and offset them against your home business income.

Business meals and entertainment expenses have been fully deductible in the past. Is it true that such expenses are only 80 percent deductible now?

Yes, and you must now substantiate a meal costing less than $25 as well as still needing a receipt for meals over $25.

I understand that business must actually be discussed at a meal for it to be deductible. What should my records include so that my deductions won't be criticized?

That's correct. Your expenses for business meals and entertainment should include:

- amount
- time
- place
- business purpose
- business relationship and what was discussed

Does that mean that if I provide dinner and theater tickets for a good customer and his wife and I don't go with them, those expenses are *not* tax-deductible?

You are correct. They're not deductible unless you are there, too.

I have just bought a $17,000 car for business use. How long will it take me to fully depreciate this car?

The highest first-year deduction of the cost of a luxury car is $2560. It will take you approximately eight years to fully depreciate your $17,000 car. Remember that the depreciation limitation is further limited to the business portion of usage.

What is the IRS interpretation of a luxury car?

A car costing more than $12,800 falls under the luxury-car rules.

I'm a small-business owner. How is my corporation being taxed?

INCOME	RATE
$0–$50,000	15%
$50,000–$75,000	25%
Over $75,000	34%

My son is interesting in working to earn some money for college. Can I employ him full-time in my firm for the summer without his having a tax liability?

By all means. Your child may earn $3000 tax free during 1990. Over the $3000, his income would be taxable. However, beware! The IRS questions excessive salaries, *especially* when they are paid to family members.

I understand that the deductibility of interest paid on consumer loans is phasing out. How fast?

In 1990 only 10 percent of interest on such consumer loans as credit cards, car and boat loans, and department-store charge cards is deductible. In 1991 nothing is deductible.

Is there any deduction for dividends?

In a word, no!

Can everyone who hires babysitters take the child-care/dependent care credit?

Only parents with children under thirteen or disabled dependents of any age may take the credit. It's usually 20 percent of expenses, totaling up to $2400 for one child or $4800 for two or more children, as of this writing. Married couples may take the credit only if *both* spouses work outside the home at least part-time or if one spouse is a full-time student or is looking for employment.

What kinds of fees are covered under the child-care/dependent-care credit?

Fees paid to a nursery school, day care center, babysitter, maid, or summer camp may qualify.

How about money paid to a relative, such as a grandparent?

Yes, that is a deductible expense as long as the relative is not a dependent of yours.

My wife and I would like to give our grandchild a $10,000 gift to begin a college fund. What is the tax status of that gift?

What nice grandparents you are! You *and* your wife may each give $10,000 a year (a $20,000 total) to anyone you wish. As for your grandchild, as long as she or he is under fourteen, any investment income from your gift in excess of $1000 per year is taxed at the child's *parents'* rate. After age fourteen, all income is taxed at the child's rate, which will be approximately 15 percent.

I would like to put some money in a custodial account for my nephew, but I'm concerned that the money will legally be his at age eighteen. He's a good kid but a little unpredictable. Could he spend the money on a Porsche at age eighteen?

Legally, yes. If you are worried about how your nephew will use the money, consider setting up a minor's trust, which lets you control disbursement of the funds until the child is twenty-one or even older. You can add a provision that extends the trust, for example, until your nephew graduates from college.

What is a Clifford trust?

In the past, a Clifford trust's earnings were taxed at a child's lower income tax rate, allowing parents to shelter income and build up some money for college. Now, all income in a Clifford trust that was set up after March 1, 1986, will be taxable to whoever set up the trust, and not the child. Clifford trusts set up before March 1, 1986, will be taxed at the parents' rate until the child is fourteen; after that, the child's rate will apply.

I have just received an unexpected phone call from a competitor offering me a 35 percent raise if I agree to start working immediately. Unfortunately, I would have to break my lease because the job is in another city. Can I write off the $1250 security deposit that I am forced to forfeit?

Yes, such a cost is considered an indirect moving expense and is deductible to the limit of $3000.

I have accepted a job nearly three hundred miles away and I've racked up many costs moving there and while looking for a new place to live. Are these tax deductible? Please say yes!

Yes. (Are you happy?) If your move is necessary for a job that you have already found, you may deduct the costs of house hunting trips, the move itself (up to specified limits), and even temporary living expenses. One important thing to remember: You don't actually have to buy a house on one of these trips for the expenses to be tax deductible, but the principal purpose of the trip must be to find a place to live.

I am about to move my family from Boston to Cleveland because of my job. Are our moving expenses deductible?

The key requirement for qualifying to write off moving expenses is that the new job be at least thirty-five miles farther from your old home than your previous job was. Obviously, you qualify! The distance between your new job and your new home doesn't matter.

If the move is to take your first job, the new house must be at least thirty-five miles away from your former home to meet the distance test.

Other qualifications that must be met to fully deduct your expenses are:

- The move must occur within one year after the date you begin work at the new location.
- You must work full-time in the general vicinity of the new location for at least thirty-nine weeks during the twelve-month period following the move.

Get IRS publication 521, *Moving Expenses,* for further details.

May I deduct the cost of commuting from my home on Long Island to New York City?

Generally you may *not* deduct the costs of traveling to and from work. However, there are exceptions:

- If you work at more than one job, you may deduct the costs of traveling from one job to another, but not the expense of getting from the second job to home.
- An employee on temporary assignment may deduct travel costs provided that the trip is "beyond the general area of his tax home." This cost is deductible even if the temporary assignment is within commuting distance of home.

May I deduct mileage expense to visit my broker or financial planner?

Yes, and you may also deduct mileage to look after investment property you own.

Every Wednesday morning I drive to a clinic for therapy that I must have since my heart attack. Is my mileage tax deductible?

Yes. The cost of gas and oil, but *not* insurance, depreciation and repairs, is deductible if your car is used for medical transportation. If you prefer, you may take a flat driving allowance of 9¢ per mile. In either case, you may deduct tolls and parking fees.

What about the cost of lodging near a clinic? My doctor is sending me to another state.

Costs up to $50 per day per person are deductible for you as well as for someone who needs to accompany you. However, the cost of food is *not* deductible.

I'm an American citizen living abroad, and I'm ashamed to say that I'm part of the statistic that estimates that more than 60 percent of the nearly two million Americans living abroad don't pay taxes. I have not paid taxes for three years and I'd like to clean up this potential problem. Can you help?

You must immediately clear up this matter because you won't get the $70,000 exclusion from U.S. taxation on foreign income unless you file a return within one year of its original due date. IRS rules for American expatriates are complex. Get professional help from one of the large U.S. accounting firms with overseas offices.

How can I find the location of an IRS overseas office?

The IRS has offices in fourteen foreign cities and part-time offices in eighty-five more cities. Check with the local embassy or consulate or write to:

Assistant Commissioner (International)
Internal Revenue Service
Taxpayer Services Division
950 L'Enfant Plaza
Washington, D.C. 20024

I work for an American company in Brussels and I am there most of the year. Do I get an income tax exclusion for part of my wages earned while overseas?

You may qualify for exclusion of up to $70,000 of wages, salary, or professional fees earned while abroad. However, to qualify, you must either be a bona fide resident of a foreign country for the full tax year or be physically present in a foreign country for at least 330 days of any twelve consecutive months. For further details, see IRS form 2555 and IRS publication 54.

May I deduct any costs associated with my volunteer work at a local hospital?

Yes, you may write off the cost of traveling to and from your volunteer work at the rate of 12¢ per mile if you drive, plus parking fees and tolls.

I'm a lawyer who charges approximately $75 an hour for consulting fees. May I deduct the time (at $75 an hour) that I spent assisting our local church with legal matters?

No, you can't deduct the value of services rendered to a charity.

I buy all sorts of raffle tickets and lottery tickets at my local church's fund raising activities. I even play bingo every week. I *never* win anything! Can I deduct the costs of these tickets and bingo cards?

Gambling losses are deductible only against winnings in a given year. Good luck!

Is there any limit on what I can deduct for charity?

You may deduct charitable contributions as long as their combined total does not exceed 50 percent of your adjusted gross income. Gifts of appreciated property are deductible only up to 30 percent of your AGI. However, if your gifts in any year exceed these limits, you may carry over the surplus deduction for up to five years. The bad news concerning charitable contributions is for those who do not itemize their income taxes. Nonitemizers lose *all* charitable deductions.

I just purchased four tickets to a charity golf tournament benefiting our local hospital. The tickets cost me $400. Is the cost of these tickets still deductible?

The cost of tickets to this event is deductible if:

- the sporting event is organized soley to benefit a tax-exempt charitable organization.
- all of the net proceeds are contributed to the organization.
- the event used volunteers for substantially all the work performed in carrying out the event.

May I deduct political contributions?

No, that deduction no longer exists.

I'm a writer. I made a lot of money this year but none for the two years before. Can I average my income?

We're sorry you asked! That provision has been repealed. And for people like you, it's less than fair.

Every year my wife and I attend an investment seminar in Nassau, Bahamas. Will the expenses related to this seminar be deductible?

No. The costs of attending nonbusiness conventions or seminars are not deductible. The law assumes that these meetings are, significantly, for personal pleasure.

Is it true that people older than seventy don't have to pay any income tax?

It's not true. People seventy and older *do* pay income tax. Some of the confusion may spring from the fact that Social Security recipients age seventy and older receive their full benefit payments no matter how much earned income they have; Social Security recipients under age seventy must pay taxes on their benefits if they surpass established income levels.

Is it true that I can avoid paying Social Security taxes on my wife's salary because I own the company?

In a sole proprietorship, your spouse's salary or wages paid to a child under the age of twenty-one, if it is deemed reasonable by IRS standards, are free from Social Security taxes. This is also true with income from an S corporation, which is a corporation that does not pay income tax at the corporate level. Profits or losses from S corporations flow directly through the company to the shareholders and avoid double taxation. All profits go to the shareholders in the form of dividends, on which no Social Security tax is due. We are not recommending that Social Security taxes not be paid for your wife or child. That is a matter to discuss with your accountant.

What is this thing that I keep hearing about called the alternative minimum tax?

The alternative minimum tax (AMT) exists in order to get a fair share of taxes from high bracket taxpayers who heavily benefit from such deductions as oil drilling investments, accelerated depreciation, incentive stock options, and other deductions. The AMT is basically a flat rate on income with certain deductions added and other adjustments made. Really, it's the least amount the government will accept from you if your income is at a certain level even though you may have enough deductions to pay no regular income tax at all.

How is the alternative minimum tax calculated?

First of all, you figure your tax bill just as you normally would with all your deductions. Second, starting from scratch again, your adjusted gross income gets increased by investment related tax preference items (an item specified by the IRS that a taxpayer must count when calculating AMT liability), such as donating appreciated property, income from certain bonds, casualty losses, passive losses from limited partnerships, and others. State and local taxes are also added to your AMT calculation.

Finally, you deduct either $40,000 for a married couple or $30,000 for a single filer. Multiply the result of this by 21 percent.

Is the final answer greater than your normal tax calculations? If so, you must pay the AMT figure. There are more rules to consider than we have mentioned here, and we strongly suggest that your AMT calculations be done by an accountant.

What steps can I take to avoid paying any alternative minimum tax?

It's important that you plan ahead. In general, although no single tax strategy applies to everyone:

- Consider making charitable contributions of appreciated property in a year that you are not subject to the AMT, that is, not having any preferences or adjustments.
- Avoid prepaying state and local income tax.
- Reduce ownership of private activity municipal bonds issued after August 8, 1986, bonds so named because 10 percent or more goes to private facilities such as sports, trade or convention facilities, airports, docks, wharfs, etc.
- Utilize passive activity losses by earning passive activity income.

I have just received a notice that "requests" my appearance at our local IRS office for an audit. Needless to say, I'm not happy about it. Do you have any tips to help me survive this interview?

The main thing is that the IRS depends on *you* for the information that may make you liable for additional taxes. Here are three guidelines:

1. Answer their questions as accurately as possible and ask for clarification when you don't understand why a question is being asked.
2. *Don't* volunteer information. Answer *only* the questions asked.
3. Don't fudge the truth. It's a crime to give false or misleading information.
4. Whenever possible, have an accountant go with you.

An audit need not be an adversarial confrontation. Be prepared, be honest, and stay cool.

I have been audited three years in a row by the IRS. I'd like to avoid four in a row! Can you tell me what write-offs trigger an audit?

Aren't you the lucky one! Only slightly more than 1 percent of all returns are audited, though the IRS has promised to audit more returns during the years ahead.

Here are some of the IRS red flags that might trigger a computer to spit out your return for further scrutiny:

1. *Certain occupations:* Occupations that offer opportunities to avoid reporting income, such as waiter, taxicab driver, beautician, independent contractor, door-to-door salesperson, and the like.
2. *Tax shelters:* These are one of the biggest causes of audits. Such items as inflated assets, deductions exceeding 20 percent of principal invested, and high promotion fees are closely scrutinized.
3. *Alimony paid or received:* There are two sides to this IRS coin. If your spouse deducts alimony payments from his or her income figure, then you should be claiming alimony income. If not, one or both of you may be audited.
4. *Charitable contributions:* For large property or cash contributions that are not clearly in the range of your income, have handy a canceled check or appraisal plus background information on the charity.
5. *Heavy business deductions:* The IRS doesn't appreciate the overestimation of hard to document business expenses and excessive home office deductions.
6. *Medical expenses:* If you want to be sure of an audit, write off the cost of a swimming pool or elevator for invalids or heart patients without *solid* medical evidence that it is needed.
7. *Loans to or from a relative.* If you deduct loan interest paid to a relative, ensure that there is a contract that specifies a reasonable interest rate.

I'm having trouble getting information about how to proceed with preparing for an audit. No one at the IRS has called me back after repeated attempts. Any suggestions?

Contact the problems-resolution office (PRO) of your nearest IRS office. Check the government listings in your local phone book. The PRO's mission is to help taxpayers who have been frustrated by the IRS bureaucracy. You must be able to prove that you've already tried to resolve your problem through normal channels. Have handy all IRS documentation and any letters that you may have sent to the IRS. The PRO is there for you.

I disagree with the IRS auditor concerning some deductions that he has disallowed. Do I have any recourse?

Absolutely. However, if you are appealing less than $5000, the appeal process may be counterproductive. You should have a competent lawyer or CPA to assist you with this process. Once you have officially protested (see IRS publication 5 for further details), your case will be assigned to an appeals officer, who will set a conference date. If you are unable to clear up the situation satisfactorily with the appeals officer, you may file a petition in the tax court and further appeal to the U.S. Court of Appeals, and even the U.S. Supreme Court. Consult your attorney or CPA for more details and stick up for your rights—but be sensible about it. Unless there's a lot of money involved, it may cost you more for professional help than your claim is worth.

I have been embroiled in a pretty serious battle with the IRS for several years now, and it looks as if I'm about to lose. Can the IRS seize all my assets?

Here is a partial list of assets that *are protected* from seizure by federal law:

- clothes necessary for the taxpayer and family
- school books that are necessary
- personal effects, furniture, fuel, and provisions up to $1500 in value
- books and tools necessary for business up to $1000 in value
- salary, wages, and other income necessary for court-ordered child-support payments
- $75 a week in wages, salary, and other income plus $25 a week for each legal dependent
- unemployment benefits
- Workers' Compensation
- annuity or pension payments under the Railroad Retirement Act or Railroad Unemployment Act
- benefits and annuities to certain armed services members
- undelivered mail

I'm not sure if I have misplaced or have never received a W-2 from my employer. The April 15 deadline is almost upon me. What should I do?

Immediately inform your employer, and request a duplicate. If it appears that the forms won't arrive on time, you have two options:

1. Reconstruct your salary, withholding, and other income information from such sources as pay stubs, monthly bank statements, etc.

   or

2. Give your best estimate and list this information on IRS form 4852, which should be attached to your return.

I'd like to get a copy of my 1980 tax return for personal reasons. Will the IRS send me a copy?

The IRS keeps copies of individual tax returns for only six years. Older returns are kept on microfiche. You can request a copy or specific information from your tax returns by filling out IRS form 4506 (Request for Copy of Tax Form or Tax Account Information). The cost is $4.25. The form can be obtained from your local IRS office or by calling the IRS toll-free at (800)-424-FORM. Instructions are included.

Is it true that the IRS provides tax preparation assistance for free? I can't make head or tail of the new forms and I can't afford an accountant.

Yes. Plenty of tax help is available from the IRS for free. The IRS Volunteer Income Tax Assistance (VITA) program includes more than 33,000 volunteer tax helpers in many cities across the country. You can get free tax assistance, including line-by-line help with your form 1040. Call the IRS toll-free information number listed in the back of your tax-instruction booklet for the VITA location nearest you. A similar program, Tax Counseling for the Elderly, is also available to older taxpayers.

Are there any free books on taxes?

Not necessarily books, but the IRS has many free publications, too many to list them all! You can obtain a complete list from your local IRS office, but here are the ten most popular:

- Publication 17: *Your Federal Income Tax*
- Publication 334: *Tax Guide for Small Businesses*
- Publication 15: *Circular E, Employer's Tax Guide*
- Publication 501: *Exemptions*
- Publication 503: *Child and Dependent Care Credit, and Employment Taxes for Household Employers*
- Publication 504: *Tax Information for Divorced or Separated Individuals*
- Publication 463: *Travel, Entertainment, and Gift Expenses*
- Publication 502: *Medical and Dental Expenses*
- Publication 521: *Moving Expenses*
- Publication 225: *Farmer's Tax Guide*

SUMMARY

As we said at the beginning of this chapter, this tax overview is just that— a brief glimpse at some of the most important facets of recent tax regulations. However, a recurring theme in this book is, Educate yourself! And nowhere in this book does that make more sense than in this tax chapter. Taxes and their impact touch every phase of our investment life. It's imperative that you always have a keen eye fixed on the effect of taxes on all our investment decisions.

- Know whether you stand to profit more from a taxable investment. Not everyone should invest tax free.
- Especially since the Tax Reform Act of 1986, investments must be looked at for what kind of return they will produce and *not* how much in losses you can write off.
- Match passive loss investments with passive income investments to derive a full benefit from each.
- Remember that you receive the same write-off from short- and long-term losses.

- Capital gains are treated as ordinary income. There is no need to hold on to an investment for more than six months in many cases.
- If you are having trouble understanding the tax laws, gets help. A good accountant will be worth his or her fee if he or she can help you save some money.
- Take advantage of the free IRS publications. They can teach you a lot.

Taxes—not the most exciting subject, but one of the most important for you and your financial well-being.

FURTHER INFORMATION
BOOKS

The Price Waterhouse Guide to the New Tax Law
Price Waterhouse
Bantam
($3.95)

Taxpayers Ultimate Defense Manual
Dan Pilla
Winning Publications

J. K. Lasser's What the New Tax Law Means to You
J. K. Lasser Tax Institute
Simon and Schuster

You Can Protect Yourself from the IRS
Sandor Frankel and Robert Fink
Fireside (Simon and Schuster)

Protecting Your Business from the IRS
Robert S. Schriebman
Dow Jones-Irwin

NEWSLETTERS

Tax Hotline
Boardroom Reports, Inc.
330 West 42nd Street
New York, New York 10036

The Kiplinger Tax Letter
The Kiplinger Washington Editors, Inc.
1729 H Street, NW
Washington, D.C. 20006

SOFTWARE

The Tax Analyzer
Intuit
IBM-PC and Apple II
($29.95)

E Z Tax Plan (tax planning)
E Z Ware Corporation
IBM-PC and Apple Macintosh
($99)

E Z Prep (form preparation)
E Z Ware Corporation
$129 for IBM-PC
$99.00 for Apple Macintosh

15

Estate Planning

Estate planning is the process of passing from this world to the next without passing through the Internal Revenue Service. ROBERT BROSTERMAN

We know what you're thinking: Estate planning . . . boring! Now wait a minute. Inflation, escalating home values, and higher salaries are just a few of the reasons why you may be worth more than you think!

At least a minimal knowledge of some of the estate planning laws and techniques we'll discuss in this chapter will ensure that your assets will be passed to whom you wish and not to the state in which you live or to the IRS, and that your family will be taken care of if something happens to you. You must realize from the onset of this chapter that once your assets have passed to your spouse, possible tax problems begin. We aim to show you how your spouse can further pass these assets to children and grand-children or anyone else without creating a taxable event.

Whether you are married or unmarried, have children or not, you must know the estate planning basics. A comprehensive estate plan allows you to accomplish more than just avoiding or diminishing the government's tax bite. It can ensure that your children are properly cared for, that your spouse receives competent business and financial direction, and that the legal costs of administering your wishes are minimized. We'll also touch on the four basic estate planning tools: trusts, wills, joint ownership, and lifetime gifts. Remember, people who fail to make provisions for the orderly passing of their assets don't suffer; their heirs do.

Why should I worry about wills and trusts? I don't own very much.

You may be worth a lot more than you think! The recent rise in the prices of homes has considerably increased the net worth of their owners. If you own a home and/or insurance policies, you are definitely worth enough to worry about a will and, possibly, a living trust.

What is a will?

A will is *your* plan of how you want your assets dispersed after your death. It designates heirs and identifies assets.

Do I need a will?

Everyone needs a will, because if you die intestate (without a will), your state law dictates how your assets will be distributed. This may not be the way you had things planned. When the state steps in, it becomes a will by default.

Do wills ever need to be changed?

Yes, wills and estate plans become outdated and should be reviewed and revised at least every five years or more often, depending on your personal situation (divorce, moving to another state, additional children, etc.).

If I die without a will, who will manage my estate?

The state court will appoint an administrator. This administrator may or may not be qualified to do the job. Children or relatives who are loved may *not* share in your assets as you had planned, and your estate may very well have to pay guardian's fees.

What is meant by probating a will?

Probate is legal lingo for proving that a will is valid. One way to reduce the much-publicized administrative delays and professional fee abuse of probate is to select the right attorney and executor.

How much does it typically cost to probate a will?

Although many states have attempted to streamline the probate process, court administration costs can be as high as 5 to 15 percent of your estate fees. A complex or contested will can, and probably will, cost more.

How long should probate take?

A will can be probated in as little as a few months, but depending on a number of factors, it may take years to process.

If I avoid probate by employing a trust, joint ownership, or other estate-planning techniques, can I also avoid estate inheritance tax?

No, you cannot.

Our lawyer has passed away. He kept an original copy of our will. Should we consider writing a new one?

Not necessarily. It is likely that your lawyer made provisions before his death that all his records and client work be taken over by another lawyer. If this is the case, consult the new lawyer. If that lawyer for some reason cannot locate your will, immediately write a new one. This situation may actually be good news. You should review your will periodically anyway, especially since tax law revisions.

My husband and I are currently writing our wills. We are thinking of naming my parents as guardians of our children if anything should happen to us. Is this a good idea?

Don't be surprised by our answer, but this is *not* a good idea. Although you'd probably be hard pressed to find anyone who would love and protect your children better than grandparents, it's generally not a good idea, simply because your parents are older. Should they pass away after you while being charged with your children's well-being, your children would be even more traumatized. We recommend a younger couple whom you know and trust.

My mother has just died and my father died several years ago. I'm the youngest of three children, born after they made up their will leaving everything to my brother and sister. Am I entitled to any of my mother's inheritance?

Yes, children born after parents' wills have been written are usually entitled to a proportionate share of the parents' estate.

My father has worded his will in an unusual way. I will inherit his estate only if I divorce my husband, whom he has never liked. I'm not about to divorce my wonderful husband! I am an only child and my mother died three years ago. What will happen to my father's estate?

It is likely that you will still inherit it. The provisions of a will cannot be "contrary to public policy." Encouraging the breakup of your marriage is not a normal thing to do!

What is the purpose of a power of attorney?

A power of attorney is the granting of a trusted person the right to handle your financial affairs. This is especially useful if you will be temporarily or permanently incapacitated.

How can I set up a power of attorney arrangement?

Many banks are able to provide the paper work relating to power of attorney for bank accounts at their institution. Your lawyer can also assist you.

How do I find a good lawyer to handle my estate affairs?

You should contact your local bar association and ask for the names of several estate planning lawyers in your area. You can also ask your accountant, family doctor, and friends for a referral.

How long should it take for an estate to settle?

That's a tough question. Some estates settle in less than a year, while other, more complex estates may take several years to settle. It takes time to deal with the IRS, creditors, and possible sales of assets to pay necessary taxes.

My dad has just died and it looks as if his estate will take a long time to settle. I am beneficiary of certain assets. Will I have to wait for the estate to settle before I receive any funds?

No. Periodic distributions can be made from the estate during the settlement period. See the estate's executor.

May I name my bank as executor of my will?

Yes, in fact many banks have trust departments that specialize in the administration of assets. However, we caution you to get to know and feel comfortable with the trust department before you take this step, and examine the bank's fee schedule and track record. Not all bank trust departments have a good record.

I have just been named executor of a close friend's estate. Because of the estate's size, I believe that it will be a difficult one to settle. Can I expect to receive a fee for my service?

Yes. Executors are paid from the estate. Fees are set in many states. A rule of thumb is that an executor's minimum fee is between 2 and 5 percent of the estate's assets.

What happens if an executor I have named is unable or unwilling to handle my estate at the time of my death?

This can be a real problem. That is why we strongly recommend that an alternative executor be named in your will.

Whom may I name in my will as executor of my estate?

The executor can be just about anyone you choose: a friend, a relative, or a bank. Make sure you consult the person you wish to designate as your executor *before* you name him or her in your will.

My lawyer says that I should carefully consider whom I name as executor because it's not always an easy job. Is she right?

Bravo! Your lawyer couldn't be more correct. The list of executor's duties is a long one, and all are important.

What are the duties of an executor?

An executor is expected to:

- provide a complete inventory of your assets, such as cash, bank accounts, securities, real estate, etc.

- collect any money owed you from employers, Social Security, outstanding loans, etc.
- notify life insurance companies of your death.
- pay off any valid debts you owe—medical bills, for example.
- prepare and file all income tax information and estate tax returns.
- distribute your estate to those named in your will.
- carefully document all receipts and disbursements to beneficiaries and the probate court.

What's the difference between an executor and a trustee?

An executor's duties end when an estate has been distributed to the beneficiaries. A trustee administers the assets in a trust for as long as the trust is in force.

Is a safe-deposit box a good place to keep a will?

Although it's very important to keep your will in a safe place, a safe-deposit box is not our first choice. Most states require the sealing of a box upon the death of its owner until the contents are inspected by tax authorities. We suggest that you keep the original in your lawyer's file, with an unsigned copy in your files at home.

My dad just passed away, but we can't find a copy of a will that I'm sure he wrote because he mentioned it from time to time. Where can we begin looking for it?

This is a tough problem. The first place to begin is to contact his lawyer to find out if he or she helped your father execute his will. If the lawyer cannot produce a will, contact your local banks to see if your father held a safe deposit box, where the will may be. You should also check with the various trust departments of local banks to see if one of them helped advise your father with various estate planning matters. Another source of information could be a close friend of your father's who might have been his confidant.

I currently live in Massachusetts. I am planning to move my family to the Southwest to take an exciting new job. Will another state recognize my Massachusetts will?

Different states have varying requirements pertaining to wills. Although a will made in one state may be recognized in another, it could be more costly to probate. Another thought to keep in mind is that a will drawn in one state but probated in another may be subject to taxes in *both* states.

Should I ever change my will?

Yes. Circumstances change concerning how you may wish your assets distributed after your death. Retirement, birth of children, and remarriage are among the reasons to rewrite your will. You should review your will on a regular basis.

Should a husband and wife have separate wills?

Yes. A wife who may not have had a career and has very few assets in her name only still needs her own will. Why? Because if her husband dies and leaves everything to her, what happens to these assets if she dies before writing her own will and specifying how the assets should be distributed? Without her own will, the state would step in and make the distribution of assets according to state law.

May I completely disinherit my spouse?

Generally, state law does not allow someone to totally disinherit a spouse. Many states require that if you are married at the time of death, you must leave a stipulated amount of your assets to your spouse. Oftentimes, the amount that the state dictates would have gone to your spouse anyway if you had died intestate (without a will).

My wife and I are about to be divorced, but I'd like to protect the assets outlined in my will during the period of the divorce proceedings. How can I accomplish this?

You may not remove your wife from your will until you are no longer married in the eyes of the law. What you may do in the meantime is to reduce her bequest to the minimum amount required by state law. Then, when your divorce decree is final, you can rewrite your will.

My lawyer says that my brother-in-law, who is one of the beneficiaries of my will, should not be a witness to it. Why?

A beneficiary should *not* be a witness or the will may be deemed invalid.

I don't want to bother with a lawyer, so I have carefully handwritten my will. Is it legal?

The answer to your question depends on the state in which you live. Some states do not recognize holographic (handwritten) wills. We highly recommend, even in your case, that you consult a lawyer, because holographic wills must also comply to specific form.

Who may write a will?

Anyone of legal age may write a will.

Must a will be witnessed?

Most states require two witnesses; some require three.

What happens if the authenticity of a will is challenged and you can't locate the parties who originally witnessed it?

That can pose a very difficult problem. It is why we recommend a self-proving will, one that was properly notarized at the time of signing.

Do my wife and I really need a lawyer to draw up our will?
Not every state requires that a lawyer draw up your will, but we strongly recommend that you seek legal help because wills must follow a specific legal form. By trying to do it yourself you might cause your heirs needless grief.

What do you think of the will kits advertised on television for very little money ($9.95) that claim to be able to show me how to draw up my own will?
Forget it! Would you perform an appendectomy on yourself to save a few dollars? A will is an important part of your estate plan. Deal with a lawyer. You and your heirs will be far better off as a result.

I've heard that owning property in joint name is a good way to avoid probate. Is this true?
If you are married and own everything jointly, it is true that those assets will pass to your spouse without going through probate. However, joint ownership is not a panacea. Some of the drawbacks are:

- Neither owner has exclusive control of the property. This could be sticky in case of a serious disagreement or divorce.
- You have no say concerning future ownership of that asset. You may not leave your share of it to someone else in your will.
- Jointly held property may be seized to pay the debts of either joint owner.
- Bank accounts jointly owned may be temporarily blocked by state tax authorities for a period of time. They may need to review the tax situation.

What is a living will?
A living will is a document that states a terminally ill person does not have to be kept alive by artificial means.

If I draw up a living will, what do I have to do to be sure that my wishes are carried out?
First, consult your lawyer to be sure that the state in which you live recognizes a living will. It's very important that your lawyer follow *all* prescribed steps to establish it.

What happens if my state doesn't recognize a living will?
Your lawyer can still draft such a document, but the lawyer and you may have to rely on precedent established by a large nearby state that allows living wills. If your living will is tested in your state, which does not have such legislation, the judge will look for precedents in a nearby state.

How often should I reexecute a living will?
We suggest a yearly reexecution in order that no judge or court will ever doubt your intention.

Who has the final decision to pull the plug on a patient who has executed a living will?

Generally, the attending physician makes the final decision. If you know that a particular physician is strongly opposed to living wills, you may want to consider changing physicians.

What is a trust?

A trust is an estate planning vehicle designed to preserve and administer property for the benefit of your beneficiaries. It is a flexible tool that can be used to minimize Uncle Sam's tax bite and achieve your objectives in the distribution of your property.

Why would someone set up a trust?

Trusts are not just for taking care of your heirs. You may set up a trust to manage your assets because you are too busy with your career to devote the time needed; you may have retired and want someone else to run your financial matters; you may be ill and unable to manage your own assets properly; or most commonly, you may want to be prepared for disability or death.

Should I consider writing a trust to provide for my wife and children for when I'm not around anymore?

Absolutely. A trust, when properly structured by your lawyer, may provide for the well-being of your wife, children, and even your grandchildren, if you are so blessed, and will even provide for you if you cannot take care of yourself. Bear in mind that a trust does not have to be run by outsiders. The trust you set up can be managed by yourself until infirmity or death makes that impossible. At that time, your spouse or children may take over the job of trustee. We are recommending a trust to help distribute your assets after death with less tax impact.

My wife and I have three children and we have written separate wills. However, how do we leave different portions of our assets to each child? One may want to go to college, and one of our sons is permanently disabled. Is there an easy way?

Yes. Check with your lawyer about a sprinkling trust, which empowers the trustee to distribute the assets of a trust on an *as-needed* basis, perhaps at different ages for each child.

What is a testamentary trust?

A testamentary trust takes effect at the death of the maker of the trust (the grantor). The beneficiaries of the testamentary trust are the heirs of your estate.

What is an inter vivos trust?

An inter vivos (living) trust takes effect when it is established and may or may not continue after death. The living trust can be revocable or irrevocable.

What is a revocable living trust?

When you make a revocable living trust, you retain control of assets in the trust that are included in your estate. You can receive income and withdraw principal. The assets then go to whomever you want—when you want them distributed, not necessarily at your death. You may manage the assets or designate a trustee to do so. A trustee would continue to act in your best interest should you become unexpectedly ill or incapacitated. You can also change the provisions of a revocable living trust at any time.

Must I put all of my assets in a trust?

Not at all. You can put any portion of your assets in one or more trusts and do what you want with what is left.

With a revocable living trust, can I avoid the probate process?

Yes. A revocable trust allows you to bypass the will process. It is more private and speedier than a will because, among other reasons, assets in the trust aren't subject to court supervision and can be distributed more quickly.

How do I set up a revocable living trust?

With the help of a lawyer, *all* your assets, including stocks, real estate, CDs, bank accounts, etc., should be transferred to the trust. It is this unwieldy process of title transfer that discourages many people from setting up this type of trust. A lawyer can ease the problem.

Who should set up a revocable living trust?

You should consider a revocable living trust if you have property, life insurance, or pension benefits, and loved ones about whom you care. In our opinion, in most instances it is better than a will.

How much does it cost to set up a revocable living trust?

It very much depends on the complexity of the trust instrument, but you can expect to pay fees of $500 to $900, in most cases.

What is an irrevocable living trust?

This type of trust is one in which you give up all rights to receive benefits from assets in the trust.

Why would someone make an irrevocable trust?

Although you lose control of the assets, you realize a tax advantage by removing assets from your taxable estate. Generally speaking, only those people for whom estate taxes are a problem and who possess sufficient other assets to ensure a comfortable life-style should consider an irrevocable trust.

My wife has not had much experience in financial affairs during our forty-two years of marriage. Now that I am ailing with a serious illness, should I consider setting up a trust for my wife?

A trust would provide that your wife's financial affairs would be handled by a trustee on her behalf if you would die or are incapacitated by an illness. However, choose your trustee wisely. Many widows have encountered problems in dealing with trustees chosen by their husbands. Better yet, teach your spouse to handle the financial affairs now, so that she can become your trustee.

I have been happily married (for the second time) for many years. I want to provide for my present wife but also for the children of my first marriage. Can a trust help me?

Yes, with a terminable interest marital trust you can stipulate the assets in the trust go to your children from the first marriage after your present wife passes away.

Should I name my bank as the trustee of my trust?

Many people name banks as trustees because they often have state-of-the-art computer systems to keep track of your trust account, generally have been in business for a number of years, and have available other services that may prove helpful. However, we strongly urge that you check out a bank's trust department before you make your decision. Many banks have a less than sterling track record of performance, and some are very expensive in their fee structure. The bank may or may not be the best trustee for your estate.

I have been named trustee of my parents' living trust. I don't have a lot of financial expertise. Can I hire a bank to help provide certain investment services to the trust?

Yes, you can, and if the performance is not to your liking or expectations, you can change advisers.

How much will the trust department of a bank charge to be a trustee?

It varies, but you should expect to pay annual fees of 5 to 7 percent of trust income and .5 to 1.5 percent of principal for the bank's services. A word of caution: Check several banks' trust departments concerning investment track records, charges for services, etc. *before* making your final decision.

What is the unlimited marital deduction?

Simply stated, this means that you are able to leave everything to your spouse without any tax ramifications, legal fees, etc.

I understand that I can leave an unlimited amount to my wife when I die, but what happens when she dies?

Unless you have employed some estate planning techniques that lessen or eliminate Uncle Sam's tax bite, if your spouse's estate exceeds $600,000, estate taxes will be due.

I don't have $600,000. Can I still reduce taxes on my estate?

One of the most commonly used techniques is to make gifts of up to $10,000 per year to anyone you wish. These gifts may include cash, securities, real estate, insurance, almost anything. However, one important point to remember: Don't give away assets that you may need at a later date.

What is the maximum tax rate on estates and gifts?

The maximum tax rate is 50 percent.

My father passed away almost six months ago. I am about to inherit one thousand shares of stock that was valued at $10 when he died. He originally paid $2 a share. The stock is currently selling for $15 a share. If I sell it, what will be my tax liability?

The cost basis for measuring capital gains on inherited stock is the price of the stock at the time of death—in your case, $10 per share. Although your father paid only $2 per share, when you sell, you pay tax only on the difference between $10 and the current price of $15. You can also price the stock at six months from the date of your father's death. Using the six-month date, the stock is $15 a share, which looks like a good deal for you. Unfortunately, the six-month date can be used only if the value of the stock goes *down* and estate taxes are reduced.

If my father gifted me stock while he was still alive, can I still use his date of death to determine the cost basis of a stock when I sell it?

No, you can't. This scenario makes for quite a different story. The tax due would be based on the original purchase price when your father bought it and not the stock's price upon his death.

Is it better for my husband to own our home or for it to be in joint name?

Some estate planning experts suggest that it's best to have a home in the name of the spouse who will die first (if you can figure that out!). If your home was wholly owned by one partner, it would pass free of estate taxes to the surviving partner as part of the unlimited marital deduction. For instance, let's say a primary residence was purchased years ago for $25,000 and at the time of death of the owner was worth $200,000. If you wanted to sell the house, the capital gains dues would be the difference between $200,000 (the price of the house at the first partner's death) and the sales price, rather than $25,000 and the sales price.

If the house was jointly owned, only half the value at the time of death ($100,000) is included in the deceased person's estate. The remaining half, plus half of the original cost would be the house's basis for the surviving spouse—a total of $112,500. If the surviving spouse sells the house for $200,000, then $87,500 would be the taxable gain (unless the surviving spouse qualifies for the once-in-a-lifetime capital-gains exclusion or defers the tax by buying a home of equal or greater value).

Could you please define *joint tenancy with the right of survivorship?*

Joint tenancy with the right of survivorship simply means that title of your home or any asset named this way passes to the surviving owner without passing through probate.

How does tenancy in common differ from joint tenancy with the right of survivorship?

Tenancy in common means that you and someone else each own 50 percent of the asset and, at the death of one of the partners, that share would then be owned by whomever the deceased designated, not necessarily the living partner.

I understand that some types of property pass directly to my heirs without going through probate. Would you please list them?

Such things as jointly owned property, U.S. savings bonds when there is a co-owner or a surviving beneficiary, the proceeds from an insurance policy where there is a designated individual named as beneficiary, and retirement plans with named beneficiaries pass directly to your heirs without going through the probate process. There is an exception: If your estate is named as beneficiary, the proceeds are included in your estate for probate purposes.

I know that in years past, gifts made within three years of death were assumed to be made "in contemplation of death" and therefore included in an estate for estate tax purposes. Is this still law?

No, with a few exceptions—such as life insurance policies—most gifts, no matter when they are made, are not included in one's taxable estate.

I am about to inherit a rather large estate from an aunt. Will I have to pay state taxes?

Although it varies by state, an inheritance tax is paid by the recipient of the estate. In an inheritance tax state, generally speaking, the closer the relationship, the greater the amount of the inheritance exempt from taxes and consequently the smaller the tax paid. In other words, you'll pay more tax inheriting from an aunt than you will from your mother. However, many states do not have inheritance taxes. Check with your lawyer.

How are inheritance estate taxes calculated?

By the size of your estate or by how much passes to an heir. Different states have different rules. In an inheritance tax state, you will pay taxes on the amount you inherit. In an estate tax state, the actual estate will pay taxes on the total before you receive your inheritance.

Is it true that many states allow you to avoid taxes on insurance policy proceeds by having the proceeds paid directly to a named beneficiary?

That is correct. Many states tax insurance proceeds only if they are actually paid to one's estate.

I've heard a-nasty rumor that some states insist that life insurance proceeds be counted as part of an estate. What states do this?

It's not a nasty rumor; it's the truth. The states that include insurance proceeds into the worth of an estate are Massachusetts, Minnesota, New York, North Carolina, Rhode Island, South Carolina, Tennessee, and Washington.

Most states exempt some of the proceeds and tax the balance of the death benefit.

I live in Massachusetts, one of the few states that adhere to the policy that life insurance proceeds be counted as part of my estate because I own the policy. Is there any way to get around this?

Yes, there is. Consider an irrevocable life insurance trust. This would allow the proceeds of the policy to go into the trust untaxed, and in most cases, your spouse receives all income from this money for the rest of his or her life as well as any principal needed to cover living expenses.

During the past twelve months, I have paid over $30,000 worth of my grandson's medical bills. I know that I'm allowed to give away only $10,000 per year to any one person. Is there a gift tax due on anything over this $10,000 amount?

There is no gift tax due if you pay someone's medical or educational expenses no matter how much money is necessary. However, to qualify for this special treatment, you must pay the bill directly. You may not give the money to someone else to have that person pay the bill.

What is a community property state?

A state that has laws that say husband and wife equally share property acquired by their joint efforts during their marriage.

Is it possible to own property separately in a community property state?

Yes. Property that was owned by either spouse at the time of the marriage or acquired during the marriage by will, gift, or inheritance remains the property of that spouse with no claim on the ownership by the other spouse unless it is in a comingled account.

If I give my wife a piece of jewelry, is that considered her separate property? We live in a community property state.

Gifts received by a spouse during marriage may be considered separate property except when given by one's own spouse. In this case, the gift becomes community property.

How about property purchased with separate funds?

It becomes separate property of the spouse purchasing it with separate funds. Similarly, property purchased with community funds becomes community property. Separate funds are basically those funds acquired before the marriage.

Which are the community property states?

Arizona, California, Idaho, Louisiana, Nevada, New Mexico, Texas, and Washington are the eight community property states. Puerto Rico has also adopted the community property system.

Who can help me devise my own estate plan?

It's important to form your own team, i.e., professionals who are experienced in putting the essential bricks into a strong financial foundation. Even an excellent financial adviser needs to have an attorney who specializes in estate planning, an accountant (CPA), and a life insurance specialist.

Where can I find a lawyer to help with my estate planning?

You can ask the trust department of your local bank for a referral for one or two estate lawyers with whom they have worked. Also, many communities have what's known as an estate planning council that lists lawyers, CPAs, insurance agents, financial planners, etc., with experience in estate planning. Check your local Yellow Pages.

SUMMARY

Using estate planning techniques is a personal and individual process best attacked by your own estate planning team. Not every professional is an estate planning expert. Look for team members with specific experience in the estate planning process who will work closely with you and with one another.

No estate plan is perfect and no estate planner has all the answers, but a good plan and talented planner will offer opportunities to help you minimize taxes and, more important, ensure that your assets are distributed to those people you wish to receive them.

Remember:

- You may very well be worth more than you think.
- Estate planning techniques are *not* just for the wealthy.
- If you don't have a will, get one today! Don't let your state decide where your assets will go.
- Get your estate planning team together. Shop around, and interview.
- There's nothing wrong with attempting to minimize the taxes due on your estate.
- Trusts can be utilized to ensure that your assets are properly distributed.

- Probate can be avoided—no delay, no excessive fees.
- A spouse may leave unlimited assets to his or her mate.
- Know where all your important papers are located, and make sure that your family knows where they are.
- Educate yourself on federal estate tax rules.
- You may make tax free gifts to anyone you wish. This will reduce your taxable estate.
- Most states have their own gift and death tax laws. Get to know them.
- The selection of an executor and trustee is a *very* important one. Don't make this decision lightly.
- Life insurance is an effective estate planning tool.
- Dying *with or without a will* guarantees the need for your assets to go through the probate process. To avoid probate, set up a living trust.

FURTHER INFORMATION
BOOKS

Family Security Through Estate Planning
Arnold D. Kahn
McGraw-Hill

The Tools and Techniques of Estate Planning
Stephen Leimberg, et al.
The National Underwriter Co.
420 East Fourth Street
Cinncinati, Ohio 45202
(800) 543-0874

Your Estate and Gift Taxes
J. K. Lasser Tax Institute
Simon and Schuster

Joint Property
Alexander A. Bove, Jr.
Simon and Schuster

Ownership
Theodore E. Hughes and David Klein
Scribner's

Estate Planning Guide
Sidney Kess and Bertil Westlin
Commerce Clearing House

The Handbook of Estate Planning (2d edition)
Renno Peterson and Robert Esperti
McGraw-Hill

Loving Trust
Renno Peterson and Robert Esperti
Viking Press

16

The Pitfalls

My greatest strength . . . is to be ignorant and ask a few
questions.
                                    PETER DRUCKER

We believe that there are no foolish questions. The worst investment a person can make is one that he or she does not understand. Even a relatively simple and completely safe investment like a federally insured certificate of deposit, if not fully understood, becomes a very bad investment. Without an understanding of what the CD is and some knowledge of the effect of interest rate movements, you can make a mistake.

Another investment problem arises because the financial community insists that unless you take some risk, you are doing your finances a disservice. Not everyone is cut out for investing in stocks and bond. Some people are best served by staying fully invested in Treasury securities and local banks. Too many people endanger their financial life by investing for higher-than-high yields and trying to double their money. The question we pose is this: Is it better to have your money working constantly at 5.5 percent for a lifetime or at 18 percent one year and −3 percent another? For those who are afraid of making investments outside of the safe zone, take heart. In the old Aesop fable it was the tortoise who won the race, not the hare.

The point of this book has been to help you the reader win that race to financial security in the way that is most comfortable to you, but with insight and understanding of the entire money picture before you begin.

We have found that investors fall into several categories: knee-jerk investors, who invest in fads; investor-phobics, who are afraid to do anything; the once-burned, who have made mistakes and never return to the fray; and finally, a rarely heard about group of people who move confidently through the minefields because they understand what they're doing. They may make mistakes. Knowledge doesn't make you infallible, but it does allow you to weather occasional errors of judgment. We hope this book will bring all investors into this small but select fold.

There are bad investments: Uncle Louie's or Aunt Lucy's stock tips; investments made strictly to eliminate taxes; placing money in a bank account because you don't know what to do; and many others.

There are also pitfalls to consider. Here's a list of the ten most common ones we've observed:

1. *Too many people act on hot tips.* The sad fact of life is that by the time you hear a real hot tip, it's probably already been heard by the professionals and acted upon. Away from the hallowed halls of Wall Street there are few hot tips. If you haven't heard it while standing on the floor of a stock exchange, then you're reacting to yesterday's news.

2. *Many investors get trampled by following the crowd.* Actually, many successful professionals make their fortunes by watching the crowd and doing just the opposite! The last person to the dinner table rarely gets a full plate.

3. *Many people fail to identify the risk they are taking before they commit their money.* How often people tell us about an investment that ended up costing them a great deal of money when they had no idea beforehand how risky the venture was. Find out the down side when talking to the professional. You'll always hear about the up side, but you want to know what the bad news can be.

4. *Far too many people make investments solely as a way to avoid paying taxes.* We believe that the only thing worse than paying income tax is having no income to tax! Investments *must* be weighed for what we can make from them even more than for how little Uncle Sam can get his hands on.

5. *Many good investments are lost because people forget to keep tabs on them.* Too many of us expect the professionals to keep an eye on our portfolios and we forget to check them ourselves. Nobody watches your money the way you do.

6. *Failure to take profits has cost many of us money at one point or another.* Don't be greedy. Set a high price and take it.

7. *Take your losses.* We hate to admit we were wrong, but when an investment starts losing money, it's most often a wise idea to cut losses and move on.

8. *Putting all your eggs in one basket is another common investment mistake.* It is most important to diversify among a number of investments for protection. The chance of six or seven different investments all going bad is far less likely than for one investment to fail.

9. *Reflex investing or jumping into something because it won't wait is a very dangerous mistake.* Advice, if it's good, is always valid. Nothing is *so* hot that it can't wait until it has been looked into and verified. We would caution all investors to pass on anything that has to be done immediately.

10. *Lack of discipline is the final mistake*. Like children in the candy store, we don't seem to be able to keep our hands or our minds on what we're doing. We seem to run from counter to counter always looking for better advice and better returns instead of being systematic and disciplined.

Putting all the pieces together for financial security is time consuming, but it's well worth the time it takes.

Index

ABOUT THE AUTHORS

Ken Dolan is a native of Boston. He graduated from Boston College and then attended the U.S. Naval Officers' Candidate School. He was commissioned ensign in November 1965 and saw duty in Vietnam in 1967 and 1968. He has held senior positions with several Wall Street firms and, in 1978, co-founded a prominent international investment banking firm. He served as vice-chairman of Petra Capital Corporation and was senior vice-president of a leading international investment firm. Mr. Dolan has appeared on the nationally syndicated PBS program *Wall Street Week* and has published numerous investment articles. He co-hosts a nightly call-in "money" program with his wife, Daria, on WOR Radio in New York City which is heard in thirty-eight states.

Daria Dolan is a native of New York and a graduate of Webster College in St. Louis. She is a former principal of a firm specializing in packaging financial service products for Wall Street firms and exchanges around the world. She has served as vice-president of a major New York Stock Exchange firm. She and her husband, Ken, co-host a daily, live, nationally televised program on the Consumer News and Business Channel (CNBC) airing in fifty states. Ms. Dolan is a frequent speaker at seminars and conferences around the country concerning investment alternatives.

The Dolans' television and radio commitments are now extensive, as are the seminars and lectures they give on financial matters throughout the country.

The Dolans live in Florida with their teenage daughter, Meredith.